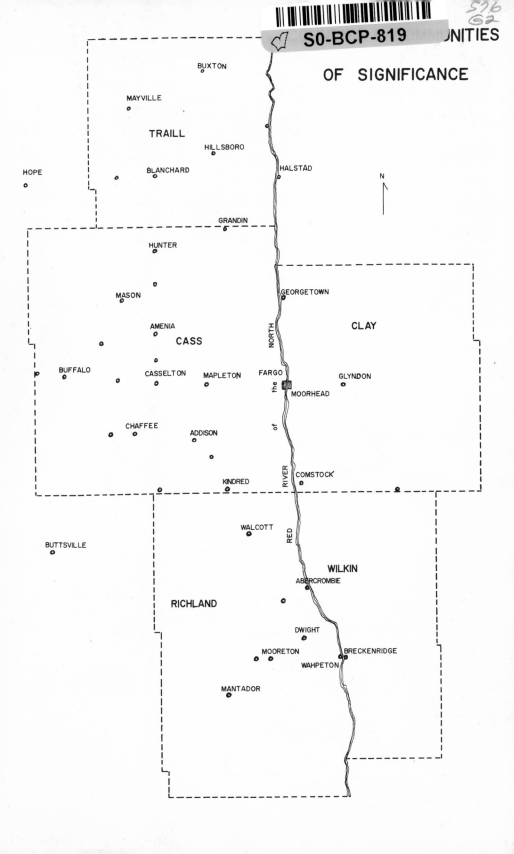

N

BUXTON

MAYVILLE

TRAILL

HILLSBORO

BLANCHARD

HALSTAD

HOPE

GRANDIN

HUNTER

MASON

GEORGETOWN

CLAY

AMENIA

CASS

NORTH

BUFFALO

CASSELTON   MAPLETON   FARGO

the

GLYNDON

MOORHEAD

CHAFFEE

ADDISON

of

KINDRED

RIVER   COMSTOCK

WALCOTT

RED

BUTTSVILLE

WILKIN

ABERCROMBIE

RICHLAND

DWIGHT

MOORETON   BRECKENRIDGE

WAHPETON

MANTADOR

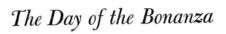

The Day of the Bonanza

By the same author:
The Challenge of the Prairie
published 1970 by
The North Dakota Institute for Regional Studies, Fargo, N.D.

The Day of the Bonanza

A History of Bonanza Farming in
the Red River Valley of the North

HIRAM M. DRACHE
Concordia College

North Dakota Institute for Regional Studies
Fargo, 1964

The publication of "The Day of the Bonanza" by Hiram M. Drache is a contribution of the North Dakota Institute for Regional Studies to the DIAMOND JUBILEE of NORTH DAKOTA STATE UNIVERSITY in 1965.

Library of Congress Catalog Number: 64-65044

Second Printing — January, 1965

Third Printing — March, 1965

Fourth Printing — June, 1965

Fifth Printing — October, 1965

Sixth Printing — December, 1965

Seventh Printing — March, 1966

Eighth Printing — November, 1966

Ninth Printing — July, 1967

Tenth Printing — February, 1968

Eleventh Printing — January, 1969

Twelfth Printing — February, 1970

Thirteenth Printing — June, 1971

PRINTED IN THE U.S.A. AT THE LUND PRESS, INC., MINNEAPOLIS

Dedicated to my parents
PAUL AND ANNA DRACHE
for their interest in scholarship

Foreword

Much of American history has been the story of the advance of pioneers into the new country to the westward. Indian traders, cattlemen, and land speculators took part in the movement but it was the farmers more than any other class who brought settled ways to the new country and made it productive of much wealth. Generally the advance of the farming frontier was the work of small proprietors, but in the Valley of the Red River of the North great farming enterprises had a part in opening the prairie wilderness.

The bonanza farms secured their lands cheaply by exchanging the depreciated bonds of the bankrupt Northern Pacific for portions of that railroad's land grant. The bonanzas had immense acreages, the capital for large-scale operations, quantities of the latest agricultural machines, and a large transient labor force. They concentrated on wheat and brought something of the methods of mass production to farming. Their spectacular operations attracted much attention, advertised the Red River Valley throughout the nation, and to a considerable degree foreshadowed the characteristics of North Dakota agriculture which have continued to the present day.

Dr. Hiram M. Drache with his energy and enthusiasm is ideally equipped to write the history of bonanza farming; he himself is not only a diligent scholar but also a farmer of long experience. Moreover, he had at his disposal the magnificent collection of manuscript materials on bonanza farming gathered by Professor Leonard Sackett and the North Dakota Institute for Regional Studies at North Dakota State University

vii

The most important records among them are those of the Amenia and Sharon Land Company. They enabled Dr. Drache to tell for the first time a detailed story of the actual operations of a bonanza farm. The Amenia and Sharon Land Company acquired some 28,000 acres of Northern Pacific land in Cass County in 1875 for about $104,000 in Northern Pacific securities. Through the skilled management of E. W. Chaffee and later his son H. F. Chaffee, the company not only carried on a large farming operation but also owned many subsidiaries—land companies, elevators, stores, grain brokerage firms, company towns, and even a part of a projected branch railroad. When the company dissolved in 1922, its gross assets and those of its subsidiaries and the men associated with it were well over $8,000,000.

The story of bonanza farming is both interesting and important —adding much new light on North Dakota history and the history of American agriculture. The labors of Dr. Drache and the support of the Institute for Regional Studies have placed all North Dakotans in their debt.

ELWYN B. ROBINSON
Professor of History
University of North Dakota

Preface

MANY INDIVIDUALS have been responsible for the completion of this history of bonanza farming. The foresighted policy of the administration of Concordia College in providing a year's leave of absence at full salary was the necessary motivation to undertake such a project. Without the free time and necessary funds granted by the college this work would have been long delayed.

Many thanks to Dr. W. C. Hunter, Professor Leonard Sackett, and Professor Dean Stallings of the North Dakota Institute for Regional Studies at North Dakota State University. It was their acquaintance with the vast amount of material in the archive of the Institute and their assistance in making it available that hastened the research work. Their firsthand knowledge of how and where the material had been collected and their contact with people acquainted with bonanza farming did much to solve some of the unanswered questions left in the records. Special thanks to Dr. Leo Hertel, editor of the Institute, for his help and services in the preparation of the manuscript for publication. And also to Mr. Oswald Daellenbach for his professional photographic work in connection with the illustrations in this book.

The willing assistance of my dissertation committee at the University of North Dakota consisting of Dr. Elwyn B. Robinson, Dr. Walter E. Kaloupek, Dr. Henry J. Tomasek, Dr. Felix J. Vondracek, and Dr. B. L. Wills with their suggestive criticisms and necessary prodding provided the stimulus to keep on working. In addition, Dr. Elwyn B. Robinson together with Dr. John L. Harnsberger, authorities on North Dakota and the Northern Pacific respectively, provided necessary leads to the sources of North Dakota's early history. Their wealth of knowledge on these

ix

subjects gave direction for probing for answers to unanswered questions. Their numerous publications provided valuable material for this subject. No writer on the bonanza era could have been more fortunate in having them for advisers and helpers.

Deepest gratitude to Ada, my wife, for her help in research, aid in correcting mechanical errors, and all the typing, in addition to keeping the family fed and clothed while trying to make chapter deadlines.

HIRAM M. DRACHE
Associate Professor of History
Concordia College
Moorhead, Minnesota

Table of Contents

List of Tables

The Day of the Bonanza

CHAPTER I

Developments Leading to the North Dakota Bonanza

"U P TO OUR own day American history has been in a large degree the history of the colonization of the Great West. The existence of an area of free land, its continuous recession, and the advance of American settlement westward, explains American development."[1] Thus wrote Frederick Jackson Turner in his famous essay on the role of the frontier in American history.

The free land of the frontier was a great motivating factor in the settlement of America. Settlers from Europe and the eastern part of America poured into the frontier, attracted by the hope of economic betterment or the chance for adventure. It was one continuous story of "beginning over again" as each new group moved west.[2]

Westward Movement

Bonanza farming in the Red River Valley of the North is a distinct phase of frontier agriculture in its westward movement across the continent. Fertile land, which provided the motivation for the westward movement, was abundant in Dakota. Bonanza farming with its peculiar techniques adapted itself well to the characteristics of the region.

The movement west and ultimate settlement of the frontier area normally took place in five or six steps. The first frontiersman was the fur trader who blazed his way into the unknown wilderness. After the fur trader came the cattleman, who, like the trader, did little to change the wilderness. If conditions were favorable the third man in the normal westward movement was the miner. The fourth man in the westward succession, the pioneer farmer, refused to compromise with nature; he conquered it and changed the wilderness. Settling on whatever land appealed to him, he broke it, erected fences and buildings, and waited for the rush of new settlers. Included in this rush was

3

the equipped farmer, the fifth man, who purchased partially improved land from the pioneer farmer and continued its development. He brought eastern civilization with him and encouraged a sixth person, the city dweller, who came to provide services. This meant the end of the frontier.[3]

The equipped farmer was most responsible for the development of every section of the country. In the Valley of the Red River of the North the equipped farmer was the bonanza farmer. This small and unique group of American farmers provides one of many distinct phases of the settlement of the West and of American agriculture.

A series of factors combined to make ideal conditions for the establishment of the bonanza farms in the Red River Valley of the North. One of the largest land grants in American history, that of the Northern Pacific Railway, and the financial failure of that road in the Panic of 1873 made a large amount of land available to holders of Northern Pacific securities at a price that easily competed with government lands under the Homestead Act. Some of the land grant was in the very fertile district of eastern North Dakota and western Minnesota in the Valley of the Red River of the North. The land was not only extremely productive, but was also treeless, stoneless, and flat, nearly all tillable, making it ideally suited for operation with large-scale machinery. Such machinery, particularly adapted to small grain, was being introduced at the time the territory was opened to agriculture. Eastern capitalists who had large holdings of deflated Northern Pacific securities were quick to realize that the only hope of recovering their investment was by securing some of the railroad's land grant and developing it. They applied business practices to agriculture and with adequate finances secured large blocks of land, professional management, and large-scale machinery to create the bonanza farms of the 1870's, 1880's, and 1890's.

National and international events made many of these enterprises extremely profitable. Europe demanded American wheat and the resultant price proved very favorable for the development of the bonanza. New milling processes adopted at Minneapolis enhanced the quality of flour ground from the premium wheat produced in the Northwest. This kept the demand active and price favorable for a number of years. The improvement of Great Lakes transportation facilities and the construction of rail lines to Minnesota and North Dakota provided the necessary means of getting the wheat to market.

The success of the bonanza system and the drama surrounding the movement advertised and dramatized the great wheat fields of the Dakotas and of the Northwest and the opportunities that appeared to

TABLE 1ᵃ. Population Growth of Northern Pacific Railway Counties in North Dakota.

County	1880	1885	1890 [b]	1900	1905	1910
Barnes [c]	1,585	6,093	7,045	13,159	15,726	18,066
Benson	...	1,255	2,460	8,320	9,363	12,681
Billings	1,323	737	170	975	2,685	10,186
Burleigh [c]	3,246	5,354	4,252	6,081	9,875	13,087
Cass [c]	8,998	21,085	19,613	28,625	31,955	33,935
Dickey [c]	...	3,897	5,573	6,061	7,412	9,839
Dunn	...	32	159	1,011	in Mercer	5,302
Eddy	...	825	1,377	3,330	3,906	4,800
Emmons	38	1,046	1,971	4,349	6,418	9,796
Foster	37	992	1,210	3,770	4,743	5,313
Golden Valley [d]	...	...	...	...	...	...
Grand Forks [c]	6,248	20,454	18,357	24,459	26,494	27,888
Grant [e]	...	...	...	...	...	...
Griggs	...	2,093	2,817	4,744	5,993	6,274
Hettinger [f]	...	...	...	...	...	6,557
Kidder	89	1,572	1,211	1,754	2,307	5,962
LaMoure [c]	20	2,072	3,187	6,048	7,715	10,724
Logan	...	336	597	1,625	4,166	6,168
McLean	...	942	860	4,791	15,245	14,496
Mercer	...	245	428	1,778	2,191	4,747
Morton	200	5,873	4,728	8,069	13,363	25,285
Oliver	...	327	464	990	2,445	3,577
Pembina	4,862	11,510	14,334	17,387	16,412	14,749
Ransom [c]	537	4,282	5,393	6,918	8,634	10,354
Richland [c]	3,597	9,043	10,751	17,387	19,379	19,659
Sargent [c]	...	3,234	5,076	6,039	7,414	9,202
Sheridan [g]	...	...	...	...	...	8,103
Sioux [h]	...	...	...	...	...	...
Stark	...	1,507	2,304	7,621	11,355	12,504
Stutsman [c]	1,007	5,632	5,266	9,143	14,580	18,189
Walsh [c]	...	12,775	16,587	20,288	20,265	19,491
Wells	...	285	1,212	8,310	9,482	11,814
N.P. Counties	30,464	123,547	137,483	211,200	279,503	358,739
All Counties	34,896	151,840	182,713	319,146	437,070	577,056

ᵃ Frank H. Hagerty, *The Territory of Dakota; An Official Statistical, Historical, and Political Abstract* (Aberdeen, S. D., 1889), pp. 55-56; North Dakota. *Commissioner of Agriculture and Labor Annual Report.* 1890, 1900, 1905-06, and 1910-12; U. S., Bureau of the Census, *Thirteenth Census of the United States: 1910 Population,* Vol. III, pp. 348-356.

ᵇ No figures for 1895 were found.

ᶜ These counties are the chief bonanza counties along the main line or branch lines of the Northern Pacific Railway.

ᵈ Part of Billings.

ᵉ Part of Morton until 1916.

ᶠ Included in Billings until 1907.

ᵍ Part of McLean until 1908.

ʰ Part of Morton until 1914.

be available to all. Settlers rushed in from everywhere, particularly from the states of Minnesota, Iowa, Illinois, Michigan, and Ohio. In addition, large numbers of Scandinavians and Germans came as a result of the European advertising and colonization campaign conducted by the Northern Pacific Railway. The bonanzas had proven themselves as an advertiser of the region beyond all expectations. From 2,405 people in 1870, present-day North Dakota grew to 182,713 in 1890 and to 577,056 in 1910. Until 1900 the larger part of the population was in the counties served by the Northern Pacific. Table I indicates the growth in population for the counties along the Northern Pacific and also for the entire state.

The particular factors that led to the creation of the bonanza and the settlement of the Valley of the Red River of the North were unique, but two basic characteristics to the westward movement and the development of American agriculture applied: free land was the great motivating force, and the farmers were the true settlers. The urge to go west was affecting so many that "some Illinois papers plaintively declare that it seems as if their state is to be depopulated by the 'Dakota fever.' Hundreds of people are leaving constantly for the world's great wheat fields and only genuine banana belt." [4] The *Fargo Argus* at that time quoted papers from Michigan, Wisconsin, Minnesota, Iowa, Ohio, and Kansas as all being worried about the great exodus to the wheat lands. Eastern railroad officials were constantly quoted as being amazed at the great numbers traveling west.

People flowed into the state as long as there was free land, but once the land was all taken, about 1915, they stopped coming. Since that time North Dakota's population has been nearly stationary or declining. The exhaustion of cheap, fertile land in other states, the large immigration of northern Europeans who liked farming and the cool climate, widespread advertising campaigns in Europe, and the high birth and low death rate of the early settlers were all responsible for the rapid settlement of North Dakota. [5]

Trends and Characteristics of North Dakota Agriculture

Because North Dakota is basically an agricultural state, any trend or characteristic of that industry reflects itself upon the entire state. One of the definite trends in North Dakota, once it was settled, was that of a nearly stationary population. The end of cheap land and a reduction in immigration put an end to the rapid growth of the state's population. Other factors aided in retarding the growth, such as the increasing size of farms, a decrease in foreign markets after 1900, the drop in birth rate, and the lack of industrialization.[6] By 1910 some counties were losing population.

High mechanization, one of the basic trends of the state's agriculture, has been due to certain characteristics of a frontier area. Population has always been relatively sparse resulting in a comparative labor shortage in the state. Even today there are only nine people per square mile. The big farms of the first few decades had to rely to a great degree on labor from other areas. The low man-land ratio, so typical of frontier areas, put particular emphasis on mechanization at a time when many new labor-saving devices were being introduced. Machinery provided for greater labor efficiency because large acreages could be handled in short periods of time and the labor force could be released until needed in another season. There was no great waste of labor as on many of the family farms where individuals are unemployed for long periods of the year. Mechanization has retarded settlement to a great extent. On the other hand, it has provided for a great deal of idleness on the cash-grain farm where livestock enterprises do not provide work in the slack seasons as on most of the Mid-Western farms.

Labor scarcity, which forced mechanization, demanded a great deal of capital to purchase the equipment and meet the payroll when necessary. Periodic labor needs required professional management which had to be well paid. Large capital investment per farm has been a characteristic of North Dakota agriculture since the day of the bonanza. A great deal of capital from out-of-state sources was necessary for many decades as North Dakota's land was being opened.

Initial investors in land in North Dakota preferred large farms. These were necessary to justify the great investment in labor-saving machinery and to gain maximum efficiency. This resulted in the concept of the large farm in North Dakota. The state has always been well ahead of the national average in acres per farm as illustrated in Table 2.

For a more accurate picture, Table 3 gives the story of the eastern tier of counties in North Dakota relative to the growth of large farms. These counties include the Red River Valley, the area of greatest concentration of bonanza farms, and represent a more nearly normal agricultural pattern in comparison with the rest of the United States. They produce all grains, have mixed livestock enterprises, and are also a sugar beet and potato area. The bonanza farms were efficiently operated by large machinery because, unlike many areas of eastern United States, there was a minimum of waste land. No woods and few hills, creeks, rivers, or stones made cultivation rapid and easy.

TABLE 2[a]. Comparative Farm Size and Numbers — North Dakota and the United States
1860-1960

Year	Total Farms	Average Size (acres)	No. Over 1,000 Acres	Per Cent Over 1,000 Acres
North Dakota				
1860[b]	123	215	.....	.....
1870[b]	1,720	176	3	.17
1880[b]	17,435	218	74	.42
1890	27,611	277	389	1.4
1900	45,332	343	1,346	3.0
1910	74,360	382	2,416	3.2
1920	77,690	466	3,944	5.1
1930	77,975	496	5,411	7.0
1940	73,962	513	6,405	9.0
1950	65,302	630	8,831	13.0
1960	54,928	755	11,364	20.7
United States				
1860[b]	2,044,077	199	.....	.....
1870[b]	2,659,985	153	3,720	.13
1880[b]	4,008,907	134	28,578	.71
1890	4,564,641	137	31,546	.69
1900	5,737,372	146	47,160	.82
1910	6,361,502	138	50,135	.79
1920	6,448,343	148	67,405	1.0
1930	6,288,648	157	80,620	1.3
1940	6,096,799	174	100,531	1.6
1950	5,382,162	215	121,362	2.3
1960	3,700,000	303	.....	.....

[a] Alva H. Benton, "Large Land Holdings in North Dakota," *Journal of Land and Public Utility Economics*, Vol. 1, 1925, p. 411; U. S., Bureau of the Census, *Sixteenth Census of the United States: 1940. Agriculture*, 111, p. 81; U. S., Dept. of Commerce, *Statistical Abstract of the United States* (1962), p. 609.
[b] Dakota Territory.

Early settlers quickly observed the adaptability of wheat to the dry, cool climate. It did not take the millers and consumers long to realize that premium wheat came from the Red River Valley where yields astounded the pioneers. Since other conditions were extremely favorable to wheat at that period, everyone turned to producing it. C. W. Thompson in his study of wheat movement said that the normal trend indicated, "Wheat production was deemed best adapted to the conditions of frontier agriculture." [7] Land was cheap so the farmer used as much of it as possible in relation to labor and capital. This led to large farms and rapid mechanization, resulting in wheat monoculture.

North Dakotans quickly became aware of the uncertainty of rainfall in the state. Rainfall is supplemented by winter snow, but nature

TABLE 3ᵃ. Farms Over 1,000 Acres in the Red River Valley
Counties in North Dakota.

Year	Pembina	Walsh	Grand Forks	Traill	Cass	Richland	Total
1910	44	20	69	52	124	32	341
1920	36	20	55	38	75	23	247
1930	46	17	55	30	80	21	249
1940	70	40	81	36	123	45	395
1950	82	73	84	45	137	42	503
1960	111	111	144	61	179	65	671

ᵃ Benton, *Journal of Land and Public Utility Economics*, p. 411; U. S., Bureau of the Census, *Eighteenth Census of the United States: 1960. Agriculture*, p. 111.

often withholds the snow during cycles of deficient rainfall. Geographers have established that in marginal areas of precipitation, such as North Dakota, there is a greater degree of variability of total precipitation than in more humid regions. Long term records indicate an overall average precipitation of 17.11 inches annually, with 15.17 inches at some western stations and a maximum of 22 inches in the extreme eastern part. Agricultural authorities in the United States have long recognized twenty inches of precipitation as necessary for satisfactory agricultural practices.[8]

Such high variability in rainfall reflects itself directly in the crop yields. North Dakota economy is subject to great fluctuations because of the high degree of risk due to the uncertainty of cash-grain income. In periods of relatively good weather and economic conditions, cash-grain farming comprises the greater share of income, but when weather and economic conditions are depressed, the farmers turn to livestock for their salvation.

Wheat, because it is the mainstay of North Dakota farms, is the greatest determining factor of the state's economic condition at any given time. North Dakota ranks high in total wheat production even though its yield per acre is one of the lowest in the entire country, often less than ten bushels per acre. Twice in the state's history, in 1900 and in 1936, the average annual production per acre was five bushels or less.[9]

North Dakotans have stubbornly clung to wheat as their major source of income, defying the risk involved in a single cash crop in a marginal precipitation area. Only during prolonged adverse periods have they tended to seek another source to supplement their income. Table 4 gives wheat acreage figures for the state and nation for the last nine decades.

North Dakota, like all of the Great Plains states, is very dependent

The Day of the Bonanza

TABLE 4[a]. Total Acres in all Farms[b] and Wheat Acreage in North Dakota and the
United States — 1880-1960

	North Dakota			United States		
Year	Total Acres	Wheat Acres	Per Cent In Wheat	Total Acres	Wheat Acres	Per Cent In Wheat
1880	3,800,656[c]	265,298	7	536,081,835	35,430,333	6
1890	7,660,333	2,709,421	35	623,218,619	33,579,514	5
1900	15,542,640	4,451,251	29	838,591,774	52,588,574	6
1910	28,426,650	8,188,782	29	878,798,325	44,262,592	5
1920	36,214,751	9,098,042	25	955,883,715	73,099,421	8
1930	38,657,894	9,969,370	25	986,771,016	61,999,908	6
1940	37,936,136	8,025,000	18	1,060,852,374	50,526,015	5
1950	41,194,044	10,202,747	24	1,159,766,020	71,161,061	6
1960	41,465,717	6,493,000	16	1,200,000,000[d]	53,024,000	5

[a] U. S., Bureau of the Census, *Sixteenth Census of the United States: 1940. Agriculture*, 111; *N. D. Ag. Statistics*, pp. 9, 17.

[b] Total acres includes farm yards, waste land, forests, and pasture land. Actual acres under cultivation is less than half of the total acres included in all farms. For the United States there were about 350,000,000 acres under cultivation in 1960. North Dakota had 19,269,991 cultivated acres in 1955. Wheat has taken one-third to over one-half of the total crop land of the state in all years.

[c] Dakota Territory.

[d] Estimate of preliminary figures.

upon the metropolitan areas on the eastern and western fringes of the Plains. Authorities on the Plains, such as Walter Prescott Webb and Carl Kraenzel, have lamented the fact that the Great Plains states are so dependent on these outside cities. Organizations within the Plains region have tried to reduce this dependency with little success. Historically, transportation in the United States has been along east-west lines. To link the Great Plains states more closely a north-south transportation system would be necessary. Such a system, however, is almost totally lacking and none is ever likely to be constructed.

The small farmer could do little to oppose the eastern monopolies while the bonanza farmer was favored by the millers, railroads, and machinery manufacturers because of his large volume of business. Favorable rates and volume discounts kept the bonanza farmer friendly with these large corporations. Many bonanzas were owned by railroad officials, bankers, congressmen, or industrialists who were not likely to criticize the monopolies. However, some bonanzas went into competition with the grain and railroad monopolies. For instance, Oliver Dalrymple chartered a Great Lakes steamer to transport his 600,000-bushel wheat crop to Buffalo in 1881, bypassing the railroads and the Minneapolis millers. It was not until H. F. Chaffee, of the Amenia and Sharon Land Company, and John Miller, of the Dwight

Farm and Land Company, united to form the John Miller Company in 1896 that any of the bonanzas made a serious attempt to circumvent the controlled marketing facilities limiting the outlet of North Dakota products.

Reliance on outside capital is typical of most frontier areas but, unfortunately, that condition has continued to exist in North Dakota. This is a contributing factor in making Minneapolis the largest farm mortgage center in the United States since parts of Wisconsin and Iowa, all of Minnesota, North Dakota, South Dakota and Montana are its hinterland. The early settler in North Dakota relied on outside capital when he purchased land from the railroad on an installment basis. He also purchased his machinery on an installment basis from the manufacturer. Capital accumulates slowly in a new agricultural community. This is particularly true in North Dakota where frequent periods of adverse weather have caused the farmers to dissipate their cash reserves for living expenses.

Throughout the years agriculture has been favorably affected by the rising value of land. Frontier history is filled with stories of great land speculators including such prominent individuals as George Washington, Robert Morris, and John Marshall in the early periods of our history. The significance of the speculator is equally important in North Dakota. The land speculator's fight to secure "the right piece of land" in anticipation of the Northern Pacific's crossing the Red River was the initial speculation in North Dakota. The *Fargo Argus* called these early speculators "boomers." There was Raffensperger, McCarther, Morton, Doty, James Holes, Thomas N. Lee, N. K. Hubbard, E. S. Tyler, James B. Power, H. S. Back, and countless other railroad officials and other men of position who made their fortunes speculating in the rising value of land.[10] These men were not disappointed. Good years that followed the opening of the territory, especially after 1876, caused land prices to rise sharply. Absentee land owners were able to secure control of a great share of the government and railroad lands because of loopholes in the existing land laws and lack of their enforcement. After some of the land was settled and prices rose, speculators had no difficulty in sub-dividing and selling their holdings for a large profit. Many of the larger land-holders did not sell their land until public pressure demanded. They were not popular citizens but little was done to prohibit their activities.

The official declaration in 1890 that the frontier was at an end, less than two decades after North Dakota was opened, caused land prices to rise more rapidly there than in older states. The American people were suddenly aware that free land could not last forever. Prices of

Red River Valley land rose from the basic minimum of $1.25 established by law to about $110 an acre by World War I.[11]

Any area to be quickly settled must have a product that can be rapidly and easily exploited by the newcomers. Because of the region's apparent lack of an exploitable commodity, people hesitated before moving into the Red River Valley. It was not until cheap lands were made available through the Northern Pacific land grant and until it became known that James Holes produced a forty-bushel wheat crop on the banks of the Sheyenne that people became interested. Eastern capitalists, however, as in previous frontier areas, were on the spot as speculators. And so in North Dakota the bonanza farm served as the chief tool of exploitation. Since large expanses of easily worked fertile acres produced wheat cheaper than elsewhere in the nation, a few exploited the area and accumulated sizeable fortunes through bonanza farming. This attracted large numbers of settlers to the state who in time became the downfall of the bonanza system because they were willing to bid the price of land to the point where it became more profitable for the bonanza farmer to sell out than to farm.

Development of Farming and Milling

"Between 1860 and 1900 over 400 million acres were added to the farm domain mostly in the Trans-Mississippi West," wrote Edward E. Edwards a historian of American agriculture.[12] The factors that produced this growth were: the use of machinery in agriculture, the free-homestead policy, improved transportation facilities, a heavy influx of immigrants which increased the labor supply, the application of science and industry to agriculture, and the expansion of foreign and domestic markets. All of these factors combined to create a large-scale agriculture in America.[13] During those years wheat growing in the country moved westward and became centered in the North Central District which included twelve states within a triangle formed by Ohio, Kansas, and North Dakota. Development of wheat production within that district is illustrated in Table 5.

Wheat production was deemed best adapted to the conditions of frontier agriculture. As land became more valuable, it had to be used for livestock production and dairying rather than wheat raising. This accounted for the shift from wheat to diversified agriculture in the states east of the Ohio in midcentury. Where land was still cheap, as on the frontier, the rent charge was low and the farmer used as much land as possible in relation to labor and capital. Wheat best answered these conditions. But later when land prices rose, the farmer shifted to greater gross income crops.[14]

TABLE 5[a]. Growth of Wheat Production in the North Central District
from 1859 to 1909

Year	Production Bushels	Per Cent of Nation's Wheat Crop
1859	95,005,130	54.9
1869	194,934,540	67.7
1879	329,550,755	71.7
1889	321,316,830[b]	68.6
1899	441,300,918	67.1
1909	505,189,796	73.9

[a]Louis B. Schmidt, "The Westward Movement of Wheat," *Readings in the Economic History of American Agriculture*, ed. Louis B. Schmidt and Earl D. Ross (New York: 1925), p. 375. (Hereafter cited as L. B. Schmidt, "Wheat.")
[b]Reduction in production due to severe drought conditions in the district.

The movement of wheat growing in Western Minnesota followed the frontier and was part of the traditional westward movement in the entire United States. By 1900 four of the nine leading wheat counties in Minnesota were in, or adjacent to, the Red River Valley: Polk, Clay, and Marshall within the Valley, and Ottertail adjacent to it.[15]

A natural result of the greatly increased production of wheat was the growth of a large milling industry in the Midwest. A happy combination of technological developments in the milling industry, of a railroad network, and of new farm machinery capable of harvesting greatly increased acreages of wheat, all appeared at the proper time to make Minnesota, and especially Minneapolis, the center of a great milling industry and to give it a reputation as a flour producer.[16] The milling industry expanded to eighty-five mills by 1860. Minneapolis, with its cluster of mills around St. Anthony Falls, was called the Mill City by the early 1870's. In 1880 the city had 436 mills and was destined to be the flour milling capital of the world.[17]

In the late sixties Alexander Faribault, the founder of Faribault, Minnesota, had called Edmond N. LaCroix from the East to his city to construct a dam and a flour mill. LaCroix had developed a new technique which was called the "shaker" or middlings purifier process. Customers gladly paid an extra cent a pound for flour made by this process. George H. Christian, a Minneapolis miller, installed such a purifier in the Washburn "B" mill in 1870 and because of the extremely high quality of his flour, was immediately able to command an extra two dollars per barrel for it. At once many millers copied the system and perfected it. The price of wheat rose twenty cents per bushel within the first year and in two years had doubled.[18]

On the heels of the discovery of the middlings purifier in the milling industry came the adoption of steel rollers and the gradual reduction technique. The steel rollers could be set more accurately, enabling the gradual cracking of the outer layers of the wheat kernel. Each successive set of rollers was placed closer together, cracking another layer of skin with the middlings purifier removing the bran after each cracking. The steel rollers not only lasted much longer, but they speeded up the milling process by preventing the outer bran layers from getting mixed with the oily kernel heart. The gradual reduction process, which had originated in Hungary, was adopted by the Minneapolis millers in 1874.

Minneapolis now had technical superiority which combined with water power, financial resources, and railroads enabled it to move into first place in the milling industry.[19] The Minneapolis millers, to overcome Milwaukee and Chicago, actively promoted the construction of the Minneapolis, St. Paul and Sault Sainte Marie and the Minneapolis and St. Louis railroads. For Minnesota and Dakota farmers resented the fact that nearly all the storage in Milwaukee and Chicago was controlled by two railroad companies and eight individuals who cooperated with each other. They also resented the grading system used in those cities for it did not take into account the superior quality of Minnesota and Dakota wheat.[20]

With the advance of the Northern Pacific Railway into the Red River Valley in 1871, the major wheat producing area began to shift from southeastern Minnesota to the Red River Valley. The above mentioned new milling processes adopted by the Minneapolis millers, which increased the value of spring wheat over winter wheat, and the development of the line-elevator system until it assumed monopolistic control over local grain markets, changed the picture in wheat production and marketing. To become more competitive, the Minneapolis Millers Association was organized to buy all the grain for the millers in that city. William H. Dunwoody headed this new organization which operated under a pooling arrangement to control prices and grading. The association was also active in the newly developed Red River Valley, attempting to secure the area's wheat for their over-expanded milling facilities.[21]

As a result Minneapolis and Duluth became the leading primary grain markets in the nation. Duluth, which had received very little wheat prior to 1876, suddenly became a lake port with an annual average shipment of 1,693,503 bushels from 1876 to 1880. From 1881 to 1885 annual consignments averaged 9,159,162 bushels, nearly all of which was handled by the Duluth Board of Trade and shipped out on the Great Lakes.

While Duluth was growing rapidly as a grain port, Minneapolis was developing as a milling center. Production of flour, which was about 30,000 barrels in 1860, climbed steadily to a peak of 20,000,000 barrels in 1915.[22]

Events Preceding Bonanza Farming

Bonanza farms were the result of a series of events in the agricultural and economical exploitation of the country surrounding the Red River of the North, a country which extended 300 miles from Lake Traverse in Minnesota to Winnipeg in Canada. The first state of exploitation leading to the eventual settlement of the Red River Valley was centered around the procurement of furs and buffalo hides. This resulted earlier in the 19th century in Lord Selkirk's settlement at Fort Garry, the subsequent founding of Pembina, and the establishment of Fort Snelling. Lumber, the basis of the second stage of exploitation, was concentrated primarily in the eastern and northern parts of Minnesota. In mid-century an awareness of the fertility of the land inaugurated the third stage of exploitation, the production of wheat. Starting in southeastern Minnesota, wheat farming moved west and north into the Dakotas.

The original activity in the Red River Valley itself came from present-day Canada. Thomas Douglas, the Earl of Selkirk, a Scotsman with substantial holdings in the Hudson's Bay Company, purchased 116,000 square miles of land in the valleys of the Red and Assiniboine Rivers in May, 1811. Selkirk was interested in promoting the agricultural settlement of the area.[23] In 1812 the first Scotch settlers appeared at Fort Garry. By 1814 the number of settlers had increased to two hundred. Life proved exceedingly miserable in this remote settlement with poor transportation to the outside world, a constant lack of food, Indian problems, and the inability to market their produce.[24]

In 1819 while at Prairie du Chien, Wisconsin, Lord Selkirk purchased 250 bushels of Scotch Fife wheat which cost a thousand pounds sterling, and had it delivered to Fort Garry. This wheat was seeded in 1820 and a good crop was harvested, the first harvest by white man in the Red River Valley. After that date the Selkirk settlers were never short of food.[25] The potato-and-wheat diet was supplemented by buffalo meat obtained from the annual hunts of the buffalo herds around Pembina.

The first significant step in the settlement of Pembina came as a direct result of the activity of the residents of Fort Garry. The Scotch settlers of Fort Garry and the Metis (French half-breeds) made annual sojourns in the Pembina region to secure their year's supply of meat from the large buffalo herds found there. These buffalo hunts started about 1812, and by 1820 the hunting party had become so large that 540 carts were used. The hunting party increased in size annually until 1840 when 1,210 carts were used to transport supplies for nearly 4,000 people and 500 dogs taking part in the affair.[26]

The second significant step in the growth of Pembina came in 1829 when John Jacob Astor's American Fur Company established a trading post in the area. In 1843 the first furs secured in the Red River Valley at the Pembina post were sent to St. Paul by Red River cart. Pembina became a frontier trading post for St. Paul and was responsible for much of the early wealth of the latter. In 1843 Norman W. Kittson, an active partner of Henry Hastings Sibley in the fur trade, broke the monopoly of the Hudson's Bay Company when he delivered four Red River cart loads of goods from St. Paul.[27]

The number of Red River carts increased annually so that by 1851 Kittson alone took sixty cart loads of goods from St. Paul. By 1854 there were 1,500 Red River carts operating between the Red River Valley and St. Paul. Their number increased to 6,000 in 1858. Each cart carried an average of 800 pounds and the carts usually traveled in trains. One such train included 800 carts and 1,300 people.[28]

Pembina grew as an outpost of St. Paul and St. Paul grew around Fort Snelling which was established in 1819 in order to prevent any further intrusion of Selkirk settlers from the north.[29] Fort Snelling served as the center of military and governmental power in this region for thirty years. As more and more settlers moved to the north and west, new frontier outposts had to be created to replace Fort Snelling. Troops from the fort traveled as far north as Pembina and as far west as Mandan to keep the frontier at peace, but the territory was too large for a single fortification. In April, 1849, Fort Ripley, near Little Falls, Minnesota, replaced Fort Snelling as the northernmost fort in the Mississippi region. In 1853 Fort Ridgely was opened near New Ulm to watch the southern Minnesota Indians. A site north of Breckenridge was selected in 1857, and the following year Fort Abercrombie was erected.[30]

Fort Snelling also made many non-military contributions to the Northwest. Industry, commerce, and agriculture all had early beginnings at the fort. In 1820 the garrison had seeded ninety acres of wheat, corn, and potatoes in addition to garden crops, all of which did well.[31]

To provide timber for the fort, a saw mill was erected at the Falls of St. Anthony in 1820. This first saw mill opened the way for the prominent lumbering industry that was to follow. The demand for flour by the garrison also necessitated the erection of a flour mill. In 1823 a government-owned and operated mill was erected at the fort at a cost of $288.33.[32]

The first important Indian cession was made in 1837 by the Sioux and Chippewa. With the fur trade on the decline and lumber interests well entrenched in the northeastern part of the state, the fertile lands of the southern half became a target for new settlers interested in wheat farming.[33] The land cession by the Sioux at Traverse des Sioux in 1851 opened the entire southern half of the state to settlement by forcing the Indians onto reservations along the Minnesota River. Later treaties in 1854 and 1855 provided for cession of much more land in the northern part of Minnesota. Failure of the government to fulfill its treaty obligations provoked the Indians into a final desperate stand in the Sioux outbreak of 1862. In that rebellion the Indians were severely beaten and in the Old Crossing Treaty of 1863 were also forced to cede the Red River Valley portion of Minnesota.[34]

To secure governmental action favorable to opening new settlements, an organized territory had to be created. Minnesota Territory, created on April 3, 1849, contained all of what is now the state of Minnesota and parts of North and South Dakota east of the White Earth and Missouri Rivers. The creation of this new territory was made mandatory when Wisconsin became a state on May 28, 1848, leaving no government to take care of the area west of the St. Croix River.[35]

Cheap, fertile land was the chief reason for the great settler's rush to Minnesota between 1854 and 1857 when 5,250,119 acres of public land were sold. This represented a several thousand-fold increase in the number of farms over the 157 that were counted in the census of 1849.[36] Land, the great exploitable commodity of Minnesota, attracted the pioneers who were also encouraged by the availability of water and trees.

The great land rush accomplished its purpose, for it had enticed sufficient settlers to arrive and to enable the territory to qualify for statehood. In addition citizens of the territory had visions that the new state would be in an ideal position to profit from the construction of a Pacific railroad. The statehood movement was pushed by them and Congress passed the enabling act on February 26, 1857. However, it was not until May 11, 1858, that Minnesota was admitted as the thirty-second state to the Union.[37]

Steamboating on the Red River

Prior to the 1870's settlers were slow in coming to the Red River
Valley. The Valley was not popular with the Indians either, even
though they recognized the richness of the soil. Sometimes they grew
maize, potatoes, and squash, all of which were luxuriant and abundant. Only about 5,000 Indians lived in northwestern Minnesota and
eastern Dakota because they did not consider the hunting and fishing in this area to be any good.[38] It was not until 1797 that C. J. B.
Chaboillez established a trading post at Pembina. The Hudson's Bay
Company, not to be outdone, sent its agent, Thomas Miller, to establish a post there in 1801 which later was extended by a settlement of Selkirk farmers. In 1823 Major Stephen Long reported that
there was a freighting business carried on by cart between the posts
at Pembina and Big Stone Lake in Minnesota. He counted only 350
inhabitants in the Pembina area at that time. In 1843 business in
Pembina became sufficiently great to cause the establishment of more
direct Red River cart routes. A military expedition to the Red River
Valley in 1849 related that the population had grown to about 1,000
south of the Canadian boundary.[39]

Two important events that hastened the settlement of the Red
River Valley occurred in 1857. First, the Hudson's Bay Company
abandoned York Factory, its great post on Hudson's Bay. It made
arrangements with the American government to transport goods in
bond through the United States via St. Paul and the Red River
Valley. This arrangement increased considerably the traffic in the
Valley. The second major event was the location and eventual construction of Fort Abercrombie on the Red River. In addition cus-
toms houses, postal roads and stations, and freight depots were erected
to handle freight for the Hudson's Bay Company and the military.
Settlers moved in and farms were opened, only to be vacated during
the Indian War of 1862.[40]

In 1857 Breckenridge was plotted to provide better facilities for
the anticipated increased trade between St. Paul and Canada. Early
in the summer of 1858 the first shipment in bond for the Hudson's Bay Company passed through St. Paul. The merchants of St.
Paul were delighted at the prospect of having a chance to handle
the approximately $5,000,000 annual trade for the Company. That
year the mail contract was also let for transportation from St. Paul
to Fort Abercrombie via St. Cloud. J. C. Burbank and Company,
who won the contract, were to provide mail service in each direction
three times weekly. The contract also specified that the company had

to provide its own road over the 160 miles from St. Cloud to the fort.⁴¹

The Hudson's Bay Company made a major contribution to the development of the Red River Valley in 1859 when it established a trading post on the Red River at Georgetown in order to make use of steam boats in transportation. James McKay, who was appointed manager of the post, was experienced in the Red River cart trade and transportation and selected Georgetown as head of navigation because the river was too uncertain for boats above that point. The Hudson's Bay Company gave J. C. Burbank and Company and Russell Blakeley a five-year contract to carry 500 tons of freight annually from St. Paul to Fort Garry. One of the early settlers near Georgetown was R. M. Probstfield who later became a prominent citizen of Clay County.⁴²

The Sioux outbreaks of 1862 raised havoc with the newly established steamboating business. Late in 1862 the Burbanks were forced to stop operation of their new boat, the *International*, which was rated at 133 tons. In 1863 and 1864 it was able to make only one round trip to Fort Garry. The Sioux outbreak, which started August 18, 1862, struck a wide area of western Minnesota. The Indian outbreak was so terrifying that in less than one week a majority of the inhabitants of twenty-three counties had vacated their homes. The scare was so intense that in nineteen counties none of the refugees had returned to their homes prior to November, 1863. And it was not until 1865 that the settlers could return with complete safety.⁴³

After a period of relative inactivity because of the Indian war, settlers began to reappear in the Valley in the late 1860's. Business had increased sufficiently so that the government extended the mail route from Fort Abercrombie to Pembina in 1867. In 1871 this service was again extended from Pembina to Winnipeg. By this time the last of the Red River carts had disappeared in Minnesota and other means of transportation had permanently replaced them. The steamboat *International*, which was once more busy carrying goods for the Hudson's Bay Company, received a competitor that year when James J. Hill placed the *Selkirk* into operation on the Red River. The telegraph line from Fort Abercrombie to Winnipeg was completed in 1871 and in the same year the Northern Pacific Railway reached Moorhead.⁴⁴

Once the railroads entered the area, steamboating expanded. James J. Hill attempted to make the best of the opportunity by securing a monopoly of the river transportation. In 1872 he bought the *International* and later organized the Red River Transportation Company.

Inhabitants of the area disliked Hill's attempts to create a monopoly but had to cope with it until the railroads were completed. In their last days the steamboats were kept busy serving as the connecting link between the railroads on the Red and Winnipeg. From December 12, 1871, when the Northern Pacific entered Moorhead, that city served as the head of river transportation until 1873. The average round trip from Moorhead to Winnipeg took ten days, according to Fred A. Bill, a clerk on the *Dakota*.[45]

James J. Hill placed N. W. Kittson in charge of the newly organized Red River Transportation Company which added the *Dakota* to its fleet in 1872, the *Alpha* and the *Cheyenne* in 1874. Other interests later added the *Manitoba* and *Minnesota* to the Red River transportation in order to compete with the Hill line.[46] Moorhead was a busy river town except in seasons when the river was too shallow and the freight had to be hauled from the railroad to Frog Point, about fifty miles north on the Red River. Frog Point, located at the foot of Goose Rapids, was the point of easy navigation to the north.[47]

The effective distance of river transportation was shortened in 1873 when the St. Paul and Pacific Railroad built its line north from Barnesville, through Glyndon, and to the Red Lake River at Crookston.[48] This moved the head of Red River transportation to Crookston until 1877 when it was replaced by Fishers Landing, nine miles down the Red Lake River. Fishers Landing had a short history as head of navigation because in December, 1878, the St. Paul and Pacific and the Canadian Pacific railroads were joined together at St. Vincent on the international boundary.[49] In 1879 James J. Hill became general manager of the newly organized St. Paul, Minneapolis and Manitoba Railroad which now established direct connections from Winnipeg to St. Paul. This fulfilled the dream of the early merchants of St. Paul who had worked for a direct route to the Red River Valley and Winnipeg.

The last international trade by steamboat on the Red River was carried out in 1881. By that time most of the boats had been taken to rivers farther north and west until railroads were built in those regions.[50]

One local phase of river transportation was of significance to the later agricultural economy of the Red River Valley and to bonanza farming. The Grandin brothers, owners of the Grandin bonanza, constructed and operated a line of river steamers to transport grain and supplies for their farm. This unique aspect of bonanza farming was possible because the Grandins possessed four miles of frontage on the Red River which enabled them to transport their wheat by river to Fargo, the nearest railroad center. The Grandin Line was well known on the Red River. When the boats were not busy hauling wheat or supplies for the farm, they served the public by carrying freight between Winnipeg and Fargo.[51] The *Daily Argus* carried many advertisements and news items about the business of the Grandin Line. Every time one of the boats came to Fargo with wheat, the day's receipts were from 9,000 to 14,000 bushels larger than a normal day's run. For several years the daily shipments were reported in the *Argus*. The *J. L. Grandin,* which had the distinction of being the first Dakota-built and owned steamer, went into operation on April 27, 1878. The *J. L. Grandin* had the largest tonnage displacement of any of the vessels used on the Red River.[52] The Grandin Line employed sixty boatmen and laborers. In its first year of operation it transported 1,500 passengers and 12,000 tons of freight, mostly machinery and grain. Its gross revenue that year was $135,-000.[53] Besides the *J. L. Grandin,* the Grandins also operated the *Pluck* and *Alsop*. In addition to the steamboats, they had four barges. All of their wheat was shipped to Fargo where the Grandins owned a 50,000-bushel elevator, for trans-shipment to the railroad. In 1881 the steamboats and barges brought 250,000 bushels of wheat into Fargo. Of this amount 150,000 bushels came from the Grandin farms and the rest from other farmers.[54]

Railroad Construction and Legislation

Important to the development of settlement, agriculture, lumbering, and flour milling in Minnesota was the construction of an adequate transportation system. Railroads and river steamboats were the early main systems of travel. Railroads were particularly important in tying the state and the Northwest to the twin cities of Minneapolis and St. Paul.

Minnesota was off to an early start in railroad construction, or at least in railroad legislation, when the 1853 territorial legislature chartered five railroads. However, due to irregularities in the passage of the Congressional land grant of June, 1854, relative to the Minnesota and Northwestern Railroad Company, no construction was started.[55] It was not until March 3, 1857, that a generous land grant for Minnesota railroads was passed. Minnesotans were anxious for railroads, but the Panic of 1857 stopped all hope of construction. Nevertheless many citizens and legislators were interested in securing help for the railroads from the state, but the state's constitution limited the state debt to $250,000, an amount entirely insufficient to help in the construction of four railroads.[56]

The construction era was short lived for by July 1, 1859, all four railroads had run short of funds. Special state bonds had sunk so low in value that they were no longer an effective aid for raising money. The state now possessed 240 miles of poorly graded roadbed and a debt in the form of special bonds in the amount of $2,275,000.[57] In 1861 a generous legislature permitted the four companies to re-acquire their property and recommence operations. However only the Minnesota and Pacific Railroad was able to make any progress. This road, originally chartered in 1857, was reorganized in 1862 as the St. Paul and Pacific Company and started operation between St. Paul and the milling center of St. Anthony.[58]

Until 1865 most of the settlers were located in the hardwood area of southeastern Minnesota because it provided the timber necessary for fuel and buildings. The forests also offered protection to man and beast, whereas the prairie sections were too remote from the markets and were believed to be deficient in fertility. The railroads changed the picture by luring farmers to the prairies. This was especially true after the farmers learned that they could improve as much prairie land in three years as they could woodland in twenty years.[59] Wheat, the most transportable farm commodity, quickly took over as the major crop.[60]

The railroads so dearly wanted by the people were no more than completed when the farmers of the state began to wage war against them. The farmers quickly linked the elevators and millers to the railroads. As early as 1868 they were attacked by the farmers as being monopolistic and corrupt. The farmers were sure that there were gross irregularities in the wheat market when in 1866 the price of that commodity jumped from a harvest-time low of $0.95 to a mid-winter high of $1.50. The railroads and elevators were accused of monopolizing the market, of incorrect weighing, freight-rate dis-crimination, and improper grading. Farmers were particularly irked by the development of the line-elevator system which, through co-operation with the railroads, virtually monopolized the local wheat markets.[61]

The disorganized farmer's complaints meant little to the railroads. Unification was necessary to give the farmers a bargaining power. This was the reasoning of Oliver H. Kelley, a Minnesota farmer who became a clerk in the Federal Bureau of Agriculture and later the founder of the National Grange. In 1867 the Grange was organized in Washington, D.C. as a secret society to promote a better educa-tional and social life for the farmer.[62]

The objections of the organized farmers were first acknowledged by Governor Horace Austin who gave special attention to the corruption in the wheat trade in his inaugural address of 1870. On March 6, 1871, the first of a series of Granger acts was passed. This law classified and put definite limitations on rates that could be charged by the railroads. It required equal facilities for all shippers. The office of railroad commissioner was created to enforce the law.[63]

After a relatively quiet year in 1872 in their opposition to the railroads, the farmers were sufficiently stirred in 1873 to organize the Anti-Monopoly Party. Although the Anti-Monopoly candidates were endorsed by the Democrats, none were elected to office. They did, however, force the Republicans to nominate a Granger sympathizer for governor and also caused that party to adopt an anti-monopoly platform. But in spite of these anti-monopolistic complaints the railroads were in no mood to compromise; not only were they failing to make money from their freight business, but they were also in a tight financial position because of the panic. The panic finally caused a cooling off for both the railroads and their opponents and a compromise law was passed in 1874. This law not only recognized the difficulties of the railroads, but repealed the law of 1871 which had proven too arbitrary and inelastic.[64]

Railroads Enter the Red River Valley

Once river transportation and adequate land routes were established and the farmers realized the great potential of the fertile soil, many of them seeded small plots of wheat which produced high yields. Only the lack of markets prevented them from raising more. Walter J. Traill, the Hudson's Bay Company agent at Georgetown, Minnesota, secured a horse-powered thresher in 1874 and offered to thresh any wheat the local farmers could produce. R. M. Probstfield and several other farmers in the area each seeded fifteen acres to wheat. Their twenty-bushel-per-acre average caused everyone to become quite excited about the agricultural prospects of the Valley.[65]

Flour milling received its first impetus in the Valley in 1874. Traill, who was also in charge of a Hudson's Bay Company post at Caledonia, North Dakota, built a fifty-barrel grist mill there, the first in the state.[66] In 1874 Henry A. Bruins, a Moorhead, Minnesota merchant, organized a stock company to erect a flour mill. This mill proved the superior quality of Red River wheat for flour by taking first premium prizes in two consecutive years at the Minnesota State Fair. This company installed the first steam elevator in the Red River Valley in 1878, the year of the first extensive wheat shipments on the river.[67]

Although steamboats and Red River carts were important to the settlement of the Valley, the railroads provided the greatest impetus. The Northern Pacific and the St. Paul, Minneapolis, and Manitoba railroads lost little time penetrating the Red River Valley. The Northern Pacific, which reached Moorhead late in 1871, laid its first tracks west of the Red River on January 1, 1872. The Northern Pacific bridge crossing the Red was opened for operations on June 6, 1872. Settlers advanced with the railroad. Unfortunately for Moorhead, speculators held lot prices there so high that many people preferred to settle across the river. Land speculation continued for about nine years but by this time Fargo had a head start.[68]

The Northern Pacific pushed road construction rapidly once it had crossed the Red River in 1872. It built ninety-three miles to Jamestown, North Dakota, in 1872 and by June 3, 1873, had completed another 106 miles to Bismarck, North Dakota.[69] The St. Paul and Pacific Railroad laid 104 miles of track in the Red River Valley in 1872, extending from Barnesville, Minnesota, through Glyndon, Minnesota, to a point north of Crookston, Minnesota. This line was not connected to any other track of the St. Paul and Pacific and, therefore, served as a branch to the Northern Pacific which it crossed at Glyndon.[70] The St. Paul and Pacific served the upper part of the Valley after 1871 when its main line was completed from St. Paul to Breckenridge.[71]

The railroads finally set the stage for a great rush to the Red River Valley and the Dakotas. Squatters had settled west of the Red River as early as July, 1871, when they learned where the Northern Pacific was going to cross the river.

During the winter of 1871-72 a rough, merry, hard-drinking gang of some six hundred lived in tents, dugouts, and log cabins by the river —Fargo in the Timber, while General Thomas L. Rosser's Northern Pacific engineering crew with their families lived in thirty or forty tents to the west—Fargo on the Prairie.[72]

By 1872 Moorhead had 800 citizens and Fargo was not far behind. The Federal census of 1870 revealed that the Red River Valley counties of North Dakota contained 2,405 people. From that core the population was destined to grow rapidly.

At this time all land west of the Red River was a part of the Dakota Territory with its capital at Yankton. The new territory was made necessary after Minnesota became a state in 1858, leaving Dakota without a government. In that year the Dakota Land Company, an organization of land speculators, created a squatter government to protect its interests.[73] Much of the political history of the territory was a direct result of the activities of certain Minnesota politicians, railroad promoters, and federal appointees who were hoping to be elevated to high office in the territory's government.[74]

During its first two decades, the population of Dakota Territory grew slowly. The territorial census of 1861 revealed 2,402 inhabitants, and only 14,181 were counted in the Federal census of 1870. Many settlers argued that Dakota would never be more than a grazing country. Railroads, gold, and bonanza farming caused a sudden growth and by 1880 the population had mushroomed to 135,000, of whom 34,896 lived in present-day North Dakota.[75]

Northern Dakota did not amount to much in the early political history of Dakota Territory. And before it applied for statehood, it had less than one-fifth of the seats in the territorial assembly as late as 1877. The most significant event in northern Dakota was the construction of the Northern Pacific Railway to the Missouri. The next most significant event was the success of bonanza farming as attempted by directors of the Northern Pacific, under the management of Oliver Dalrymple.[76] The drama of the bonanza farms furnished the railroad with excellent propaganda for its colonization program. Once people started to move into northern Dakota in greater numbers, political fever for division and statehood gathered momentum, which climaxed in 1882 when separate conventions were held in Fargo and Sioux Falls.[77] Northern Dakota, with its rapidly increasing population, gained a step toward separate statehood in the fall of 1883 when the territorial governor, Nehemiah G. Ordway, and his son, the territorial auditor, moved their offices to Bismarck. Although the long and bitter struggle for statehood continued, this move proved to be a strong factor in the division of the territory. When Congress finally made the decision for the creation of two states on February 22, 1889, everyone in the Dakotas seemed too pre-occupied with drought, depression in farm prices, and foreclosures to be overly excited.[78]

The Great Dakota Boom

Once the success of bonanza farming was apparent, northern Dakota became the center of a great boom. This great boom in American frontier agriculture and railroad construction was concentrated primarily between the years 1879 to 1886, reaching a peak in 1883 and 1884.[79] The promotional activity of the Northern Pacific Land Department under its commissioner, James B. Power, had much to do with starting the boom. Getting rid of its land grant, securing settlers, and creating business were important aspects of early American frontier railroads. In America railroads were the explorers of the frontier and not just another mode of transportation as they were in Europe.[80]

J. B. Power, the land agent of the Northern Pacific Railway, stated that "men, capital and energy . . . rapidly converted the raw prairie into a great field of waving grain." What he forgot to mention was how three of the four above elements got to Dakota.[81] The boom in eastern Dakota was a unique combination of railroad expansion, land colonization policies, and agricultural advancement.[82] Harold Briggs, an authority on the boom, wrote: "The greatest factor in the up-building of Dakota next to her vast expanse of public lands, has been the railroad. . . . Without good transportation facilities . . . the boom could not have taken place."[83] The local papers were filled with both praise and rebuke of the railroad, but they and the local citizens clearly recognized that without the railroads they would probably not have been there. The settlers flowed in, claims to public land were filed, the prairie sod was broken, towns were built, and the population increased rapidly.

In 1871 the Northern Pacific Land and Immigration Departments were created to sell the lands and fill them with people. Every corner of Europe and eastern America was made aware of the potential of the Dakota prairies. Attractive installment arrangements on land sales, free transportation to Dakota for all land purchasers, and other enticements were offered.[84] In spite of these inducements, people were timid about buying land in far-off Dakota. The Panic of 1873 slowed down most of the activity on the frontier. But once the general economy of the country improved and the railroad recommenced construction, the Great Dakota Boom started.[85]

The two most direct causes of the boom were the great demand for hard, red spring wheat demanded by the new milling processes developed in Minneapolis, and construction of a new railroad across the northern prairies by James J. Hill. Other contributing causes of the boom were the rise of land values in eastern states, the fertility of the soil as dramatized by the bonanza farms, the immigration of many Norwegians to the Dakotas, the manufacture of new machinery conducive to large-scale farming, and a revival of the speculative and adventurous spirit of the citizens, causing a nation-wide boom and a movement to the frontier.

The combined result of the above factors was a dramatic rise in the filings at the United States Land Office in Fargo. From almost a complete standstill prior to 1876, weekly filings during the spring and summer months of 1880 averaged nearly one hundred, covering about 12,000 acres of land. The peak of claim filings was reached in 1882 and 1883 as indicated in Table 6. The peak finally leveled off in 1884. Business in the U.S. Land Office in Fargo dropped sharply after that because most of the available good land was taken.

A more complete picture of land taken from public domain in the entire Dakota Territory during this period is given in Table 7.

Railroad lands were sold just as rapidly as the public domain was taken up, but more was sold in larger blocks to speculators and bonanza farmers. Even before the Panic of 1873, sales were considerably larger than the 80-and 160-acre plots secured under the Homestead acts by settlers on the government lands. After the panic, individual sales to eastern capitalists were extremely large so that the tracts

TABLE 6[a]. Claims in Fargo Land Office during Peak of the Boom.

Week Ending	Total Claims	Total Acres
April 7, 1882	417	66,720
April 28, 1882	426	68,160
June 9, 1882	542	86,720
June 30, 1882 ....'......	612	97,920
Dec. 1, 1882	359	57,440
March 2, 1883	298	47,680
April 7, 1883	316	75,360
April 14, 1883	403	61,480

[a] *Fargo Argus.* All reports cover a one-week period. These reports were found within a day or two of each of the dates used here.

TABLE 7[a]. Public Land Taken in Dakota Territory
from 1877 to 1889

Year	Acres
1877	213,000
1878	1,378,000
1879	1,657,000
1880	2,269,000
1881	2,673,000
1882	4,360,000
1883	7,317,000
1884	11,083,000
1885	4,548,000
1886	3,075,000
1887	2,076,000
1888	1,881,000
1889	2,383,000

[a] Briggs, *NDHQ*, IV, 81.

sold by the railroads were about triple the size of those made by the government.[86]

The newly constructed railroads connected the wheat fields of Dakota to the great milling center of Minneapolis. They not only provided the link between remote northern Dakota and the eastern areas of the United States, but brought employment opportunities, a source of cash income for the farmers, a chance for commercial agriculture, and hope of progress for the new area. James J. Hill, who was well acquainted with the Red River Valley and North Dakota through his experience in steamboating, provided the greatest railroad network for the state.[87] In 1879 Hill had become the manager of the St. Paul, Minneapolis, and Manitoba Railroad which had just taken over the property of the St. Paul and Pacific Railroad. The reorganized railroad controlled by Hill and his associates possessed 657 miles of track and two million acres of land in Minnesota. In its first year of operation the Hill line earned a million dollars over expenses.[88] Hill was now prepared to extend his railroad to the Dakotas.

In 1880 the Manitoba Railroad, as Hill's line was called, crossed the Red River at Grand Forks. In the next four years rapid extension of lines took place including one from Fargo north to Neche on the Canadian border, a second from Wahpeton north to Park River, a third from Wahpeton west to Milnor (now owned by the Northern Pacific), and a fourth from Grand Forks west to Devils Lake.[89] The Northern Pacific, not to be outdone, was just as active. It had completed 200 miles of road to Bismarck when construction stopped because of the Panic of 1873. In 1879 it crossed the Missouri and in the following year reached the Montana border. A line of forty-three miles was built from Casselton via Blanchard to Mayville in 1880 and 1881 which was traded in 1883 to the St. Paul, Minneapolis, and Manitoba Railroad in return for forty miles of track from Wahpeton to Milnor. The Fargo and Southwestern branch was built from Fargo to Lisbon in 1882 and extended to La Moure in 1883, a total of seventy-seven miles. That same year thirty-six miles of track were laid from Sanborn to Cooperstown, sixty-nine miles were officially opened from Jamestown via Carrington to Sheyenne, and another thirteen miles from Carrington to Sykeston. In all, the Northern Pacific had nearly 650 miles of road in operation in the state at the end of 1884.[90] These two railroads had done their share in creating the boom.

The new lines greatly increased the freight potential of the railroads. Wheat, the prime product of Dakota, was the chief outbound cargo. The real drama of the boom in Dakota is illustrated in the wheat shipment figures. In 1874 the Northern Pacific carried only 144,000 bushels of wheat while 10 years later it carried 5,777,000. The St. Paul and Pacific carried only 2,292,000 bushels in 1874. Its successor, the St. Paul, Minneapolis and Manitoba, carried 20,697,000 in 1884. The bulk of the Northern Pacific wheat was hauled to Duluth while Minneapolis received the greater portion of the wheat from the Manitoba line.[91] The rise in freight tonnage shipped from Fargo corresponds well with the wheat shipments. In 1877 the Northern Pacific accepted 24,783,621 pounds of freight; by 1882 this figure rose to over 213,000,000 pounds.[92] Northern Pacific tonnage continued to rise so that by 1886 the total handled by the road on North Dakota shipments alone reached 1,311,550,000 pounds and 2,548,712,000 in 1892.[93]

Land held the key to the economy of northern Dakota. The big task was to get it opened and producing. By 1882 northern Dakota was way ahead of its chief rival, the southern part of Dakota Territory (now South Dakota) for in that year South Dakota had 2,858,-678 acres on the tax rolls in contrast to 4,372,801 for the northern state. Railroad lands sold to private individuals were supposed to be placed on the tax lists at once, and much more land in northern Dakota had been "proved up" than in southern Dakota.[94] In the fiscal year ending June 30, 1882, one-third of all homesteads filed in the entire United States were in Dakota Territory, more than in Minnesota, Kansas, and Nebraska, which ranked second, third, and fourth.[95] Wheat acreage in northern Dakota, which amounted to only a few scattered plots in 1873, reached 2,000 acres by 1875, and 145,-506 in 1879. In 1884 when the construction of the major railroad lines were finished in eastern Dakota, wheat was seeded on 1,000,000 acres and within five years this had increased to 2,655,991 acres. Wheat acreage had expanded to 4,030,061 acres by 1900 and to 8,-345,416 acres by 1910. Acreage expansion leveled off gradually after that date, reaching an all-time high of 11,372,000 acres seeded in 1933.[96]

The Great Dakota Boom produced a population explosion. The rapid increase in population is illustrated in Table 1 above. When the railroad crossed the Red River, it, along with most of the 2,500 settlers, was infringing upon certain rights still retained by the Sisseton and Wahpeton Indian tribes in the area. In 1872 a new agreement was signed in which the tribes explicitly gave up their rights in the Valley. The agreement was so arranged as to give the Northern Pacific control of the townsite of Fargo.[97] Legal recognition of the claims of the early settlers was not given until June 3, 1874.[98] The

first sizeable building in Fargo was the railroad office which was converted to the Headquarters Hotel in April, 1873. On January 2, 1874,
the Northern Pacific filed the first plat of the townsite of Fargo.[99]
From this start the town grew rapidly, reaching 7,394 in 1885, while
northern Dakota grew from 2,405 to 152,199. After the boom slack-
ened, many counties and towns actually lost population. Some towns
died completely. The end of the boom came not so much because of
dry years, as because of the lack of speculative excitement which had
caused it in the first place. The end of the boom was more psycho-
logical than economic.[100]

The Great Dakota Boom had served its purpose well in North
Dakota history. In 1890, six years after its climax, the population of
the state had reached 190,983. There were fifty incorporated towns
and villages and numerous school systems, railroads, post offices,
churches, flour mills, newspapers, and banks. If anything, the speculative fever of the boom had caused an over-expansion of facilities.[101]
There cannot be any doubt that the real beginnings of the Great
Dakota Boom had its roots in the land grant to the Northern Pacific Railway. This most generous of all land grants was the key
to the boom; by using the great abundance of land as a means of
securing a railroad, it linked the two essential features of the boom
together.

FOOTNOTES

[1] Frederick Jackson Turner, "The Significance of the Frontier in American History."
The Turner Thesis Concerning the Role of the Frontier in American History, George
R. Taylor, editor, Problems in American Civilization (Boston, 1949), p. 1.

[2] Ray Allen Billington, *Westward Expansion: A History of the American Frontier*
(New York, 1949); p. 2.

[3] Turner, pp. 8–11.

[4] *Fargo Argus*, April 4, 1882.

[5] J. M. Gillette, "Study of Population Trends in North Dakota," *North Dakota Historical Quarterly*, IX (April, 1942), pp. 179-193. (Hereafter, cited as NDHQ).

[6] *Ibid*, p. 190.

[7] C. W. Thompson, "The Movement of Wheat Growing: A Study of a Leading State,"
The Quarterly Journal of Economics, XVIII, (1904), p. 573.

[8] R. F. Engelking, C. J. Heltemes, Fred R. Taylor, *North Dakota Agricultural Statistics*, North Dakota Agricultural Experiment Station Bulletin 408 (Fargo, 1957),
p. 99, (Hereafter cited as *N. D. Ag. Statistics*). Frank J. Bavendick, *Climate and
Weather in North Dakota* (Bismarck: North Dakota State Water Conservation
Commission, 1952), pp. 52-53.

[9] C. J. Heltemes and Baldur M. Kristjanson, *Handbook of Facts About North Dakota Agriculture*, NDAES Bulletin No. 357 (Fargo, 1950), p. 11; *N. D. Ag. Statistics*,
p. 17; "1958 Yield Summary, Major Crops," *Doane Agricultural Digest*, Vol. 22, Jan. 2,
1959, p. 2.

[10] *Fargo Argus*, Oct. 26, 1880, Sept. 24, 1881, Sept. 28, 1881, Oct. 12, 1882, Oct. 16,
1882, Oct. 19, 1882, and April 13, 1883.

[11] In 1961 some of the original Dalrymple bonanza was sold for $175 to $200 per
acre in section lots.

[12] Edward E. Edwards, "American Agriculture — The First 300 Years," *Yearbook of Agriculture, 1940: Farmers in a Changing World*, ed. Gove Hambidge (Washington: U. S. Government Printing Office, 1940), p. 237. (Hereafter cited as Edwards, "American Agriculture.")

[13] *Ibid.*, p. 237.

[14] Thompson, *Quarterly Journal of Economics*, XVIII, 575.

[15] *Ibid.*, p. 572.

[16] James J. Hill, "History of Agriculture in Minnesota," Minnesota Historical Society, *Collections*, VIII (1898), p. 276. (Hereafter cited as MHS, *Collections*.)

[17] George D. Rogers, "History of Flour Manufacture in Minnesota," MHS, *Collections*, X, pp. 38-39.

[18] Joseph LaCroix, "1871–1890 Towards Finer Flour: The Middlings Purifier," *With Various Voices, Recordings of North Star Life*, ed. Theodore C. Blegen and Philip D. Jordan (St. Paul, 1949), pp. 164-166; Rogers, MHS, *Collections*, X, pp. 45-49.

[19] Theodore C. Blegen, *Building Minnesota* (New York, 1938), pp. 263-264; Rogers, MHS, *Collections*, X, pp. 45-49.

[20] Henrietta M. Larson, *The Wheat Market and the Farmer in Minnesota 1858–1900* ("Columbia University Studies in History, Economics and Public Law," Vol. CXXII, No. 2; New York, 1926). pp. 68-69.

[21] Larson, *The Wheat Market*, pp. 118, 134; Blegen, p. 265

[22] Larson, *The Wheat Market*, p. 127; Blegen, p. 276.

[23] John Harnsberger and Robert P. Wilkins, "Transportation on the Northern Plains: 1, The Genesis of Commerce," *The North Dakota Quarterly*, XXVIII (Winter, 1961), p. 21.

[24] William Watts Folwell, *A History of Minnesota* (St. Paul, 1921), Vol. 1, pp. 213-214.

[25] J. H. Shepherd, "History of Agriculture in the Red River Valley," *History of the Red River Valley Past and Present* (Grand Forks, 1909), Vol. 1, p. 196

[26] Marcus L. Hansen, *Old Fort Snelling 1819–1858* (Minneapolis, 1958), p. 38.

[27] George B. Winship, "Forty Years Development of the Red River Valley," *History of the Red River Valley: Past and Present*, Vol. 1, p. 74; Harnsberger and Wilkins, *The North Dakota Quarterly*, XXVIII, p. 24; Elwyn B. Robinson, "A History of North Dakota" (unpublished manuscript, copy in possession of author, University of North Dakota, Grand Forks, N. D.), Chapter vi, pp. 3-4, 7.

[28] Harnsberger and Wilkins, *The North Dakota Quarterly*, XXVIII, pp. 24-25; Robinson, Chapter vi, p. 7.

[29] Harnsberger and Wilkins, *The North Dakota Quarterly*, XXVIII, p. 21.

[30] Hansen, pp. 50-52.

[31] *Ibid.*, p. 28.

[32] Rogers, MHS, *Collections*, X, p. 37.

[33] Blegen, p. 116; James M. Goodhue, "The Treaty of Traverse des Sioux," *With Various Voices, Recordings of North Star Life*, p. 45.

[34] Blegen, p. 140.

[35] Folwell, Vol. I, p. 246.

[36] *Ibid.*, p. 360.

[37] Folwell, Vol. I, pp. 389, 392; Vol. II, pp. 1, 3, 11.

[38] Warren Upham, "The Settlement and Development of the Red River Valley," MHS, *Collections*, VIII (1898), pp. 11, 17.

[39] James M. Heifort, "Steamboating on the Red River" (unpublished Master's thesis, North Dakota Agricultural College, 1960), pp. 15-22; LeRoy R. Hafen and Carl Coke Rister, "*Western America: The Exploration, Settlement and Development of the Region Beyond the Mississippi* (2nd ed.; New Jersey, 1950), p. 530.

[40] John Lee Coulter, "Industrial History of the Valley of the Red River of the North," North Dakota State Historical Society, *Collections*, Vol. III (1910), p. 552. (Hereafter cited as NDSHS, *Collections*.)

[41] Russell Blakeley, "Opening of the Red River of the North to Commerce and Civilization," MHS, *Collections*, VIII (1898), p. 150; John Harnsberger and Robert P.

Wilkins, "Transportation of the Northern Plains, p. 11: Steamboating North of Fargo," *North Dakota Quarterly*, XXIX (Spring, 1961), pp. 58-59.

[42] George N. Lamphere, "A History of Wheat Raising in the Red River Valley," MHS, *Collections*, X (February, 1905), pp. 16-17; Fred A. Bill, "Steamboating on the Red River of the North," *NDHQ*, Vol. II (January, 1928), pp. 106; Winship, Vol. I, p. 75.

[43] Blakeley, MHS, *Collections*, VIII, 59; Folwell, Vol. II, pp. 109, 124; Robinson, Chapter vi, p. 12.

[44] Blakeley, MHS, *Collections*, VIII, pp. 57, 63; Harnsberger and Wilkins, *North Dakota Quarterly*, XXIX, p. 63.

[45] Harnsberger and Wilkins, *North Dakota Quarterly*, XXIX, pp. 64-65; Edith S. Moll, "Moorhead, Minnesota Frontier Town 1871–1915" (unpublished Master's Thesis, North Dakota Agricultural College, 1957), p. 5; Blakeley, MHS, *Collections*, VIII, p. 65; Bill, *NDHQ*, Vol. II, p. 210.

[46] Bill, *NDHQ*, Vol. II, pp. 215-216.

[47] *Ibid.*, pp. 202-207.

[48] Winship, Vol. I, p. 89.

[49] Blakeley, MHS, *Collections*, VIII, p. 66; Heifort, p. 56.

[50] Heifort, p. 56; Harold F. Peterson, "Some Colonization Projects of the Northern Pacific Railway," *Minnesota History*, X (June, 1929), 143; Winship, Vol. I, p. 92.

[51] *Fargo Daily Argus*, Sept. 3, 1880.

[52] Bill, *NDHQ*, Vol. II, p. 216.

[53] Heifort, p. 59.

[54] Interview of Leonard Sackett with Hilstead, North Dakota Institute for Regional Studies, North Dakota State University, Fargo, North Dakota; Grandin Papers, File 269. Hilstead was a Grandin employee. No first name was used. (The bulk of the material for this thesis came from original sources on deposit at the Institute at North Dakota State University Library, Fargo, North Dakota. Hereafter cited as NDIRS.) Coulter, NDSHS, *Collections*, Vol. III, p. 576; *Fargo Argus*, June 5, 1882, p. 7.

[55] Folwell, Vol. I, p. 329.

[56] *Ibid.*, Vol. II, pp. 44-49.

[57] *Ibid.*, pp. 52-57.

[58] Blegen, p. 244; Folwell, Vol. II, pp. 328-330; Vol. III, p. 2; Larson, *The Wheat Market*, p. 57.

[59] Folwell, Vol. III, p. 63.

[60] *Ibid.*, p. 62; Larson, The Wheat Market, pp. 55, 57.

[61] Blegen, pp. 295-296; Merrill E. Jarchow, *The Earth Brought Forth, A History of Minnesota Agriculture to 1885* (St. Paul, 1949), p. 59; Larson, *The Wheat Market*, pp. 77-80.

[62] Larson, *The Wheat Market*, pp. 104-106.

[63] Folwell, Vol. III, pp. 40-43, 74; Jarchow, p. 171; Larson, *The Wheat Market*, p. 108.

[64] Larson, *The Wheat Market*, pp. 110-111.

[65] Lamphere, MHS, *Collections*, X, pp. 12-13.

[66] Fred A. Bill, "Early Steamboating on the Red River," *NDHQ*, IX (January, 1942), 70.

[67] Harold E. Briggs, *Frontier of the Northwest: A History of the Upper Missouri Valley* (New York: Peter Smith, 1950), pp. 510-511.

[68] Moll, p. 5.

[69] Henrietta M. Larson, *Jay Cooke, Private Banker* (Cambridge, 1936), p. 399.

[70] Larson, *Jay Cooke, Private Banker*, p. 369.

[71] Folwell, Vol. III, p. 442.

[72] Robinson, Chapter vi, p. 36.

[73] Howard Roberts Lamar, *Dakota Territory 1861–1889: A Study in Frontier Politics* (New Haven, 1956), pp. 43-44.

[74] *Ibid.*, pp. 70-71, 124, 143.

[75] *Ibid.*, p. 148.

[76] *Ibid.*, p. 191.

[77] *Ibid.*, p. 237.

[78] *Ibid.*, p. 238.

[79] Harold E. Briggs, "The Great Dakota Boom, 1879-1886," *NDHQ*, IV (Jan., 1930), p. 78.

[80] Peterson, *Minnesota History*, X, p. 127.

[81] J. B. Power, "The First Wheat Farm," *The Northwestern Farmer and North Dakota* (May, 1905), p. 4.

[82] Stanley N. Murray, "Railroads and the Agricultural Development of the Red River Valley of the North, 1870–1890," *Agricultural History*, XXXI (Oct., 1957), p. 57.

[83] Briggs, *NDHQ*, IV, pp. 79-80.

[84] J. B. Hedges, "Colonization Activities of the Northern Pacific," *Mississippi Valley Historical Review*, XIII, pp. 314-321.

[85] Robinson, Chapter vi, p. 41.

[86] James B. Power to A. H. Barney, Jan. 11, 1881, found in Power *Letterbook*, NDIRS, File 309.

[87] Robinson, Chapter vii, p. 12.

[88] *Ibid.*, p. 11.

[89] *Ibid.*, p. 12.

[90] H. V. and H. W. Poor, *Manual of Railroads of the United States* (New York, 1885), p. 201.

[91] Robinson, Chapter vii, p. 4.

[92] *Fargo Argus*, March 10, 1880, April 18, 1881, Aug. 6, 1881, and Feb. 26, 1884.

[93] Dakota, Railroad Commissioners, *Annual Report*, 1886; N. D. Railroad Commissioners, *Annual Report*, 1892.

[94] *Fargo Argus*, March 1, 1882.

[95] *Fargo Argus*, Aug. 29, 1883.

[96] Coulter, NDSHS, *Collections*, Vol. III, p. 589; Hagerty, p. 60; *N. D. Ag. Statistics*, p. 17.

[97] Robinson, Chapter vi, p. 33.

[98] *History of the Red River Valley, Past and Present*, Vol. I, p. 491

[99] *Ibid.*, p. 489.

[100] Robinson, Chapter vii, p. 25.

[101] *Ibid.*, p. 27.

CHAPTER II

The Northern Pacific Land Grant and Its Influence Upon Land Speculation

As MENTIONED before the Northern Pacific land grant was the key factor in the establishment of bonanza farms along the Red River Valley. When the financing of the construction of the Northern Pacific Railway became a difficult problem Jay Cooke's banking firm was called to the rescue. But even that powerful organization was unable to sell Northern Pacific securities fast enough to cope with the reckless spending of the road's directors. And so Cooke's firm went into bankruptcy, touching off the Panic of 1873.

Just prior to the fall of Cooke, James B. Power, the prime mover of the bonanza scheme, appeared on the scene. Power and certain directors of the railway wanted large, specialized farms to dramatize the fertility of Dakota soil in order to hasten settlement. Since the railway could not wait for the normal flow of homesteaders to settle the region a bond-land exchange program was started which enabled the company to dispose of its land and at the same time reduce its bonded indebtedness. Men with access to large amounts of capital were attracted by the opportunity of buying fertile land at an extremely low price. It was these eastern capitalists who later became owners of most of the bonanza farms.

Already since the 1840's Americans had been dreaming of a northern railroad to the Pacific. In 1845 Asa Whitney, a New York merchant with an interest in the China trade, presented his plan for the construction of a northern railroad to Congress. Whitney, often called the "Father of Pacific Railroads," suggested that Congress set aside a strip of land sixty miles wide from the western shore of Lake Michigan to the Pacific Coast.[1] Congress turned down Whitney's proposal as impractical. However, the settlement of Oregon, the acquisition of California as a result of the Mexican War, the pressures of lobbyists and speculators, and the precedents established by the land-grant acts of

1850 and 1862 were too much of a temptation. On July 2, 1864, Congress chartered the Northern Pacific Railway Company. The act granted "every alternate section of public land, . . . designated by odd numbers, to the amount of twenty alternate sections per mile, on each side of said railroad line, . . . through the territories of the United States, . . . ten alternate sections of land per mile of said railroad whenever it passes through any state." [2] This Northern Pacific land grant was extremely generous, for it was double in acreage per mile over any other grant. Since the Illinois grant of 1850 and all others that followed provided that the minimum price of public domain, within the land grant, should be raised to $2.50 per acre, the United States lost no cash income because of the grants. [3]

Shortly after the Illinois grant, Congress, in the regular army appropriation bill of March, 1853, commissioned the War Department to make surveys to determine "the most practical and economic route for a route for a railroad from the Mississippi River to the Pacific Ocean." [4] Isaac I. Stevens, governor of Washington Territory, was in charge of one of the five military parties sent out in 1853. He was to explore the region between the 47th and 49th parallels. The results of his thorough survey were used a decade later by the War Department as a preliminary route to be actually followed. [5]

Financing the Northern Pacific Railway

Financing a railroad across the vast unsettled areas of the Western United States presented a new problem to the railroad builders. There were no states to back the new railroad securities, and foreign investors were unwilling to speculate on roads in unsettled areas. The Federal Government, with experience in national transportation dating from 1806, believed that the "vast public domain . . . could be used as security for the inducement of private funds." [6] Congress had specified "that no money should be drawn from the treasury of the United States to aid in the construction of said Northern Pacific Railroad." [7] The original Northern Pacific grant was for 47,000,000 acres of which 10,700,289 acres were in North Dakota, covering nearly one-fourth of the state's area. [8] The Northern Pacific did not satisfy all requirements and in a final decision received only 38,916,338 acres. [9]

The early incorporators, under the leadership of Josiah Perham, believed that the public would subscribe to the Northern Pacific bonds. Section I of the Northern Pacific charter provided that the capital stock of the company be one million shares of one hundred dollars each. The public, however, would not buy them when it could secure government-endorsed bonds of the Union and Central Pacific. [10] Because of the inability to raise funds, the Northern Pacific appealed to Congress three times for a postponement of its starting date, which was eventually set for July 2, 1870.[11] In the meantime, a reorganization of the board of directors of the Northern Pacific greatly strengthened that body with important personages in American transportation in an effort to aid in the financial campaign.[12]

The Northern Pacific had approached Jay Cooke, the prominent American banker, as early as 1865 to supply construction funds and sell its stock. Cooke, still busy in refinancing the government and not optimistic about speculative, but highly profitable, railroad financing, declined to do business with the Northern Pacific. Still unable to secure the financing, the directors again approached Cooke in 1869. This time Cooke was more receptive. He made a preliminary contract with the company on May 20, 1869. This was not binding until his firm had made a thorough survey of the route of the railroad in order to determine the feasibility of the enterprise. Cooke's personal engineer, Milnor Roberts, who surveyed some of the route, reported his complete findings in the fall of 1869.[13] Roberts' report not only convinced Cooke of the feasibility of the project, but it also aroused the interest of the public in the Northern Pacific country.[14] Cooke's partners, William Moorhead, Pitt Cooke, and Harris Fahenstock, all were opposed to the Northern Pacific project because they believed it would take several years before any profits could be made by the railroad. They were convinced that the only bonds that could be sold would be to individuals who would buy on the personal recommendation of Jay Cooke, who had a reputation for honest investing. To secure the support of his partners, Cooke was forced to modify part of the original contract for financing the Northern Pacific.[15] The major points regarding finances in the supplement to the preliminary contract were as follows:

The eighteen shares into which the whole interest was divided were increased to twenty-four, of which Jay Cooke and Company were to receive twelve.

A land company was to be organized in connection with the railroad to own and improve town sites, etc., whose interests should be divided into twenty-four parts, Jay Cooke and Company receiving twelve.

Five million dollars were to be raised within thirty days to enable the company to commence and complete at once its line to the Red River.

The increase in the number of shares made the $80,001,000 divisible as follows: $93,400 to each immediately and $40,500 to each upon the completion of each section of twenty-five miles.

The $80,001,000 is the amount to be held by the twenty-four shares. Of the $100,000,000 in capital stock to be issued, Jay Cooke and Company were to receive $19,999,000 as a bonus.[16]

The signing of the contract on January 1, 1870, between Jay Cooke and Company and the Northern Pacific enabled construction to commence on February 15, 1870, and also provided the spark for pressure on Congress to revise the charter. On May 26, 1870, Congress passed a bill which permitted the Northern Pacific to mortgage its railroad and telegraph line and to issue bonds secured by such property.[17]

Jay Cooke put his reputation and personal friendship at stake to secure support in the halls of Congress, among the country's newspapers, and even in the White House.[18] Jay Cooke was more than a mere broker of Northern Pacific bonds. He was an interested and ardent supporter of its cause and the Northern Pacific country. He not only sold the bonds, but advanced the capital of his own banking house. Jay Cooke had a reputation of being very cautious in investing in any untried venture. But he liked investing in transportation and that, combined with previous favorable experience, plus the great government backing, made the Northern Pacific look like "a sure thing."

The Northern Pacific was the biggest single business enterprise undertaken in the United States up to that time, surpassing any of the other railroads and the Erie Canal. Cautious as Cooke was, he was sure that his experience in financing during the Civil War would aid him in what he considered a venture of similar national significance. Cooke visualized people flooding into the great Northwest, willing to pay a good price for the land. The same people would also provide heavy traffic for the railroad. The public, however, never became as enthusiastic about the prospects of the Northern Pacific country or the railroad bonds as Jay Cooke thought it would. European investors, having a mania for government securities at the time, showed a similar reluctance toward railroad bonds.[19]

After construction had started in 1870, the road did not stop at the Red River, as some of Cooke's partners had hoped, but pushed across the river in 1872. By June 3, 1873, it had reached the Missouri River. At this time the railroad again turned to Cooke for more money. His pioneering instincts, speculative interests, and love for the Northwest overcame his banker's caution as he struggled to sell bonds in Europe and America.[20] However, Cooke could not go to Europe himself to sell the bonds because he had to press necessary legislation through Congress. Therefore, he sent George B. Sargent, manager of his banking and real-estate interests in Duluth, abroad. Unfortunately, Sar-

gent was not the salesman that Cooke was and before any great success could be attained in Europe, the Franco-Prussian War started,
plunging Europe into panic. This had a great effect on the future of
the house of Jay Cooke and the Northern Pacific Railway.[21]

A new campaign to sell bonds was started in 1871. By May 2, 1871,
over $350,000 had been spent for advertising them. The public was
interested in the 7.3 per cent interest, but other railroad bonds paid
an equal or higher rate of interest. And in addition these other railroads were operating in settled areas and had already sufficient traffic to have a stimulating effect on the value of their securities. By the
fall of 1871, Cooke warned officers of the railroad that they would
have to stop waste and perhaps curtail construction if the bonds did
not sell. Cooke was worried because the only people who purchased
the securities were those who bought them on his personal recommendation. He felt a great moral responsibility for these bond sales.
The deteriorating trust of his business partners, who had never been
too favorable to the Northern Pacific project, a personal quarrel with
his church over high church tendencies, and the death of his wife, all
in 1871, greatly weakened his spirit just at a time when the sale of
bonds was proving most burdensome and cut down his decisiveness
and confidence of former days.[22]

The demand for funds became greater than even Jay Cooke could
furnish. The railroad officers however continued purchases beyond
their contractual limits with Jay Cooke and Company and refused to
heed the banker's warnings. Because of over-extension in Northern
Pacific bonds, the bank was finally unable to meet its commitments
and Cooke was forced to close his doors on September 18, setting off
the Panic of 1873. Cooke's firm did not fail because of any irregularities in its activities and an audit after the firm's failure indicated total
assets of $15,875,120.04 and liabilities of $7,937,409.26. The greatest
weaknesses in his firm were over-investments in relatively non-liquid
railroad securities and over-extension of credit to the Northern Pacific. On November 26, 1873, the courts adjudged the firm bankrupt.[23]
With Jay Cooke no longer able to help, construction of the railroad
came to a standstill until new avenues of financing were available.
The Northern Pacific had to turn to its biggest asset, the generous
land grant, to get relief from its financial distress.

James B. Power and the Sale of Northern Pacific Land

As mentioned before the Northern Pacific received 25,600 acres of
land for each mile of railroad it constructed from the Red River to
the Pacific coast. Jay Cooke and the railroad officials had computed

the average value of the land at five dollars per acre. This sum should have been more than adequate to pay for the entire cost of construction.[24] Cooke and all the others were assuming that the land could be quickly disposed of and money from its sale would assure continuous progress. Prior to his contract with the Northern Pacific, Cooke had issued a circular that laid down his ideas for selling and colonizing the land. The railroad adopted his basic ideas, one of which led to the formation of the land department under the chairmanship of Frederick Billings. So great was Cooke's faith in the land and so heavily did he rely on its quick sale that some contemporaries felt that this optimism was the chief reason for his failure.[25]

And so in the final end the inability to sell the land, the lack of business for the railroad on account of the sparse population, and a heavy interest load on the bonded indebtedness prompted the railroad's officials to search for a scheme that would relieve the financial burden and save the company. Early in 1871, John S. Loomis, land commissioner for the Northern Pacific, submitted a plan for the promotion of immigration and land settlement. Loomis was also president of the National Land Company which was then selling and settling land along the Kansas Pacific Railroad. To aid in land sales, a Bureau of Immigration was created under the leadership of Major George B. Hibbard.[26]

An important early figure in the development of northern Dakota was James B. Power. He came to the Northern Pacific in 1871 as chief clerk of the Minnesota Division. In 1873 he was made general agent of the land department and promoted to land commissioner in 1875.[27] Power was well aware of the general opinion that Dakota was no place for human beings, that nothing could grow there, that the winters were too severe and the summers too dry. Because of this common misunderstanding of the region, Power had to use every possible means to prove that the area was productive and, at the same time, he had to try to rescue the railroad. According to him the land of the Northern Pacific had to be opened rapidly if the railroad's investors were to have any hope of recovering their money. More and more settlers would have to break the sod and build communities. In 1872 Power traveled as far west as Valley City. It was a dry year and he began to doubt that the area would ever attract settlers. But he did not voice his personal opinion. In 1875 he traveled to the Little Missouri in western Dakota, where he also felt that this region was no good for cultivation and not very good for ranching. Here he recognized the difficult task before him. But again he remained silent and it was not until much later before he dared reveal his true impressions about the country.[28]

In addition his task was made more difficult by the stand taken by the directors to protect the railroad's interest. Power said: "The directors of the road are inexorable in their policy to develop the country and to prevent absorption of their land grant by men rich enough to hold it unimproved for a future large advance in value." [29]

While the great land grant of the Northern Pacific was a chief source of hope, it also inspired doubts and lack of confidence among many of its officials. Some doubted the value and salability of the land; others doubted the need for the land department. In defense of the land department, Power, who by now had changed his original opinion and had become convinced of the fertility of the land, wrote to Frederick Billings, chairman of the Northern Pacific Board of Directors:

Many things are yet required to bring our Land Dept. up to the standards that it can reach and I am very anxious to see it obtain the recognition that is its due, far from the commencement of our work, it has appeared to me that there has been a disposition on the part of other Departments of the road to consider the Land Dept. a "necessary evil" but know that very soon it will be acknowledged that we have not only saved the road but made it in all its departments a grand success.[30]

Power had to keep his own faith in the enterprise as well as convince the doubting officers of its feasibility. Although Billings was aware of the fertility of some of the western land, he did not share Power's feeling about its general potential. He was interested only in speculation. In the spring of 1875 Power approached Billings again and tried to convince him:

[I have] strong faith that "dirt" on the line of the N. P. is a good thing to handle and in the end will prove profitable. Scarcity of money, low prices and grasshoppers is a combination which coming all at one time, has a tendency to make things look down at present. We are at our worst times but I do not fear the future.[31]

Selling over 10,000,000 acres of company land in North Dakota was made more difficult by the availability of public domain. It was only natural that settlers would take the less costly government land. But these railroad officials, who now partially accepted Power's opinion, were not dismayed by this competition. One official wrote: "It does not matter very much to the company whether settlers locate upon our lands, or upon government lands. What we want to do is secure the rapid settlement and development of the lands tributary to our line."[32] By now rather than oppose the tendency to settle government land, the railroad officers reasoned that once it was settled, railroad land would be enhanced in value. In 1876 Power wrote to Billings:

I am making every effort to get settlers on the gov't lands and beginning to see good results from the work. Prospects for rapidly increasing settlement and enlarged area of cultivation were never better since the opening of our road there [Fargo] this spring. A good crop this season will settle the question for us and bring choice selected lands into active demand. Already there is considerable movement in this direction.[33]

Agreement on settlement was fine, but as one bonanza operator recalled years later, "We needed something larger than the small fields of the homesteaders to attract farmers of means and to give the road something to carry."[34] For that reason, the Northern Pacific spent vast sums of money to stimulate farm settlement, promote agricultural success, and expand its facilities to all parts of the Valley.[35] The Northern Pacific was interested in a commercialized agriculture, which not only expanded rapidly between 1876 and 1886, but also proved extremely profitable.[36]

Not all the information about the Northern Pacific country was favorable. As mentioned before Power had had reservations of his own. He had kept his ideas to himself but made some references in personal correspondence to officers of the railroad. Power and the railroad interests in general were disturbed by the dry years from 1864 to 1876 in the Red River Valley and the Dakotas and also the extensive locust damage between 1873 and 1877 in areas east and south of the Red River Valley in Minnesota. This dampened interest in settling that region. In 1876 Power wrote that the "hoppers" had done extensive damage as far east as Becker County and that they were still working in the Valley. He estimated that yields "would still average at least 20 bushels per acre. If the Red River Valley is cleaned out it is going to be a serious drawback to us." At the same time, he wrote of a "senseless Indian panic" in parts of Ottertail County which caused settlers to leave "by the scores," the results of which, Power thought, "will determine whether our work next year will be easy or hard."[37] In the following year a new source of opposition appeared in the form of adverse propaganda.

Major John Wesley Powell of the United States Geological Survey had urged in the 1870's that the western prairies be preserved as a national resource. In 1877 Major Powell read his essay, "On the Public Domain," to the convention of the National Academy of Sciences in Washington, D.C. In this talk, which received much publicity, he bluntly stated that he considered everything west of central Minnesota as a great arid region which could not support a large population. Angry at such talk, though he himself had shortly before held a similar opinion, Power wrote the St. Paul *Pioneer Press* that if Powell wanted to deter immigration, he would be greatly disappointed because his facts were "so far from the truth that everyone knows they are false." [38]

Power's letter to a friend in Washington, D.C. was even more caustic:

Major Powell may be a first class "rock sharp" but it is clear that as a judge of agri. value of western lands he can be written "an ass." Practical men looking for lands, prefer talking and to take the judgment of one who digs in the soil, even if he can neither read or write, rather than the opinion of a school of such specialists as Maj. Powell. The game is hardly [worth] the powder, yet as the press has published his absurdities, he may if time permits, [make] his answers through the press. [39]

With such information as Powell's being circulated, the difficulty of selling the land grant was increased. This could be overcome only by an intensive advertising campaign by the railroad.

The land department under Power tried every known scheme to sell its land. It offered land to settlers at 20 to 60 per cent off the list price, depending on the number of acres the farmer could put under cultivation within a specified time. Thus, the land contracts were written to encourage cultivation as rapidly as possible. [40] As an added inducement, settlers could buy on the installment plan with 10 per cent down and the balance divided over seven annual payments and carried at 7 per cent interest. The railroad also sold for cash and particularly encouraged bondholders to trade their bonds for land. The bonds were convertible at $110 in exchange for land. This was very attractive to the bondholders and, at the same time, enabled the railroad to reduce its indebtedness. [41] Power realized, however, that it would take more than attractive financial arrangements and the homesteader's small fields to draw sufficient capital and settlers to open the land and create business for the railroad.

It was decided that a large-scale advertising campaign should be activated to get settlers. Power, as land commissioner for the Dakota division, used every avenue open to him to advertise the Northern Pacific country. He had been nursing the idea of developing a spectacularly large farm for dramatic advertising. In Thomas H. Canfield of the board of directors of the Northern Pacific, he secured an ardent supporter of the large-farm scheme. Canfield suggested to the other directors that they establish such large farms in the Red River Valley to "raise wheat and prove by results what the land was worth, incidentally advertising the railroad." [42] However, neither Canfield nor Power was able to convince the directors of forming a pool in an effort to start such a farm.

Discussions on creating a large farm were intensified by the news of a bumper wheat crop produced by a homesteader near the Sheyenne River west of Fargo. This farmer had produced 1,600 bushels of No. 1 Scotch Fife wheat from 40 acres which sold for $1.25 a bushel. The local citizens went wild and eastern papers gave it much publicity. Visions of a $32,000 income from a $400 farm stimulated the purchase of bonds in exchange for land.[43]

By making use of the bumper wheat crop on the banks of the Sheyenne, Power was able to interest General George W. Cass, president of the Northern Pacific, in starting a large farm. Cass, together with Benjamin P. Cheney, another director, cashed in their bonds and in 1874 authorized Power to select land for them. The first selection, near present-day Casselton, was 10 sections for Cass and 8 for Cheney, a total of 11,520 acres.[44] Not all of the land was purchased directly from the Northern Pacific. Power corresponded frequently with Cass and Cheney relative to securing land from claimholders of government land and even purchased some with Indian or soldier's script.[45] When operations began, there were 13,440 acres in this original bonanza.[46] The Northern Pacific now had its large farm for advertising and making headlines.

An intensive advertising campaign was carried on both in Europe and America. To facilitate the handling of immigrants and settlers, the land office of the road was moved from New York to St. Paul and an immigration bureau was opened in Portland, Oregon. Agencies to secure immigrants were established in most western European nations. By 1883 there were 831 local agents in the British Isles alone, and 124 general agents, with many local agents under them, in Norway, Sweden, Denmark, Holland, Switzerland, and Germany. There were 632,-590 copies of Northern Pacific literature distributed from Liverpool during that year, and over 60,000 letters of inquiry were received by the Portland and St. Paul offices.[47] Advertising in Canadian and American newspapers was just as intense as in Europe.

In the spring of 1877, Power wrote: "We are advertising the Red River Valley well and effectively and letters indicate that we will have a good many well-to-do-farmers coming in this season to take up gov't and non-resident lands near road and station." [48] That same year Power sent each agency selling Northern Pacific preferred stock a thousand copies of a special edition of the *Fargo Times* which he said he had "cooked directly to immigration." [49] When the bonanzas were well established, Power asked the operators for their results which he submitted to leading eastern farm papers. He also asked for any information that would make "spicy" reading for immigrants.[50]

Newspapers and pamphlets were not the only means of advertising the great "Nile region of America," as some called Dakota. In the fall of 1880, the *Fargo Weekly Argus,* which was active in promoting the area, carried this item:

Mr. Land Commissioner James B. Power of the Northern Pacific Railroad being one of the sort of officials who never lets his right hand know what his left hand doeth, so to speak, has been hard at work for six weeks or more, arranging a special car to go down into the deserts of New England carrying specimen productions of the great wonderland of the New Northwest from Canaan to Egypt, as it were.[51]

This special car was, in fact, a complete exhibition train sponsored by the Northern Pacific to carry products from the Valley throughout eastern United States.

Power's promotional efforts proved successful; he turned financial disaster into a "bonanza" for those who adopted his scheme. Before he was finished, railroad bondholders were recovering their money, new settlers were moving in, land was being gobbled up at an unprecedented rate, and the population of Dakota was swelling beyond all imagination. It was one of America's great agricultural booms. Railroad expansion, combined with land colonization and agricultural advancement. The Panic of 1873, the shift from subsistence to a one-crop commercial agriculture, and the work of James B. Power gave the Red River Valley of the North a unique place in agricultural development.[52]

Disposal of Northern Pacific Land

There is little doubt that the great amount of land which was made available through the Northern Pacific land grant was in itself a "bonanza" for the speculator, the "land sharp," or "boomer" of that era. This spectacular phase of American agriculture was born out of the financial crisis of 1873 and the failure of the Northern Pacific. The railroad, in desperate financial straits, and with a great amount of unsalable land in its possession, decided on a gigantic land disposal program. Under this program, land could be secured in three basic ways, cash purchase, time payment, and bond exchange. In each case the price of land was determined by the method of purchase.[53]

The Northern Pacific needed a plan to save itself from its great interest burden on its depreciated securities, minimize the loss to the stock and bondholders, and at the same time open the Northern Pacific country for settlement. After 1873 the railroad was unable to raise money for new construction and on January 1, 1874, it failed to make interest payments on first mortgage bonds and dividends on its preferred stock. The bonds, which were to pay 7.3 per cent annual interest, had fallen in market value to below twenty dollars. The railroad was desperate to get out from under this heavy interest burden. Most bondholders rushed to sell their holdings for whatever they could realize from them, but some of the larger investors were unwilling to liquidate at a loss. In this dilemma all bondholders were encouraged by the board to exchange their bonds for land. Bonds were to be honored at $110 if exchanged for land. By setting the value of a bond at $110, the railroad was actually giving a bonus of 10 per cent over the face value of the bonds. The bond-land exchange was even more attractive because after 1873 the market value had fallen to less than 20 per cent of the face value of the bonds, hence, they could be sold for cash only at a great loss. Individuals with only a few bonds were not interested in going west just to save their investment, but the offer was appealing and profitable to the large bondholders. They did not have to go west because they could trade their bonds for large tracts of land, making it economically feasible to hire a manager and the necessary labor. This was exactly what James B. Power hoped would happen, for he was sure large, commercial, specialized farms would succeed. Power also hoped that such large-scale operations would do more to dramatize, and hence advertise the area than could be done by small farmers and homesteaders.

An advertisement in the *Fargo Weekly Argus* proved that the bond-land trade was open to all and was no under-the-counter operation: Railroad lands can be purchased with Preferred Stock of the company, which at its present market price brings the cash cost of land to a very low price. Reduced rates of Fare to Land Hunters. Low rates of fare and Freight to Settlers. Dec. 21, 1880, James B. Power, Land Commissioner.[54]

On September 28, 1875, the Northern Pacific was reorganized and the old first mortgage bonds were exchanged for preferred stock in the new company. The preferred stock, as was true of the bonds, were convertible to land at the rate of $110.[55] Between the Panic of 1873 and its reorganization in September, 1875, the railroad made every effort to get bondholders to convert their bonds into land. The adverse financial status of the country discouraged investment in new ventures. During this period, the bonds declined to about $9 or $10. At reorganization, the market value of the new preferred stock was $8 and common stock was $1.50.[56] Preferred stock and land were available to meet the demands of those desiring to use the stock-land exchange. Power, in correspondence with Frederick Billings, now a vice-president of the Northern Pacific and one of the most active speculators among the directors, wrote: "Pft. stock is sold by different parties here [Fargo] and at points on the line and there is considerable competition among the different dealers, holding prices down to eastern quotations, so that sales have within the past 30 days ranged from 12½ to 13½".[57] From the low of $8 at reorganization, market value of the preferred stock rose to $14 and $16.66 during 1877.[58] In 1878 for example Oliver Dalrymple made a considerable investment in land by using Northern Pacific preferred stock which had cost him $38 per share.[59]

Reorganization had little immediate effect on the actual value of the preferred stock. The average market value was only about $15 between September 29, 1875, and August 31, 1878.[60] With recovery continuing at a gradual rate from September 1, 1878, to June 30, 1879, the price of preferred stock averaged about $28, ranging from $18 to $50 and from July 1, 1879, to June 30, 1880, the average was $44.83. By November 30, 1880, the average market value had reached $53.[61] Financial conditions continued to improve. By 1882 those who had purchased Northern Pacific bonds and stocks from Jay Cooke and Company had received $1.56 for each dollar invested.[62]

The stock-land exchange proved the best way for the road to dispose of land. Between September, 1875, and August, 1878, over 70 per cent of the sales were to stockholders. Most of the large farms were a direct result of this conversion option, for nearly half of the 1,240,363 acres disposed of in that period went to 40 persons.[63] In the period from January 1 to June 20, 1874, the Northern Pacific accepted its old first mortgage bonds with a par value of $206,400 in exchange for land, in contrast to total cash sales of only $17,000.[64] In October, 1877, Power wrote to George Stark, a vice-president of the road, that he had received stock and cash for 83,192 acres, and had sold an additional 125,000 acres to easterners "for which the stock has not yet been received".[65]

The price of public domain had a direct bearing on the price of railroad land. If the railroad wanted to make cash sales, it could not ask too much more than the price of public domain, which was $2.50 per acre within the land grant and $1.25 beyond the grant. But the railroad could not wait until all public domain was occupied. To sell, it had to be competitive with the government. The cash price of railroad land in Dakota was also determined by the closeness to the Red River and the main line of transportation, assuming quality was a constant factor. The price of $1.25 per acre on public land beyond the grant affected only the more remote railroad sections. Most of the early settlers preferred to locate between the Red and James Rivers and within six or eight miles of the rail lines. The basic price range of the railroad land was from $2.50 to $10 per acre.[66]

Some land was held in reserve by the railroad in anticipation of future needs or increased value. For example, the company would not sell land within the limits of Fargo unless the purchaser promised in the contract to build a home or a place of business for himself within a specified time. The same was true for farm lands near villages along the line. In January, 1874, Power wrote to Major George G. Hibbard of the land department:

Friend Hibbard, the only tracts we have left in the immediate vicinity of Fargo that will be sold and those only for actual cultivation are . . . 320 acres at $8.25 . . . 320 acres for $8.50 . . . 320 acres for $10.50 an acre. [There are others that] I do not care to sell now at any reasonable figure, the amount of cultivation contracted for in that vicinity will enhance values to an extent that makes a reservation of some tracts a prudential measure.[67]

The railroad made a great profit from sale of this reserve land. Although the road had plotted Fargo in 1874, it speculated with certain lots for several years. In 1880, it auctioned thirty-four lots for $30,230, the highest lot bringing $2,375.[68] Within a decade after the railroad's construction in Cass County, improved farm land within five miles of the line sold for as much as $25 per acre.[69]

Buyers were willing to pay a higher price for land when they could pay with stock. This competition caused the price of both land and stock to rise. From June 15, 1872, to September 30, 1873, the date of the Cooke failure, land prices averaged $5.58 per acre. From October 1, 1873, to September 28, 1875, the date of reorganization, sales averaged $5.04.[70] Railroad land sold slowly in the early years due to the competition from public domain. Prior to July 1, 1874, only 130,929 acres had been sold out of the total of 743,941 acres the railroad had received of its grant to that date.[71]

It was not until the first important bonanza sale to Cass and Cheney was consummated that land sales began to speed up. This purchase was important, not only for the dramatics associated with its size, but also because it showed the value of the bond-conversion feature. The actual cash cost per acre for Cass and Cheney varied from $0.46 to $0.60.[72] The Grandins later purchased land at a cash cost of $0.43, and their last purchase in September, 1877, cost them $0.16 per acre. This was made possible by purchasing preferred stock at $15 and trading it for land listed at $1.23 per acre.[73] This was an exceptional purchase, for even at the low point of the bonds or the preferred stock, most of the land cost between $0.37 and $1.65 per acre. Power estimated that from September 29, 1875, to August 31, 1878, the average cash cost of most of the land was $0.65 per acre, based on a land price of $4.38 and an average market value of the stock at $15.[74]

After the initial bonanzas were established, the demand for preferred stock increased moderately. Power said that this was "encouraging [the] stock owners to hold, and discouraging speculators from buying." [75] After 1878, when most of the close-in and choice land was taken, people were less willing to convert their stocks for land. The market value of the stock averaged $28 during much of 1878 and 1879. To offset the rising value of stocks, the railroad was forced to reduce the list price of land to $1.50 and $3.50 per acre, making the cash cost through conversion from $0.50 to $1.35 per acre.[76]

When the market value of the stock reached $50 by June, 1880, and only more remote western land was available, it became necessary to reduce the list price of land again to maintain sales. Power had forecast this in the spring of 1879.[77] At that time he wrote to an eastern broker: "The demand for stock here [Fargo] for conversion into land has almost entirely ceased and I have not kept posted on quotations. . . . Where is the pft. going to? Our general interests are helped by its advance, but land sales will be materially reduced by its enhanced value." [78]

By 1880 the railroad found it more difficult to sell its land at the higher list price and reported that most of the sales were "in bulk on the extreme limits of the grant and lower grades near the road. West of the James River and culled lots inside of the 'takings' during the past eight years, . . . under ordinary circumstances unsalable at any price to either settler or speculator." The average list price was reduced to $2.53, but because stocks had risen to $53, the cost price of land had increased to $1.34 per acre.[79] When the list price of land had dropped to an average of $2.22, Power informed Billings: "Our best lands are now so far from track that it is not easy to sell. Settlers will not go to those remote lands so long as gov't lands nearer road are open for entry. We can sell only to speculators and . . . low figures must be given to attract attention." [80]

A short time later Power predicted the end of the stock-land trade:

The present average price of stock makes these lands [between the Sheyenne and James Rivers] range from $1.50 to $1.75 *cash* cost, and unless the purchasers can work up some scheme by which they can be settled, and their product brought to the road by other than wagon transportation I cannot see other than very slow advances in value for them.[81]

Not all land sales by the stock transfer method were to bonanza farmers or speculators. Groups desiring to settle a single community could purchase large blocks of land. The land department had encouraged entire groups from eastern states to settle in communities along the line. Power made references to such groups as early as 1874 when several Canadian families made a joint application for fifteen sections of land. By making a single application, they were sure of getting a large block for their own community and also have priority in securing bonds for the purpose of conversion.[82] One of the earliest community promoters was an Englishman, Richard Sykes, who represented an English syndicate that purchased 45,000 acres northwest of Jamestown, near present-day Sykeston, for the purpose of developing the land and settling the area.[83] A Mr. Davenport, an "Iowa capitalist," secured the cooperation of Jamestown citizens and purchased a block of twenty-two sections west of that village. Davenport erected buildings, drilled wells, broke the sod, and then offered it to tenants or buyers in small farms.[84] Within a year after the purchase, the land was being advertised as improved farms for sale or rent.

A close check of the movement of settlers over the Northern Pacific as given in the *Fargo Argus* reveals that there were many communities settled by such promotions. As soon as branch lines were built and the outlying land became more accessible, other groups did the same. A group from Grand Rapids, Michigan, settled in Grand Rapids, North Dakota. Two groups, one from Piper City, Illinois, and the other from Canada, settled at Buffalo. Amenia, Oriska, Sanborn, Mardell, Cooperstown, Carrington, and Tower City were created by community transfers. An eastern syndicate purchased 32,000 acres in Burleigh County in 1883 for $5 an acre list price.[85] In May, 1884, an Iowa syndicate secured 30,000 acres in one unit northwest of Carrington.[86]

One of the last community purchases through stock exchange came in 1884 with the settlement of LaMoure. Land along the southwestern branch out of Fargo had risen to $7 an acre, but by securing a block of stock at $48 on the market and trading it in on land, the cost price for this land was only $3.06.[87] Some community projects failed, but those were few compared to the many successful settlements.

Many purchasers of railroad land were private settlers of limited means. Some purchased railroad land to enlarge their homesteads. Although the railroad was anxious to dispose of its land through the stock-exchange plan for financial reasons, it would have preferred to sell it in small lots, on time payments, to individual settlers. To sell land in large blocks and still keep out the speculator was a real problem. The Northern Pacific officials foresaw that speculators would bring no general development along the road and would do little to bring freight traffic. Land buyers had to be induced to cultivate. In 1874 Power recommended a "plan of offering reductions from appraisals in proportion to the amount of cultivation the purchaser would agree to make, this becoming part of the consideration in contract." [88] Under this contract, individuals could buy up to 320 acres from the Northern Pacific but were required to settle on and improve the land. The general terms of the contracts were 10 per cent down and a 10 per cent payment on the principal each year, plus 7 per cent interest on the unpaid balance. On purchases of very small farms, one-sixth down was required with the balance in five annual payments, plus interest. [89] A rebate of 25 per cent was given to all purchasers on the acres actually broken within two years. [90] Additional incentives up to 60 per cent discount were given when land was put under cultivation. The railroad attempted to fit a land policy to every pocketbook. [91]

Many who purchased railroad land on the installment basis had difficulty making the payments or failed to live up to other terms of the contract, such as settlement and cultivation. The Northern Pacific was extremely lax in the enforcement of contractual requirements because it was interested in good public relations and encouraging, rather than discouraging small settlers. However, it occasionally was severe with those who were slow in making payments. Power once remarked that the only time his department had a balance was on the day it opened for business. Because collections were so slow, he made frequent excuses for not being able to transfer more funds from his department. Foreclosure notices were occasionally sent to scare the purchasers into making their payments, even though the railroad had little intention of repossession. [92]

The Grandins secured their farm under most unusual circumstances. They lived in Tidoute, Pennsylvania, where they were active in lumber, oil, and banking enterprises, but had no money invested in the Northern Pacific. However, Jay Cooke and Company had borrowed from the Grandin bank and when Cooke's firm closed its doors, the Grandins were left holding an $88,600 note. Cooke offered to set-

tle for ten cents on the dollar or give the Grandins $60,000 face value
of Northern Pacific bonds which, after 1875, were converted to preferred stock. By taking the bonds and exchanging them for land, the
Grandins had a chance to realize full recovery on their loan. However,
with their other extensive holdings, they were not willing to get into
farming unless it proved profitable and not too time consuming. It
was decided that before they would take Cooke's railroad bonds,
John L. Grandin should go to Dakota to determine the value of the
land.[93]

In May, 1875, John L. Grandin arrived in Fargo to inspect the
land. He made the acquaintance of Colonel H. S. Back, a Fargo realtor and boomer who had extensive knowledge of land in the entire
Valley. Back understood the true richness of the soil north of Fargo
along the Elm and Goose Rivers, where he took the dubious John L.
Grandin. On their journey north from Fargo, they met a settler who
was living in a dugout cave along the river. Grandin was so impressed
with the settler's small patch of wheat that he decided immediately
to take the bonds and purchase land.[94]

Back and Grandin traveled around the area to select the desired
land. They had difficulty distinguishing between railroad and government sections because they were unable to find the surveyor's corner
posts which had been rubbed off by the buffalo. However, they located a baseline post with rocks piled around it. Back and Grandin
secured permission from the Moorhead office of the Department of
Interior to measure out the land Grandin had decided to purchase.
With the aid of a compass, and a handkerchief tied to the spoke of a
buggy wheel, they measured thirty-six railroad sections (odd num-
bered) in two townships. A wagon loaded with cedar posts followed
and a new post was placed at each corner of the sections measured.
At this time Grandin also secured four government sections with the
use of Sioux half-breed scrip, making his original purchase nearly
26,000 acres. By using scrip, the Grandins secured public domain for
$2.20 per acre.[95]

Grandin returned to Pennsylvania where he discovered that the
market value of the preferred stock had dropped from $22 to $10.50.
He immediately purchased 1,000 shares and wired Oliver Dalrymple,
whom he had met while in Fargo, to select more land farther north
on the Goose River. When this transaction was complete, the Grandins possessed 41,764 acres.[96] The land which Grandin had selected in
the first purchase was listed at $4.50 per acre, but by promising to
erect buildings and develop 2,500 acres at once, a $1.50 rebate per
acre was granted.

The Grandins, who had the largest bonanza in the Valley, eventually secured over a hundred sections, most of which came from the Northern Pacific. They secured forty-three sections about thirty miles north of Fargo between the Elm and Goose Rivers which included four sections bordering the Red River. A second holding of twenty-six sections was secured six miles farther north on the Goose River near Hillsboro. The third, and best-known Grandin farm, containing thirty-six sections farther west on the Goose River, was called the Mayville farm. The Grandins also owned land east of the Red River near Halstad and Georgetown, Minnesota.[97]

The Baldwins had the only major bonanza not formed directly from the Northern Pacific land grant. It was located primarily in Dickey County, around Ellendale, North Dakota. This farm was started by George Baldwin of Appleton, Wisconsin, in 1890 when many of the great bonanzas were already beginning to disappear. He took advantage of the depressed economic condition of the homesteaders and purchased land directly from them, mostly in quarter section (160 acres) units. His cost per acre ranged from $1.25 to $3.25 with most quarter section homesteads costing from $200 to $500.[98]

Significance of Public Domain to the Bonanzas

Bonanza owners acquired public domain by various methods. By collusion with migrant settlers or with bonanza employees, the owners could secure large holdings of government land within a short period of time. A homesteader could secure title to his land six months after filing his claim by commuting, which meant paying the full $2.50 per acre within the land grant or $1.25 beyond the grant. Other homesteaders purchased their land under the pre-emption laws. Between 1871 and 1890, 29,000 settlers and homesteaders purchased 4.6 million acres under the pre-emption law or by commuting. In 1890 settlers or speculators had started to acquire over 11.6 million acres on original entries for which they would make final proof.[99] Much of the land owned by bonanza operators was purchased direct from pre-empters or homesteaders, either before or after they had secured title. This was possible through relinquishment, which was legally recognized by the government.

Land was often secured by questionable and illegal means, but the abuses were so widespread they were difficult to prevent. Many well-founded tales relate of men who homesteaded sections in the names of their mules or hired men.[100]

Not all land secured from homesteaders was given up voluntarily. Power was always on the lookout for land that had been claimed, but was not being properly managed by the claimants. The chief essentials of securing land in this manner were a close contact with those in the government land office, a roving self-styled land inspector, and a good attorney. It was the "duty" of the "inspector" to report to the government land office any claimant who was not living up to his contract. Then the government officials notified the claimant that he was in danger of losing his claim. About that same time, a land agent would appear at the homesteader's farm offering to purchase it for cash. With proper timing, the temptation of a cash offer and a little pressure from the land office or attorney, the defaulting homesteader could be induced to sell. He almost always realized a profit, but still did not get the full market value because individuals did not care to bid against a bonanza operator, particularly if his land surrounded the homestead involved. Many homesteaders actually operated with the intention of doing what has been described above.[101]

Bonanza owners tried to obtain scrip to purchase government land for the purpose of making their farms solid blocks. Scrip had been used in March, 1876, to secure three government sections which made part of the Cass-Cheney bonanza a solid block.[102] Power, who was working for Cass and Cheney, had secured this scrip in small amounts.[103] Indian scrip was quickly taken and was virtually out of existence by the end of 1877.[104]

Speculation and Large Land Purchases

Much of the early economic history of North Dakota revolves around speculation in real estate. Speculation in land was desirable because it helped attract settlers. Speculators in North Dakota were typical of those found everywhere on the frontier and especially along the route of the Northern Pacific. This was new country; it had possibilities. The psychology of speculation prepared the way for the "Great Dakota Boom." Great profits from buying and selling land could be made if enough people came to Dakota to create a demand for it. It is unfair to say that the Northern Pacific wanted speculation; it wanted farmers. The farmer was the chief motivator of speculation and its major beneficiary.

It is difficult to distinguish between those who were pure speculators and actual settlers who were motivated by speculation. Any individual who invests in land is a speculator of sorts for he hopes his land will be rising in value while he is farming it. This speculation is desirable for it has been the major factor of success for many farmers. Most investors in the Northern Pacific country must be considered speculators, including homesteaders, bonanza farmers, city real-

tors, or land buyers who had no active interest in farming. These
people did exactly what those in any other era would have done.

The price of farm land rose as a result of railroad construction, immigration, and good weather. In March, 1876, Power predicted that
land values would double in one year if the Cass-Cheney-Dalrymple
operations proved a success. Confidence in rising land prices caused
railroad officials to buy government as well as railroad land.[105] After
the government land along the main line was taken, the price of railroad land rose rapidly, especially in the more densely settled areas.
The stimulus of rising land values caused many people to purchase
land far beyond their ability to cultivate or pay for.

Land prices started a natural spiral upward from the first rumor
that a railroad was going to be built. The struggle to find out where
the railroad was going to cross the Red River dramatizes speculation
at its height. Boom psychology was caused by professional "boomers"
who bought land for resale at a profit after they had done a thorough
job of advertising, or "booming" their purchase. The *Fargo Argus*
gave a typical case of booming:

In the spring of 1881 Dr. Glasgow sold two lots to Mr. McCarther
for $400. On the same day McCarther sold these lots for $450 to E.
Page. In August Page sold them to a Mr. Benton for $700. On No-
vember 15, Mr. F. Mackey bought them for $900. He planned to
build a house on one lot and sell the other for $900.[106]

Speculators soon began selling some of their land at greatly increased prices. One of the first large sales by a speculator-farmer was
that of R. Hadwin who owned more than twelve sections in the
Wheatland area, twenty-five to thirty miles west of Fargo. Hadwin
secured his land in 1876 at a list price of $4.50 per acre (his actual
cash cost is not known). After breaking the prairie and harvesting
two crops, he offered two sections, with the crop, for $28 per acre. His
advertisement appeared in the *Argus* on June 23, 1880, and on July 7
an article in that paper stated he had sold two sections with crop for
$33,600 ($26.25 per acre). This was a 600 per cent increase in the list
price of four years earlier.[107] Hadwin planned to develop and sell all
of his land in this manner. At the time of this sale, he stated that he
had three sections which were being improved and seven sections
which he planned to make into farms with the intent of selling them
on the next big rise in land prices. Hadwin had broken the sod and
worked the land so that the buyer could receive an immediate income
without much additional expense. The two crops he had harvested
off that land repaid him for those efforts.

Some speculators did not break the sod. They were content to wait and take their mark-up in price when the demand increased. W. A. Kindred, a Northern Pacific employee, was one of those who was satisfied with the natural price rise. Kindred paid no more than $0.50 to $1 actual cash cost per acre on land purchased during the stock-land exchange. By April, 1881, he had sold 11,000 acres in northern Cass County for $63,000. This represented at least a 600 per cent profit for having the patience to wait for the price to rise.[108] S. C. Dalrymple, Oliver's brother, broke the sod on his farm and held it until 1881 when he sold 2,200 acres for $20 an acre. He paid as high as $1.40 cash cost per acre, but even at that price he profited greatly.[109] In March, 1882, S. C. Dalrymple made another sale of 2,160 acres near Mapleton to General George Howe, an oil producer from Bradford, Pennsylvania, for $37 an acre. Land near Eldridge, west of Jamestown, that had been broken but not cropped, was available at $18 per acre in lots of 640 acres.[110] As far west as Bismarck, land values were increasing sharply. Part of the Clark farm, four miles east of that city, was sold to Colonel S. P. Magill for $25 per acre.[111] The Amenia and Sharon Land Company sold unimproved land in southwestern Cass County for $10 to $12.50 per acre.[112]

After choice government and railroad land was less readily available, settlers began to buy from speculators. The speculators subdivided their large holdings which they sold in small lots for all the market would bear and offered extensive financing to lure buyers. Power managed the private holdings of several of the railroad directors who were speculating in land. When approached by prospective purchasers, he would often offer privately held lands rather than company holdings. In 1877 Power wrote: "I have control of some very choice tracts of land in the Red River Valley . . . owned by eastern parties for sale from $4 to $10 per acre on long-time and easy payments.[113]

Large blocks of Northern Pacific land were sold to speculators who were interested only in the price rise. Power lists those who were interested only in speculation in a letter to A. H. Barney, chairman of a special land commission created at the time of his, Power's, release. From June 15, 1872, to September 30, 1873, no exceptionally large purchase was listed. The 6 largest buyers secured 13,831 acres for an average of 2,305 acres, in contrast to the settlers' 123-acre purchase. A total of 46,119 acres were sold at an average price of $5.85 per acre.[114]

From September 30, 1873 to September 29, 1875, a total of 483,141 acres at an average price of $5.04 was sold to 1,220 purchasers, but of that amount, 304,965 acres were sold to only 23 purchasers. The average purchase of these 23 buyers was 13,259 acres. The first and largest purchase to Charlemagne Tower contained 28,240 acres in contrast to the average sale of 303 acres for the small buyers.[115]

After the reorganization of the railroad in 1875 the list price from September 29, 1875, to August 31, 1878, was $4.38 and a total of 1,240,363 acres were sold. Power stated: "About 500 actual settlers who purchased 80 to 320 acres, the balance were sold to small holders [of stocks] or speculators." Nearly half, or 587,270 acres, was sold to 40 persons for an average purchase of 14,682 acres. The other 1,458 buyers averaged 447 acres each. Some of the big purchases at this time were: J. Dunlop, 10,900 acres, improved and settled by Scotch Canadians; F. Billings, 28,672 acres; improved by Mosher; J. Mosher, 19,020 acres, improved, all occupied in small farms.[116]

From September 1, 1878, to June 30, 1879, 362,344.77 acres were sold for an average list price of $4.51. Of this amount, 150,595 acres were sold to 12 buyers for an average of 12,550 acres. The other 315 buyers averaged only 747 acres. Power said that rising stock and land prices discouraged the speculators at this time. Large buyers listed were: Frank Semple, 5,640 acres, George W. Christian, 28,060 acres.[117]

The period from July 1, 1879, to June 30, 1880, saw a total Dakota sales of 224,842.51 acres averaging $2.61 per acre going to 242 buyers. The 10 largest buyers secured 112,115 acres or 11,211 acres each, while the other 232 averaged 550 acres. The largest buyers at this time were: Carrington and Casey, 17,222 acres; Steele and Small, 11,628 acres; with a later addition of 27,620 acres for a total of 48,000; J. W. Pence, 32,960 acres, 52,120 purchased later for a total of 85,080.[118]

During the final period from July 1, 1880, to November 30, 1880, there were 173 purchases for 440,651.41 acres. Of those, 25 purchasers secured 371,474 acres for an average of 14,860 acres. The others settled for 572 acres each. The list price was reduced to $2.53 per acre causing a sharp rise in sales. Large buyers were: Carrington and Casey, 18,560 acres which were added to their previous purchase for a total of 35,782; J. B. Colgate, 12,646 acres; Griggs and Foster, 35,756 acres; F. J. Cooper, 34,080 acres; F. J. Buxton, 5,760 acres.[119]

Big buyers not otherwise listed were: Charles M. Reed, 14,300 acres; Howell D. Clark, 25,500 acres; Charles W. Hassler, 17,500 acres; Norman H. Galusha, 15,300 acres; B. S. Russell, trustee, about 20,000 acres; H. S. Back, 7,000 acres; Cochran and Newport, total unknown; R. J. Green, total unknown; Davenport Farms, S. L. Glaspell, 10,240 acres; and R. Hadwin, 7,680 acres.[120]

In all of these transactions the Northern Pacific was successful in selling its land. Up to 1878 the average land sale to individuals was

576 acres, considerably larger than the claims made by seekers of government land, and an indication that the road had helped foster a new phase of farming. Northern Pacific land sales to November 30, 1880, totalled 2,851,314 acres and averaged $4.08 per acre list price.[121] On May 31, 1881, the railroad reported that it had only 13,760 acres left to sell in Cass County. The list price by this time had risen to $7 per acre.[122] At that time it had sold most of its land south of the main line for 100 miles west of the Red River.[123] The week ending March 23, 1883, was probably the top week in Northern Pacific land sales in North Dakota when 508,608 acres, or nearly 5 per cent of the total grant, were sold. In that same week, 43,840 acres were secured by settlers of public domain through the Fargo Land Office.[124]

Activity in the land department declined rapidly after 1883. In the year ending June 30, 1884, only 268,395 acres were sold in the Dakota Division. Sales dwindled and little choice land was available. The railroad reported it had only 6,029.86 acres remaining in the state as of June 30, 1908.[125]

Power was a leading speculator who profited by financing his land sales. When he sold, he did so in the smallest plots possible and nearly always on the installment basis. To one buyer Power wrote: "Sec. 1 adjoining Station of Mapleton is for sale only on the following terms, $10,000 . . . Terms $2,000 down, balance on five or seven years time in equal annual payments at 10 pr. ct. yearly interest." [126]

Some of the speculators relied on others for financial assistance. Oliver Dalrymple, one of the greatest land speculators who was penniless when he came to Dakota, secured much land from other speculators who financed him. He did not worry how much his debts were as long as he could increase his land holdings, counting on time and rising land prices being in his favor. He started his accumulation of land the day he became involved in the Cass-Cheney farming operations. One of his purchases was from Frederick Billings early in the spring of 1878 for two sections of land. Dalrymple stated frankly that he had only a limited amount of cash but he did have spare teams and equipment to get the land under cultivation at once. He offered $0.75 down per acre and the balance on terms, but Billings, through Power, demanded $1 per acre down. Because some settlers were willing to buy parts of the land involved for $7.50 per acre, Dalrymple consented to pay $6.66 per acre, $1 down and the balance to be carried at 10 per cent payable in 5 equal payments.[127]

Some directors of the Northern Pacific made a personal profit from the financial crisis of the road and the development of Dakota. Many early state and railroad leaders were involved in speculation. Towns and counties of the state named after these men are recognition of their position and influence in early history. Early in 1876 Power advised Billings to make application to purchase certain government sections. "Buy sections 10 and 14 Twp. 139 R 52. They are nearest the road and both good tracts. These lands will cost you $1.87 per acre, including all land office fees and recording papers." [128] Billings bought and sold constantly and was interested only in short-term profits, never indicating any desire to get into farming operations. Several times Power attempted to encourage him to enter farming but never with any success. Billings held his land until settlers came in and developed the government sections. This automatically enhanced its value. He then sold on time with low down payments and a high interest charge for an easy profit.[129]

At this time Power wrote:

I . . . think your lands will in time bring your figure, the govt. secs. in 138/52 are being well taken by actual settlers and now we can expect some demands for your lands in that twp. next year as well as for these in 139/52. Your N. P. investment is going to be a better thing in its present shape than it ever could be by remaining in Bonds or Pfd. stock.[130]

Men such as Billings had invested heavily in Northern Pacific securities and had lost much when the road collapsed. This was their chance to recover.

Railroad officials had first choice of new land before sales were opened to the public. After discussing in detail several areas where land was still available, Power requested of Billings: "If concluding not to buy, please advise early that the Tp. [township] may be put in open market again." [131] A short time later Power informed Billings that he had reserved some more land for him.[132]

Charlemagne Tower of Philadelphia was a leading speculator in railroad lands. In 1871 Tower had purchased $56,000 worth of Northern Pacific bonds in Jay Cooke's pool. He had done so on the belief that the land which secured the bonds was a good investment. By June, 1872, he had secured $250,000 worth of bonds and was elected to the board of directors of the railroad.[133] Tower was one of the first large buyers of company land. He traded bonds for more than 105,000 acres along the railroad. Of that amount, 65,877 acres were in wheat lands of the Red River Valley and the other 40,000 acres were in farm and timber land of Washington Territory. Tower purchased most of his land through Luman H. Tenney and Company of Duluth and Glyndon, Minnesota.[134] In Barnes County he had fifty-eight sections which stretched fifteen miles along the main line. Power, writing to

Tower, said that everyone asked why there were no settlers on that strip of land. Power advised him to offer some at a low price on easy terms to get it settled. It would then become income property as far as the Northern Pacific was concerned and also help increase the value of Tower's other land. Later Tower encouraged settlement, but he withheld much land waiting for the natural price rise. Reselling at a profit was his sole aim. In Minnesota he paid an average $4.40 list price per acre (cash cost not determined) and sold for from $7 to $10 on easy terms at 10 per cent interest.[135]

Local citizens were aware of speculation by railroad officers and were critical because they wanted to do the same. When the officials of the Northern Pacific raised the minimum price of land from $2.50 to $5 an acre, people along the line opposed it as a misuse of the land grant and said it was playing into the hands of speculators which would divert settlement to other parts of the country. The public said the railroad officers, many of whom owned from 30,000 to 50,000 or more acres, were trying to enrich themselves. The officers defended themselves by replying that conditions had warranted a rise in land prices but Power had opposed it.[136]

The *Fargo Argus* of that day seldom printed information unfavorable to the Northern Pacific or its officers. The editor was a friend of many of the officers and was fully aware that the prosperity of Fargo hinged, to a great extent, on the blessing or curse that the railroad bestowed on it. However, news occasionally did appear about speculation and the fight which developed among various officials of the company. Headlines reading, "Key directors of N. P. in great land speculation ring. Blame Power and Kindred" was the first hint that something was wrong.[137] At this time Power was released by the Northern Pacific. The land-price feud was the major reason for his release, but there were also personal disagreements. Power was replaced by his bitter enemy, Colonel R. M. Newport. An editorial from the *Jamestown Alert* stated that Colonel Newport thought he was putting himself in solid with the Northern Pacific management by raising land prices and also by trying to break up Kindred and Power. The *Argus* stated: "His $5 an acre plan apparently cost the company thousands of dollars."[138] The road revised its price down to $4 an acre which, the paper said, "pleases none of the parties concerned."[139] The *Argus's* closing comments on the feud were:

Henry Villard, of the Northern Pacific road, is quoted as saying, "If C. F. Kindred is a thief, so are we all, for we have all bought land with bonds which is all he has done, and as we are stockholders we would not be likely to steal from ourselves." This is the whole case in a nutshell as reported by the editor of the *Argus*.[140]

A factor which encouraged individuals to speculate in land was the low or complete absence of a land tax. There was a definite refusal to make tax payments, even in cases when assessments were made. Some of these "non-payments" were legal; others were not and court cases were necessary to determine who was right. Some settlers had to pay back taxes on land purchased from the railroad but the company did not pay taxes on the grant. Protests were frequent and to the point. As the *Fargo Argus* pointed out:

> The fact is, the county [Cass] officers discriminate in favor of the railroad company, and that is all there is to it. If the odd sections belong to the railroad, then those lands should be taxed. If the company do [sic.] not own them, how do they sell the lands and give warranty deeds? Too [sic.] thin gentlemen.[141]

There was a great deal of Granger legislation against the railroad in an effort to secure taxes. H. S. Back of Fargo and Asa Sargent of Traill County were credited with originating the first railroad taxation bill. This took much courage because the Northern Pacific had been a great benefactor to the area and was very powerful. Back defended himself by stating that it was "legitimate taxation on property amply able to pay."[142] Representative E. P. Wells of Stutsman County was not particularly interested in taxing the railroad, but wanted to place a heavier tax on the absentee land speculators who controlled 400,000 acres of land in that county.[143] A clear decision as to when taxes should be levied against former railroad land was not made by the courts until 1883. The land grant was not taxable initially, but when it became taxable remained a point of dispute. Title was not always immediately passed to those on the "inside" who purchased land, and in this way it was kept off the tax rolls.[144]

Comments about taxes shed much light on how important this was to the land speculator. Power, who had just paid $92.16 taxes on sections 10 and 14, T. 139, R. 52 ($0.072 per acre), wrote to Billings:

> It is well your odd secs. are not taxable, yet the high rate is the result of so little property in the country that can be taxed. The question that perplexes the county officials very much and resident owners of taxable property who are carrying the burden of county expenses and making every effort to compel the authorities to test the question of right to tax odd Secs. and I would not be surprised to see some move in that direction next season.[145]

Power, as a large land owner, had his tax worries too. To B. W.

Benson, his attorney at Valley City who was handling certain land sales for him, he wrote:

Now as to taxes. All are paid except 1885 and 1886, those of 1885 are without doubt illegal and do not have to be paid and in due time an order of the court will be obtained that will clear the records. Those of 1886 are exactly in same condition unless the N.P.RR. Co. paid their survey fees *before* the date when the 1886 taxes were assessed.[146]

Property was put on the tax list when the Northern Pacific surveyed the land and paid the survey fee. Power advised railroad officers not to sell their land "until the odd Sec. become taxable . . . at the same time, however, be ready to take advantage of a rush and unload while demand is warm." [147] This is a clear indication that individuals were securing title to land but still preventing it from being placed on the tax rolls. To Kindred, in the land department office, Power wrote that Billings did not want to sell any land for less than original cost, commissions, plus 10 per cent extra but "I think however that the determination of the tax question will settle his [Billings] views; if the tax levy of last year holds he will want to unload about as quick as he can." [148] In regard to that levy, Power advised all concerned that "the tax is too excessive to pay without first being fully assured that it cannot be contested." [149] Later, Power contacted his superiors and advised that a Northern Pacific attorney "Col. Gray wrote to contest taxes in Dakota on the grounds of being excessive and irregular as well as that under present laws of the U.S. any odd Sec. were not taxable." [150]

Many of the larger land holders, including Cass, Cheney, Billings, Power, and Dalrymple, joined in a protest of the tax levy. As a result, the Cass County commissioners granted a one-third to one-half reduction in the 1878 levy and an abatement of penalty and interest. Power warned that future reductions would probably not be so likely because Judge Stearn's decision in the Morrison case "Is being taken by the officials in Dakota as a good law upon which they evince a disposition to stand." [151] Power very wisely commented to Billings:

Not to influence your decision but to advise you on the sentiment of the people. I would say, that considerable unfavorable comment is made because you do not pay, not that you are the only delinquent but because your position is one that makes you the "shining mark" —the question seems to now resolve itself to one of policy and I do not wish to advise, but will be governed by your wishes and if payment is to be made will effect the best settlement possible in all the counties.[152]

Because of the advent of taxation, the land owners who were able to retain their holdings were those who developed bonanzas. The speculators sold their land rather than be faced with the obligation of an annual tax. Land taxes proved to be a factor in the eventual control of the land of northern Dakota. At a later date it was also income and corporation taxes that caused at least one of the great remaining bonanzas to discontinue operations.

FOOTNOTES

[1] Margaret L. Brown, "Asa Whitney and His Pacific Railroad Campaign," *Mississippi Valley Historical Review*, XX (1953), p. 211.

[2] U. S., *Statutes at Large*, XIII, 367.

[3] Hafen and Rister, p. 515.

[4] Eugene V. Smalley, *History of the Northern Pacific Railroad* (New York, 1883), p. 51.

[5] *Ibid.*, pp. 79-97.

[6] John L. Harnsberger, "Jay Cooke and Minnesota: The Formative Years of the Northern Pacific Railroad 1868-1873" (unpublished Ph.D. dissertation, Dept. of History, University of Minnesota), p. 2. (Hereafter cited as Harnsberger, "Jay Cooke and Minnesota.")

[7] U. S., *Statutes at Large*, XIII, 367.

[8] Benton, *The Journal of Land and Public Utility Economics*, Vol. I, p. 3; Harnsberger, "Jay Cooke and Minnesota," p. 45.

[9] Benjamin H. Hibbard, *A History of the Public Land Policies* (New York, 1924), p. 264.

[10] U. S., *Statutes at Large*, XIII, p. 365.

[11] Smalley, pp. 125-132; U. S., *Statutes at Large*, XV, p. 255.

[12] Harnsberger, "Jay Cooke and Minnesota," pp. 41-42.

[13] Ellis Paxon Oberholtzer, *Jay Cooke: Financier of the Civil War* (Philadelphia, 1907), Vol. II, pp. 153-158.

[14] Larson, *Jay Cooke, Private Banker*, p. 263.

[15] Harnsberger, "Jay Cooke and Minnesota," pp. 50-52.

[16] Oberholtzer, Vol. II, pp. 158-160.

[17] *Ibid.*, p. 158; Larson, *Jay Cooke, Private Banker*, pp. 288-295.

[18] Larson, *Jay Cooke, Private Banker*, pp. 292-294; Harnsberger, "Jay Cooke and Minnesota," pp. 59-63.

[19] Larson, *Jay Cooke, Private Banker*, pp. 281-283.

[20] Larson, *Jay Cooke, Private Banker*, p. 283; Harnsberger, "Jay Cooke and Minnesota," pp. 69-71; Hedges, *Mississippi Valley Historical Review*, XIII, 313-314; John L. Harnsberger, "Land, Lobbies, Railroads and the Origins of Duluth," *Minnesota History*, XXXVIII (Sept., 1960), 91-92.

[21] Harnsberger, *Minn. Hist.*, XXXVIII, 92; Larson, *Jay Cooke, Private Banker*, pp. 295, 299.

[22] Larson, *Jay Cooke, Private Banker*, pp. 328-329, 341-349, 356-357.

[23] *Ibid.*, pp. 350, 413.

[24] Harnsberger, "Jay Cooke and Minnesota," pp. 234-235.

[25] Benton, *The Journal of Land and Public Utility Economics*, Vol. I, p. 3.

[26] Hedges, *Mississippi Valley Historical Review*, XIII, 314-315.

[27] Power to Helen G. Putnam, Jan. 5, 1895, NDIRS, File 309.

[28] James B. Power, "Bits of History Connected with the Early Days of the Northern Pacific Railway and the Organization of its Land Department." NDSHS, *Collections*, Vol. III (1910), p. 343.

[29] "Dakota Farming," *Cultivator and Country Gentleman*, XLI (June 1, 1876), p. 340. This is one in a series of many articles by Power submitted to farm magazines of that day. His Letterbooks contain copies of many of his letters to the editors.

³⁰ Power to Billings, June 20, 1874, NDIRS, File 309.

³¹ Power to Billings, April 13, 1875, NDIRS, File 309. Power not only had faith in Dakota, but had come to love it. Personal notes in his Letterbooks clearly portray his strong feelings toward the "N.P. Country," as he called it.

³² Hedges, *Mississippi Valley Historical Review*, XIII, p. 331.

³³ Power to Billings, June 8, 1876, NDIRS, File 309. Power is referring to the opening of the road in the spring of 1876 after service had been nearly at a standstill in the winter season.

³⁴ *Fargo Forum*, Jan. 18, 1927, p. 1. An interview with Robert Reed, manager of the Amenia and Sharon Land Company after 1912.

³⁵ Hedges, *Mississippi Valley Historical Review*, XIII, p. 341.

³⁶ Murray, *Agricultural History*, XXXI, p. 58.

³⁷ Power to Billings, July 15, 1876, NDIRS, File 309. For more details on the grasshopper plague, see Harold E. Briggs, "Grasshopper Plagues and Early Dakota Agriculture, 1864–1876," *Agricultural History*, VIII (Jan., 1934), pp. 51-63; also J. A. Munro, "Grasshopper Outbreaks in North Dakota," *North Dakota History*, XVI (July, 1949), pp. 147-153; Folwell, Vol. III, pp. 99-110.

³⁸ Power to Editor, St. Paul *Pioneer Press*, May 8, 1877, NDIRS, File 309.

³⁹ Power to Max Woodhull, Washington, D.C., May 5, 1877, NDIRS, File 309.

⁴⁰ Power, NDSHS, *Collections*, Vol. III, p. 345.

⁴¹ Harnsberger, "Jay Cooke and Minnesota," pp. 352-353.

⁴² *Fargo Forum*, June 4, 1951. A reprint of an article dated Jan. 20, 1879.

⁴³ Power, NDSHS, *Collections*, Vol. III, p. 344.

⁴⁴ Coulter, NDSHS, *Collections*, Vol. III, p. 570. The original transaction to George W. Cass (N.Y.C.) took place June 2, 1874, on 6 sections in Township 139 and 1 section in Township 140, Cass County, for $20,620.22. The B. P. Cheney (Boston) transaction was on June 3, 1874, and included 5 sections in Townships 151 and 152, Cass County, for $14,489.15. NDIRS, Grandin Papers, File 450; Power to Billings, June 20, 1874, File 309. These figures represent an apparent cash outlay of $4.60 and $4.52 per acre respectively, but considering the depreciated condition of the Northern Pacific bonds at the time, the cash cost was about $0.50 or $0.60 per acre.

⁴⁵ Power to Cass, May 4, 1876, NDIRS, File 309; Power to Cheney, Aug. 12, 1876, Aug. 19, 1876, Sept. 5, 1876, File 309.

⁴⁶ Power, NDSHS, *Collections*, Vol. III, p. 340.

⁴⁷ Hedges, *Mississippi Valley Historical Review*, XIII, 329-330.

⁴⁸ Power to Billings, April 12, 1877, NDIRS, File 309.

⁴⁹ Power to Beebe, Nov. 3, 1877, NDIRS, File 309; Power to C. B. Wright, Nov. 3, 1877, File 309.

⁵⁰ Power to J. L. Grandin, Sept. 22, 1877, NDIRS, File 309; Power to Dalrymple, April 12, 1877, NDIRS, File 309. Among those receiving materials from Power were the editors of *Country Gentleman* and E. B. Chambers of Chicago who was preparing some maps and atlases for Rand and McNally. Power to *Country Gentleman*, May 10, 1877, File 309; Power to E. B. Chambers, Oct. 10, 1877, File 309.

⁵¹ *Fargo Weekly Argus*, Sept. 1, 1880.

⁵² Murray, *Agricultural History*, XXXI, pp. 58-59.

⁵³ Harnsberger, "Jay Cooke and Minnesota," p. 252.

⁵⁴ *Fargo Weekly Argus*, Dec. 22, 1880.

⁵⁵ Oberholtzer, Vol. II, pp. 531-532.

⁵⁶ Power to A. H. Barney, treasurer of the Northern Pacific, Jan. 11, 1881, File 309; Oberholtzer, Vol. II, p. 533.

⁵⁷ Power to Billings, Jan. 22, 1878, NDIRS, File 309.

⁵⁸ Coulter, NDSHS, *Collections*, Vol. III, p. 587.

⁵⁹ *Fargo Argus*, July 14, 1883. This was still a cheap way to buy land for by exchanging the stock for land at $110, the cash cost per acre was somewhere between $0.86 and $1.47 based on land prices between $2.50 and $4.

⁶⁰ Power to Barney, Jan. 11, 1881, NDIRS, File 309.

⁶¹ *Ibid.*

⁶² Oberholtzer, Vol. II, p. 536.

⁶³ Power to Barney, Jan. 11, 1881, NDIRS, File 309.

⁶⁴ Power to Billings, June 20, 1874, NDIRS, File 309.

⁶⁵ Power to Stark, Nov. 13, 1877, NDIRS, File 309.

⁶⁶ Coulter, NDSHS, *Collections,* Vol. III, p. 587.

⁶⁷ Power to Hibbard, Jan. 17, 1874, NDIRS, File 309.

⁶⁸ *Fargo Argus,* June 9, 1880.

⁶⁹ *Fargo Argus,* April 13, 1883.

⁷⁰ Power to Billings, June 20, 1874, NDIRS, File 309; Power to Barney, Jan. 11, 1881, File 309.

⁷¹ Poors, VII, 638; VIII, pp. 363-364.

⁷² Record of Northern Pacific Railroad land sales found in the Grandin Papers, NDIRS, File 450.

⁷³ Grandin Papers, NDIRS, File 450.

⁷⁴ Power to Barney, Jan. 11, 1881, NDIRS, File 309.

⁷⁵ *Ibid*

⁷⁶ *Ibid.*

⁷⁷ Power to Billings, April 28, 1879, NDIRS, File 309.

⁷⁸ Power to Chas. D. Barney and Co., May 7, 1879, NDIRS, File 309. They were brokers in Philadelphia, not to be confused with A. H. Barney, Northern Pacific official and recipient of many other letters.

⁷⁹ Power to Barney, Jan. 11, 1881, NDIRS, File 309.

⁸⁰ Power to Billings, May 8, 1880, NDIRS, File 309.

⁸¹ Power to Billings, Aug. 11, 1880, NDIRS, File 309.

⁸² Power to Billings, June 23, 1874, NDIRS, File 309.

⁸³ *Fargo Argus,* Nov. 24, 1881, Feb. 9, 1882, p. 1; Walter E. Spokesfield, *The History of Wells County North Dakota and Its Pioneers* (Jamestown, N. D., by the Author, 1928), pp. 45-47.

⁸⁴ *Fargo Argus,* April 18, 1882, July 5, 1883.

⁸⁵ *Fargo Argus,* Nov. 24, 1881, Sept. 19, 1883.

⁸⁶ *Fargo Argus,* May 2, 1884.

⁸⁷ *Fargo Argus,* May 3, 1884.

⁸⁸ Power to Barney, Jan. 11, 1881, NDIRS, File 309.

⁸⁹ Hagerty, pp. 79-80.

⁹⁰ *Fargo Argus,* April 30, 1881.

⁹¹ Harnsberger, "Jay Cooke and Minnesota," p. 253.

⁹² Power to Billings, Nov. 4, 1880, NDIRS, File 309.

⁹³ Grandin Papers, NDIRS, File 450.

⁹⁴ Grandin Papers, NDIRS, File 450.

⁹⁵ Grandin Papers, NDIRS, File 450. A brief history of the Grandin farms by John L. Grandin, April, 1892. Other figures in this file indicate that probably 27,520 acres, including the Indian scrip purchase, were obtained.

⁹⁶ Grandin Papers, NDIRS, File 450.

⁹⁷ Coulter, NDSHS, *Collections,* Vol. III, pp. 574-575. The Grandin records, as copied from the journals of the Northern Pacific, indicate that they secured 72,975.24 acres from that company in addition to 2,560 acres from the government, for a total of 75,535.24 acres (118 sections). The Mayville farm, their last purchase, only cost them $0.16 per acre by securing the stock at $15 and trading it in on land listed at $1.23. The last 17,226.48 acres were secured at a cash outlay of $2,750. The Grandin purchases from the Northern Pacific were as follows: June 8, 1876, 41,764 acres @ $3.00, $64,252.92; October 12, 1876, 3,216 acres @ $3.00, $9,964,83; December 19, 1876, 5,409 acres @ about $4.00, $21,300.00; August 30, 1877, 5,359.76 acres @ $3.73, $20,000.00; September 14, 1877, 17,226.48 acres @ $1.23, $21,300.00. The dollar figure is not accurate as advance payments and interest accrued was involved. The price per acre is the price listed by

the Northern Pacific. Moorhead *Daily News*, Sept. 12, 1912; Grandin Papers, NDIRS, File 148; Grandin Papers, File 450.

⁹⁸ Benton, *The Journal of Land and Public Utility Economics*, Vol. I, p. 409. Material on the Baldwin farm has just been released by the Baldwin family. Several tons of records are on deposit at the NDIRS in Fargo.

⁹⁹ Robinson, Chapter vii, pp. 21-22; Hibbard, p. 387.

¹⁰⁰ Alva H. Benton, *Cash and Share Renting of Farms*, North Dakota Agricultural Experiment Station Bulletin 171 (Fargo, Feb., 1924), p. 39. Hereafter cited as Benton, *Cash and Share Renting*. It is difficult to determine how much land bonanza owners secured by this method because such deeds are not often recorded in diaries or journals.

¹⁰¹ Power to Cass, May 4, 1876, NDIRS, File 309; Power to Cass, May 4, 1876, File 309, a second letter; Power to Cheney, Aug. 12, 1876, Sept. 5, 1876, File 309.

¹⁰² Power to Cheney, March 10, 1876, NDIRS, File 309.

¹⁰³ Power to Cass, Feb. 17, 1876, NDIRS, File 309.

¹⁰⁴ Power to Billings, Dec. 1, 1877, NDIRS, File 309. The scrip referred to here came in several forms, all legally negotiable. There were military bounty scrip, Sioux and Chippewa half-breed scrip, and agricultural college scrip. Professor E. B. Robinson in his "History of North Dakota" reports that not more than 100,000 acres were involved in all scrip transactions. Other references to the use of scrip on the bonanzas are Power, NDSHS, *Collections*.

¹⁰⁵ Power to Billings, March 10, 1876, NDIRS, File 309.

¹⁰⁶ *Fargo Argus*, Nov. 16, 1881. The favorite comment of the editor of the *Argus* after every such article was, "Let the boom go on." McCarther, a Fargo banker, was one of many whom the *Argus* editor called a "boomer"; he had boomed several towns along the Northern Pacific but became most famous in Fargo.

¹⁰⁷ *Fargo Argus*, June 23, 1880, p. 8, July 7, 1880, p. 4.

¹⁰⁸ *Fargo Argus*, April 11, 1881.

¹⁰⁹ *Cultivator and Country Gentleman*, Vol. 47, July 13, 1882, p. 549.

¹¹⁰ *Fargo Argus*, July 5, 1883.

¹¹¹ *Fargo Argus*, November 8, 1882, p. 3.

¹¹² The Stickney-Smith farm of 1,920 acres with a full set of buildings including elevator and side track, was sold in November, 1882, to Trace Jordan of Butler County, Ohio. A stock company, created to purchase this farm, had operated it for five years and grossed $150,000. The company claimed that the total cost of land, breaking, and buildings was $29,000, which was probably a very high estimate. This farm sold for $42,000. *Fargo Argus*, Nov. 16, 1882, p. 3. An editorial in the *Argus* stated that land in Cass County, improved and within five miles of the railroad, was averaging $15 to $25 per acre, while unimproved was going for $8 to $15. Partly improved farms within ten miles of the railroad were selling at the $15 level. *Fargo Argus*, April 13, 1883. However, as late as 1889, some improved land could still be bought for $20 an acre. Hagerty, pp. 79-80. In 1878 the Grandins had sold two sections to their brother-in-law, S. S. Blanchard, for $0.50 per acre. In 1888, they repurchased that land for $12.50 per acre and, in addition, paid full cost for the improvements. This represents a 2,500 per cent gain in price in ten years. They sold 1,855.51 acres of their original purchase in Kragnes Township, Clay County, Minnesota, in 1911 for $120,608.15, or $65 per acre. This was sold to Daniel P. Wild of De Kalb, Illinois, and represents well over 100 per cent increase in price for each year the land was held. Clipping from the Moorhead *Daily News*, May 25, 1911, Grandin Papers, NDIRS, File 148.

¹¹³ Power to John Douglas, Winona, Minn., Nov. 13, 1877, NDIRS, File 309.

¹¹⁴ All large sales are lumped together and may include bonanza farms but they cannot be distinguished in the records. Power to Barney, Jan. 11, 1881, NDIRS, File 309.

¹¹⁵ *Ibid.*

¹¹⁶ *Ibid.*

¹¹⁷ *Ibid.*

¹¹⁸ *Ibid.*

¹¹⁹ *Ibid.*

The Day of the Bonanza

[120] *Ibid.* This is a far from complete list but clearly indicates that there were numerous large-scale buyers. The land sales described above are all enumerated in Power's letter to Barney in defense of his actions as land commissioner and may be somewhat partial on Power's behalf, but there is no reason to doubt the accuracy of the figures.

[121] Power, NDSHS, *Collections*, Vol. III, p. 346.

[122] *Fargo Argus*, Aug. 30, 1881, Dec. 27, 1881.

[123] Coulter, NDSHS, *Collections*, Vol. III, p. 588.

[124] *Fargo Argus*, March 24, 1883.

[125] Poor, XVIII, 721, XLIII, 1263, XLVIII, 1453.

[126] Power to T. M. Hadwin, Casselton, Nov. 30, 1877, NDIRS, File 309.

[127] Power to Billings, March 5, 1878, NDIRS, File 309; Power to Dalrymple, March 14, 1878, File 309; Power to Billings, March 19, 1878, File 309.

[128] Power to Billings, Jan. 12, 1876, NDIRS, File 309.

[129] Power to Billings, Dec. 1, 1877, NDIRS, File 309.

[130] Power to Billings, Nov. 17, 1877, NDIRS, File 309.

[131] Power to Billings, Aug. 11, 1880, NDIRS, File 309.

[132] Power to Billings, Oct. 29, 1880, NDIRS, File 309.

[133] Power to Barney, Jan. 11, 1881, NDIRS, File 309; Leonard Hal Bridges, *Iron Millionaire* (Philadelphia: U. of Penn., 1952), p. 100.

[134] *Cultivator and Country Gentleman*, XLI, p. 340; Bridges, p. 109.

[135] Power to Tower, June 26, 1878, NDIRS, File 309; Bridges, p. 110.

[136] *Fargo Argus*, April 16, 1881, NDIRS, File 309.

[137] *Fargo Argus*, April 20, 1881, NDIRS, File 309.

[138] *Fargo Daily Argus*, June 2, 1881.

[139] *Ibid.*

[140] *Fargo Argus*, Oct. 23, 1882.

[141] *Fargo Argus*, March 10, 1880.

[142] *Fargo Argus*, Aug. 27, 1880.

[143] *Fargo Argus*, Feb. 18, 1881, Feb. 28, 1881; Spokesfield, p. 80.

[144] *Fargo Argus*, Sept. 29, 1880, Nov. 14, 1882, Feb. 1, 1881, Oct. 6, 1885. In 1879 the legislative assembly of Dakota Territory passed a 2 per cent annual gross earnings tax effective for the first five years of a company's operation, and 3 per cent rate thereafter. This tax was to be paid in lieu of all other taxes on roadbed, right-of-way, station grounds, track, rolling stock, tools, furniture, telegraph lines and equipment, and fuel. "All property not above enumerated, subject to taxation, shall be treated in all respects, in regard to assessment, equalization, and taxation, the same as similar property belonging to individuals whether said lands are received from the general government or from other sources." A third of the property tax was to go to the general fund of the territory and the remaining two-thirds paid to the counties in proportion to the number of miles of main track in each county. Territory of Dakota, *Laws of the Thirteenth Session of the Legislative Assembly*, 1879, C. 46, sec. 24. For the fiscal year ending November 30, 1888, the Northern Pacific paid $93,873.18 property taxes to the territorial and county governments. Hagerty, p. 85.

[145] Power to Billings, Jan. 12, 1878, NDIRS, File 309.

[146] Power to B. W. Benson, April 29, 1887, NDIRS, File 309.

[147] Power to Billings, Jan. 11, 1878, NDIRS, File 309.

[148] Power to Kindred, Nov. 1, 1878, NDIRS, File 309.

[149] Power to Cheney, Nov. 17, 1878, NDIRS, File 309.

[150] Power to Billings, Jan. 6, 1879, NDIRS, File 309.

[151] Power to Thomas and Benton, Jan. 15, 1880, NDIRS, File 309; Power to Billings, Jan. 30, 1880, File 309. Thomas and Benton were Fargo attorneys. Information given in various letters indicates something about the amount and rate of taxes paid by these big land holders. Taxes in 1876 for Cass, 1760 acres in T. 139, R. 51, T. 139, R. 52, and T. 140, R. 52 assessed at $5,434 were taxed for $86.88 or $0.049 per acre. Power to Cass, Jan. 10, 1877, File 309. Billings, on Sec. 10 and 14, T. 139, R. 52 valued at $3,840, paid taxes for 1876 of $61.44 or $0.045 tax per acre. Power to Billings, Jan. 10, 1877,

File 309. In 1877, the tax on that land was $96.16 or $0.072 per acre. Power to Billings, Jan. 12, 1878, File 309. Total tax in Cass County in 1878 for Cheney was $2,069 on $45,300 valuation; for Cass $3,084.84 on $58,012 valuation, and for Billings $1,000 tax valuation unknown but on about 16,000 acres. Power to Cheney, Nov. 17, 1878, File 309. Traill County taxes on 3,916.64 acres for 1879 was $293.70 or $0.075 per acre. The taxes for 1878 were dropped. In Richland $91.06 or $0.0525 per acre. Power to Billings, Jan. 30, 1880, File 309.

[152] Power to Billings, Jan. 21, 1880, NDIRS, File 309.

CHAPTER III

James B. Power and the Rise of
the Bonanza Farms

BONANZA FARMS served their purpose well, for they clearly demonstrated the great opportunities available on the prairies of northern Dakota. They introduced a new style of frontier agriculture, copying the techniques of the rapidly growing American industrial economy. The construction of a vast railroad network and the simultaneous increased European demand for American agricultural products provided the necessary stimulus for rapid settlement of the Red River Valley and cultivation of its fertile land. The bonanzas by their very size were the source of many legends and stories which were circulated in magazines and other various publications throughout the country in the 1880's and after. Through them Dakota became known as the land of the bonanza farms. Although few in number, the bonanzas also exerted a great influence on the early development of northern Dakota. The men associated with them were active in most phases of the State's early years. The most outstanding of all was James B. Power, the father of North Dakota agriculture. Power was not only the originator of the bonanza idea, but was important in the development of the livestock industry, new seeds, and other innovations in the State's agriculture.

John L. Coulter, an early North Dakota economist associated with the Agricultural College, called the bonanzas "demonstration farms." He said that they were so satisfactory that the "very best settlers" from other states flocked to the area by the thousands.[1] The bonanzas were farms of large-scale commercialized agriculture. In 1877 Power wrote that the big change introduced by the bonanza was "the large investment in land and cultivation to wheat by capitalists." He was the person most responsible for this change and thoroughly understood what was taking place.[2] The bonanza combined a vast amount of capital, big machinery, professional management, and cheap labor with the fertile prairies of North Dakota which suited themselves perfectly to such large-scale operations. In its days it was the most advanced form of commercialized agriculture. An article unfriendly to the bonanzas described them as "a combination of the most powerful social and economic forces known to man."[3] "In the lexicon of the Dakota farmer, there is no such word as 'hoe',"wrote William Allen White in a series of articles about the great businesses of that day.[4]

The bonanzas were a one-crop farming operation. The operators of the bonanzas bought cheese, butter, meat, and most other food from small surrounding farms or from Minnesota and Iowa. Through bonanza farming commercial agriculture gave the railroads a two-way business. Wheat production in the Red River Valley rose rapidly from 4,500 bushels per 100 inhabitants in 1879 to 11,500 bushels per 100 inhabitants in 1884.[5] Walter R. Reed said: "At first these farms were almost invariably straight wheat farms. They did not even raise oats for their horses, figuring they could buy oats cheaper than they could raise them. Some farmers of the valley made big profits raising oats for the bonanza farms."[6]

In many ways the North Dakota bonanza farms were unique to American agriculture of the 1870's, '80's, and '90's. They were unique in that they were carried on in an extremely business-like manner using strict managerial supervision, had a large investment both in land and machinery, and had to have access to a large periodic labor supply. No experience or knowledge of farming was required of the labor force because supervisory help directed them. Bonanzas employed the factory technique of mass use of large-scale uniform machinery for greatest efficiency. They used the latest and most advanced methods available and sometimes innovated new ones. Because of their size they secured advantages in dealing with machinery manufacturers, grain companies, and financial and transportation agencies. Finally, the bonanzas were unique because their influence was all out of proportion to their number and acreage in the agriculture of the Red River Valley.

Legends of the Bonanza

The operational records of the bonanzas had an immediate value, for Power and the Northern Pacific officials hoped that the bonanza farms would serve as the basis of a great promotional campaign to dramatize the potential of the area. But in their expectations they had not counted on the many wild stories about the bonanza farms that were written or passed by word of mouth to other parts of the country. These newspaper accounts, letters, and fantastic stories had a much greater effect on the easterners than any promotional campaign of the Northern Pacific. The company, however, was not adverse in encouraging these stories; it was all part of the "boomer" psychology that had overcome the region.[7]

The very word bonanza created excitement. Bonanza implied lucky strike, big fortune, and stories of drama. Everyone dreams that he will someday strike a bonanza. In the Red River Valley there are countless stories about the big bonanza farms. These stories just grew a bit better each time they were told. Each year the bonanzas became a thousand acres larger; the furrows another mile longer. The following are some of the tales passed about in the day when the bonanza was a reality. In the fall of 1882, for example, the *Fargo Daily Argus* carried the following article from the *Cincinnati Commercial:*

Fargo is the favorite residence of a bonanza farmer. A little explanation of that title seems pertinent. When a man secures 1,000 to 20,000 acres of wheat lands and gets them under cultivation, he will have an annual net profit of from 10 to 15 dollars an acre. He is then said to have a bonanza, the possession of which entitles him to the rank of bonanza farmer. But there are all grades of bonanza farmers from the struggling private in the ranks with only 1 or 2 thousand acres of wheat up to the bonanza king with many thousands. This distinction may account for the prevalence of military titles, for generals, colonels, majors, and captains do much abuse [*sic*].Anything below a captain is considered small potatoes and don't count. Private Dalzell must secure a brevet before he can measurably expect any distinguished man's autograph "in this neck of the woods." There is no position in the world I would more cheerfully undertake to fill than that of a BONANZA FARMER. During most of the year he lives in town in his own house or stops at the best hotels, smokes the best cigar, is full of good stories and takes life in an easy, jolly way, which would be decidedly refreshing to the heavy-hand "Ohio farmer." The farmer is the true aristocrat here—the man of means and elegant leisure. You never hear him talk of the "money bags of Wall street" or bloated monopolies.[8]

The *Argus* commented that the author of the account was "a greasy Fargo lawyer," William F. McNagney. This story is an exaggeration but not beyond the limits of the "gospel truth" as far as the residents along the Northern Pacific were concerned.

The tallest tale of the bonanza has to do with the length of the furrow. A good example of the furrow stories in circulation in our time reads as follows:

I was born at Casselton on 8th November in the year 1879. My father worked near Casselton for two or three years, back in the '70's of the past century. He worked for a man by the name of Dalrymple, and according to my father this man Dalrymple had the biggest farm that ever lay out of doors. My father told me that this Dalrymple once set up stakes, for him to strike out a land of breaking, and he went along with four horses on a walking breaking plow, and plowed a furrow that was over 40 miles long, and so straight you could snap a chalk line in it from one end to the other without touching either side. They headed in a northwesterly direction and plowed straight for two days. When they stopped that night Dalrymple asked my father if he thought they had gone far enough and he replied, "I hope you don't go any farther, or we may never get back," and this is how the town of Hope got its name, it being near there that they turned back at the end of the furrow.[9]

Some furrows were even longer than the one leading to Hope. Another article of the eighties entitled "Furrows Were Long, But" reported: "I've seen a man on one of our big farms start out in the spring and plow a straight furrow until fall. Then he turned around and harvested back."[10]

In practice, the normal field of operation was a section. "You plow a furrow a mile long and you can afford to turn around," implying that there was little waste of time in turning around when the furrow was that long. It was common, however, for the plow teams to work around the section instead of across, making an initial round of four miles with the minimum in turning time. It was seldom possible to have a field larger than one section as most farms were not contiguous sections because of the checkerboard system as created under the railroad grant.[11] Dalrymple's stock answer to questions about long furrows and big fields was that "When the plowing commences in the spring, the men go out in gangs, each gang taking 640 acres."[12] A captain was assigned to each gang of ten or twelve plows. In the morning of the first day they would make two rounds, or eight miles, around a new section, and three rounds in the afternoon. In one week's time a gang could plow a section. The tales add much romance to the bonanza story, but even the truth of a four-mile round was beyond the imagination of most people living east of the Mississippi and the Red River, for farmers who operated farms of one-eighth to one-quarter sections.

Bonanzas: Their Size and Number

No authorities have ever definitely established the minimum acres necessary for a farm to be classified as a bonanza. Some early studies have used 1,000 acres as the minimum requirement. John L. Coulter stated that by 1880 there were 82 farms in the Valley of over 1,000 acres and most of those contained 4 to 6 sections. He implied that there may have been several large farms created after that date because the bonanza system was just getting a good start, but, in his opinion, a bonanza was at least 1,280 acres. He implied that 5 sections or 3,200 acres was a more correct minimum. In concurrence with Coulter, this study has established 3,000 acres as the minimum size for a bonanza. This limits the total number of farms that can be classified as bonanzas to ninety-one. The 1,000-acre minimum is too low because the 1890 census listed 323 farms of over that size which would make such farms rather general.[13] William Allen White, in writing about the bonanzas in 1897, used 7,000 acres as the average size of these large farms He does not reveal how he arrived at this figure as he did not make a list of any farms.[14] White's article has proven so reliable that it is safe to assume that this figure has a good basis.

Local newspapers of the day of the bonanza give the impression that every other farm was a bonanza, for the term was applied to anything larger than a garden. It was all part of the boom psychology that was so prevalent in Dakota during the bonanza era. The papers wanted everyone to believe that the Red River of the North was the Nile of America and that every settler had made a bonanza in wheat. This was in part the result of the Northern Pacific's promotional scheme to attract settlers to the region, a promotion which succeeded beyond the dreams of its creators. It not only attracted settlers but it created a lasting impression in the minds of many that Dakota was the home of big capitalistic farmers. The popular belief was that North Dakota abounded with bonanza farms and it took several decades to destroy that impression.[15] Writing in 1899, Power, the originator of the bonanza farming system, stated that the eastern one-fourth of North Dakota, which includes much of the Red River Valley, contained 23,038 farms which covered 6,760,000 acres for an overall average "including all the bonanza farms" of only 293 acres. He said: "This certainly disproves the idea that we are a state made up of bonanza farms only." [16]

Local papers did much to create the impression that Dakota was the land of big farmers. Once it was rumored that Standard Oil Company was buying wheat land with an attempt to gain a corner on the market. The Fargo *Argus* editor commented that Red River Valley farmers "will laugh at this measly million acres as any of 2 or 3 second-class bonanza farmers could clean out such a job in 20 minutes."[17] Local papers also made a comparison with big farms elsewhere in the nation. California bonanzas, which had their start sometime during this period, had one farm that exceeded 60,000 acres. This was larger than the biggest farm in North Dakota in 1880 which was the 50,000-acre Grandin farm. In another respect, however, North Dakota did not have to take second place. Dalrymple had the distinction of having the largest single cultivated unit under one operation, 28,000 acres.[18]

The Cass-Cheney farm, which is generally recognized as the first bonanza, was purchased in 1874. Oliver Dalrymple, its manager and later owner (his contract provided for gradual acquisition of the land), so overshadowed the original owners that it was incorrectly called the Dalrymple bonanza from the beginning. It was not until after 1900 that the last of the original bonanza was secured by the Dalrymple family. In 1896 Dalyrmple actually owned 30,000 acres, but the greatest size of the entire family's operation is uncertain and very likely may have totaled 100,000 acres with as much as 65,000 acres under cultivation. Dalrymple himself reported that he had "in excess of 35,000 acres" under cultivation at one time. The 65,000-acre figure probably included all the land operated by many Dalrymples at the same time which was not necessarily under Oliver Dalrymple's management.

Among his relatives farming in Dakota were S. C., R. A., S. N., W. F., and Grout Dalrymple and Oliver's sons, William and John S. S. C. Dalrymple opened a large farm, later purchased by the Howe brothers. He also went to Gardner and opened a second large farm which he sold to W. A. Scott. R. A. Dalrymple owned a large farm near Gardner while S. N. Dalrymple, a brother of Oliver, had a large farm six miles from Casselton. Another brother, C. C. Dalrymple, owned a farm near Kelso. Grout Dalrymple possessed land in the same general area.[19] W. F. Dalrymple was manager of that portion of the Grandin farm which was under the general management of his brother, Oliver. W. F. Dalrymple reported that in 1883 they had 30,000 acres under cultivation.[20]

The Dalrymple bonanza was stabilized at 22,000 acres about 1908 after reaching its peak in 1896. It was operated in ten units by William and John S. until 1917 and was later sold.[21] Nearly all of the land was repossessed by the family in the 1920's and 1930's so that in 1955, John S. Dalrymple owned about 25,000 acres and William about 5,000 acres in addition to land they rented.[22] The 3,840-acre Alton farm near Casselton served as Oliver Dalrymple's headquarters. The original bonanza contained 13,440 acres.[23]

The second big bonanza was the Grandin operation created in 1876. It was subdivided into four separate farms, one northwest of Mayville, another west of Hillsboro, another near the village of Grandin, all in North Dakota, and a final purchase near Halstad, Minnesota. The Grandin brothers had 118 sections of which 114 were secured

from the Northern Pacific and 4 purchased from the government totaling 75,535.24 acres. In 1912 the *Moorhead Daily News* credits John
L. Grandin with the ownership of 72,000 acres of land in North Dakota but does not refer to any Minnesota holdings.[24] The Grandin
farms were subdivided and sold quite rapidly after 1894. In November, 1894, they advertised fifty-five sections for sale on the crop-payment plan.[25] It was not until 1946 that the Grandin family disposed
of their last land in the Red River Valley.

Among all the bonanza farms in Dakota the Amenia and Sharon
Land Company was an outstanding one. It was incorporated under
the laws of Connecticut in 1875 by forty stockholders who pooled
their Northern Pacific stock to purchase 27,931.66 acres.[26] The Amenia and Sharon farm was located in Cass County although it owned
the alternate sections of nearly two townships in Stutsman County.
Eventually the Amenia and Sharon came to own over thirty subsidiary farming, elevator, livestock, and finance enterprises. It also owned
two towns and at one time a railroad. It actually had over 42,000
acres under cultivation at its peak which very likely meant that it
was the largest bonanza in that respect since Dalrymple's maximum
acreage under cultivation cannot be positively established. At one
time the Amenia and Sharon possessed altogether 58,350 acres. The
Amenia and Sharon's story is one of integrated large-scale agriculture
with excellent management. The farm held together until 1923 when
the major stockholders decided to subdivide it. A large amount of
land is still held by descendants of the original stockholders.

West of the Amenia and Sharon farms on the Barnes County line
were the lands of Charlemagne Tower, a railroad official who made
the first big purchase of Northern Pacific lands totaling 28,240 acres.
It was operated as a big unit with 3,000 acres under cultivation by
1880.[27] Tower made additional purchases later which ran his total to
36,877 acres in North Dakota alone.[28]

Next to Tower's land in Stutsman County near Jamestown was the
Spiritwood bonanza. This farm, consisting of 19,700 acres, was owned
by Cuyler Adams, Charles Francis, and B. S. Russell, trustee. The
first purchase was made in May, 1878, for 15,000 acres of land. At
least six other purchases were made which brought the total beyond
200,000 acres.[29] A syndicate owned Spiritwood with B. S. Russell handling the business and Cuyler Adams doing the managing. In the late
1880's the farm was sold in subdivisions because it was no longer
profitable.[30]

Farther west along the Northern Pacific near the present town of
Steele in Kidder County were the Steele and Troy farms. These farms

each contained about 10,000 acres. Power referred to these as the Steele and Small farms with an original purchase of 11,628 acres and subsequent additions bringing the total to 27,620 acres. Later purchases from the government increased the total to 48,000 acres. This bonanza moved in 100 families and dispersed them on the land to get as much under cultivation as quickly as possible. They had a store, blacksmith shop, and even a stage line.[31]

In Burleigh County near Bismarck was the 9,900-acre Clarke farm. The *Cultivator and Country Gentleman,* however, credited Howell D. Clark (not Clarke) of Ohio as being the possessor of 25,500 acres.[32] Forty miles north of Bismarck was the 23,000-acre bonanza of John F. Betz, a Philadelphia brewer, who planned to grow barley for his brewery.[33]

In Wells County near the present town of Sykeston, Richard Sykes established what could be called a bonanza community. Sykes purchased 45,000 acres from the Northern Pacific in 1881. He planned to settle that area but reserved a big bonanza for himself as part of the development.[34] Sykes, in cooperation with Walter J. Hughes, purchased an additional 23,000 acres in La Moure County in 1882. They attempted to break 10,000 acres that year.[35] The syndicate which Richard Sykes represented was headed by Lord Francis Sykes of near Manchester, England. Its purpose was to make extensive investments in foreign lands. Walter Hughes, the manager, used oxen to break 3,000 acres in 1882. The Sykes-Hughes farm, as it later became known, was rented to J. A. Field in 1889.[36]

In the vicinity of Carrington in Foster County was the bonanza of Carrington and Casey from Toledo, Ohio. This farm, which contained 35,782 acres, was purchased early in 1880.[37] Griggs and Foster purchased 35,756 acres in 1880 but no account has been found as to how they developed their land.[38]

In Griggs and Barnes counties south of Cooperstown was the big bonanza of the Cooper brothers of Chicago. This farm, which was purchased late in 1880, contained 34,080 acres. It was quickly put under cultivation with 5,880 acres in production in 1881. The brothers later enlarged their farm to 37,000 acres. Buildings were constructed, and livestock and grain were shipped in as soon as the land was purchased.[39]

Richland County in the southeastern corner of the State had several large bonanzas. The Fairview farm (sometimes called the Adams farm) was owned by J. Q. Adams and later inherited by his son, W. P. Adams. This farm, located south of Mooreton, contained at least

9,600 acres of which 9,000 were eventually cultivated. From the beginning it was heavily oriented toward sheep raising.[40]

Also in Richland County farmed the Downings, neighbors to the Adamses and their good friends. Their farm, referred to as the Downing or the Mooreton farm, was the headquarters of the Downing operation. It was owned in part by J. F. Downing of New York. There were 5,000 acres in the Mooreton unit and 4,600 acres near La Moure in La Moure County. F. A. Bagg, manager of the Mooreton unit, became a big bonanza operator in his own right at a later date.[41]

Mantador in Richland County was the home of the Keystone farm owned either by a Mr. Soule or C. H. Janke. The entire 6,080 acres were under cultivation and in addition a school section was rented for pasture.[42] A reference to the Clifford farm in Richland County gives the impression that it may have been the same as Keystone farm.

Antelope farm, owned by Hugh Moore and located near Mooreton, contained 17,300 acres.[43] Antelope farm was one of the better known early farms and was in full operation by 1878. The least known of the bonanzas in Richland County was the Woodruff farm owned by Trask and Woodruff.[44] Power's correspondence in 1882 with a Joe Woodruff in regard to a purchase of hogs is one of the few clues to this farm.

Best known of all the bonanzas in that area was the Dwight farm, owned by the Dwight Farm and Land Company, headed by Congressman John W. Dwight of Dryden, New York. It had twelve stockholders who were in an advantageous position to secure land. Two of them, Charles Cady and John Miller, both of whom were superintendents, became later political leaders in North Dakota. John Miller, the State's first governor, became president of the Dwight Farm and Land Company in 1896. In the same year he founded the John Miller Company, a grain commission firm in Duluth.[45] Purchases from the railroad amounted to 17,000 acres scattered throughout 9 townships of Richland County.[46] The company set out to double its holdings by securing government lands and succeeded in building up to 27,000 acres in Richland County alone.[47] An additional 32,000 acres were secured in the Finley area of Steele County, making a total of 60,000 acres under the supervision of the company and Miller.[48] This farm was divided into three units, but only the headquarters farm at Dwight had buildings of any size. After 1900 the land was gradually sold so that by January 1, 1909, there were only 6,720 acres in Richland and 4,800 acres in Steele County remaining.[49] John Miller was virtual owner of the Dwight farms at the time of his death. The stock was worth $336 per share, and the total net worth of the company in 1909 was $413,865 with 11,520 acres of land remaining. If the land had been retained and stockholders had not withdrawn assets, the company would have easily amassed a million-dollar surplus.[50]

In the 1890's George Baldwin bought quarter sections of land for $200 to $500 per unit from farmers who were in trouble. In all, he acquired 75,000 acres which were divided into 4 ranches, as he preferred to call them. The Baldwin farms centered around Ellendale in Dickey County but also extended into La Moure County.[51]

The Watson farm was well known among the bonanzas of Cass County. Lewis E. Watson—factory owner, oil man, and congressman from Pennsylvania, purchased forty sections in 1878 which were divided into three units. The 1893 atlas of Cass County reveals that there were 34 complete sections within the Watson farm as well as numerous partial sections for a total of over 23,000 acres. These lands were all in Eldred, Watson, and Highland townships of Cass County.[52]

In Ransom County, the town of Buttsville serves as a reminder of the big Buttz bonanza. Three brothers, Major, D. H., and John Buttz, owned more than 36,000 acres of land in Ransom, La Moure, and Barnes counties. This land was purchased a little later than most of the other bonanzas. In the spring of 1882 they purchased the last of their sixty sections. That year under the management of John R. Buttz, they had 4,000 acres in wheat. D. H. Buttz constructed a 45,000-bushel warehouse in 1882 along the newly laid Northern Pacific tracks and Buttsville (originally spelled Buttzville) was founded. Major Buttz was a lawyer in South Carolina.[53]

Addison Leech, a capitalist from Pennsylvania, came to Cass County in 1880 and purchased land twelve miles south of Fargo.[54] He secured 1,600 acres for $16.50 an acre.[55] Before he finished buying land that year, he had secured a total of 7,300 acres, most of which was in Warren Township of Cass County. He later bought an additional 40,000 acres in western Cass and eastern Barnes counties.[56] In spite of the rather high price that Leech paid for his land, he was able to produce a large enough crop in the first year to pay for his land and still have a net profit of $8 per acre.[57] In 1893 Leech sold his farm to James Kennedy, a large construction contractor in Fargo. Kennedy, however, was not too interested in the management of the farm. His major concern was that the farm should provide feed and shelter for the horses needed in the construction business. No business records were kept on the farm's operation. Francis Sterling Colwell was manager of the farm. During his period of service the farm size was reduced to 5,280 acres.[58]

John B. Raymond, also referred to as Delegate Raymond, had his start by using some veteran's benefits to secure land. By 1881 he had 6,000 acres 12 miles north of Fargo.[59] Raymond had 2,000 acres in crop in 1881. He purchased some of his land for as much as $8.50 an acre. He made a profit in his first year on a twenty-five-bushel wheat yield. In 1883 Captain Chase purchased a one-third interest in Raymond's bonanza. It was expanded to 15,000 acres.[60] The *Cultivator and Country Gentleman* credits J. B. Raymond of Cass County with having 6,000 acres in wheat for that year.[61]

In addition to the Grandins, Traill County had two well-known bonanza operations. One was the Blanchard farm owned by S. S. Blanchard, a brother-in-law of J. L. and W. J. Grandin. In 1878 Blanchard secured his first land from his brothers-in-law at $0.50 per acre. Until 1892 it was operated as a part of the Grandin farm, when three additional sections were purchased. It then became a separate operation and was called the Blanchard farm. This farm was located west of Hillsboro near Blanchard.[62]

The other farm in that vicinity belonged to Datus C. Smith, sometimes called Date Smith. This farm, called the Belle Prairie farm in its early years, was later renamed Cloverlea farm. It was started by Smith in 1879 with a loan from his father's friend, Marshall Field, the Chicago merchant.[63] The farm contained five sections in Blanchard Township of Traill County. Smith was a very progressive, scientific farmer specializing in the production of seed crops, especially clover. He did much to promote the use of clover as a sheep and cattle feed. A very well written brochure advertised his farm, using Cloverlea as a trade name.[64]

Two other farm names appeared in the NDIRS files that logically must have been in Traill County. In 1881 Power mentioned the 5,760-acre farm of F. J. Buxton. No other record has been found regarding that farm. If it was in Traill County, it is only logical to assume that it was near the present village of Buxton.[65] A second such farm which was listed as being in Traill County was the Hillsboro farm. This farm was credited with having 40,000 acres. It was definitely not part of the Grandin operation because it is mentioned as one of the big bonanzas in 1878 in addition to the Grandin farm.[66]

John Dunlop purchased 10,900 acres from the Northern Pacific late in 1875. Power reported that Dunlop had adopted the long-term lease system and by 1880 had all of his land improved and settled by Scotch Canadians. The Dunlop farm was centered in Cass County around Mapleton.[67]

Just west of the Dunlop farm between Mapleton and Casselton was the J. Mosher bonanza. Mosher secured 19,020 acres of railroad land and used the same system as Dunlop. He quickly improved the land and leased it to tenant farmers. Mosher, who came from New York, had a large operation of his own in addition to his tenant farm. He attempted to interest Frederick Billings in a bonanza operation. He improved some of Billings' land but never succeeded in getting Billings to start a big farm.[68] G. S. Scofield and Brothers of Cass County were known to have 3,840 acres in wheat in 1882. One brother's name was Frank. These men came from New York.[69]

Other large operators in 1882 were W. H. Wright who had 3,500 acres of wheat seeded in Cass County, J. B. Chapin who had over 9,600 acres seeded to wheat in Cass, Traill, and Barnes counties, and J. W. Morrow of Cass County with 5,500 acres of wheat.[70] Brooks and McKnight of St. Paul, Minnesota, were owners of a 4,000-acre farm in Cass County in 1876. J. S. Bryse of New York and Clement Smith of Kentucky had a 3,500-acre farm in 1876, half of which was in wheat and the other half was being used for feed for their herd of purebred cattle. Power secured a pass for Clement Smith for the year 1877 on the Northern Pacific and referred to him as one of the "big farmers in Dakota." He made the same remark about Henry Williams, a large farmer located within three miles of Dalrymple Station, a short distance west of Casselton. In 1882 Williams sold his farm to R. J. Green who paid $60,000 down and the balance of an undisclosed amount on time payments. Green owned land near Spiritwood in Stutsmen County in addition to extensive holdings in Burleigh, McLean, Cass, and Ransom counties.[71]

J. G. Brown, a Minneapolis gas works operator, owned a large farm in Traill County. This farm was referred to as the Rand and Brown farm and also as the Brown and Preston farm. It consisted of at least 4,480 acres. The Preston brothers were from New York.[72] Robert Hadwin, an Englishman who came to the Valley from Canada, settled in the Wheatland area. He purchased his first land in 1876 and by 1880 had over 2,100 acres in wheat. In 1880 he owned 12 sections or 7,680 acres of land. He improved the land and sold parts of his farm in 1880 when he was paid $26.25 an acre for 1,280 acres.[73] The *Fargo Argus* had more news comments about Hadwin than any other bonanza operators except the Grandins and Dalrymple.

Colonel H. S. Back owned considerable land in Richland County. He had at least 7,000 acres in one farm and had succeeded in break-

ing 1,000 acres when he ran out of cash. In March, 1880, the *Fargo
Argus* reported that he had sold half interest in his 18,000-acre farm
in Richland County to Hugh Moore of Newburgh, New York.[74] The
Davenport farms near Jamestown were started in April, 1882. Davenport came from Iowa. He purchased a very large acreage, improved
the land, and then subdivided it for renting purposes or for sale.
S. L. Glaspell was the manager of the Davenport operation.[75]

Captain Thomas W. Hunt purchased six sections west of Blanchard
in 1882. The Hunt farm was one of the first to use steam power for
plowing. Hunt formed a syndicate with other large farmers who
called themselves the Aurora Farming Company with headquarters
in Fargo. Others in this syndicate were the previously mentioned Scofield brothers, and Brown, Preston and brothers. There were also
Field and Lieters near Grandin, Wieble, and Thompson of Philadelphia, Rieker, Wild, and Emerson, all of Ohio, and the von Steinwehr brothers of Connecticut.[76] Little is known about some of these
operators. Emerson was a manufacturer of carriages from Cincinnati,
Ohio. His bonanza was located near Blanchard. Forty-seven head of
mules furnished the power for the farm and a pair of "fancy driving
horses" helped provide Emerson with recreation.[77] However, the most
of these farms do not meet the 3,000-acre requirement set by this
study but combined under the Aurora Farming Company there was
more than 20,000 acres.

Stephen Gardner sold a 3,140-acre farm to a Mr. Mairs in 1881.
Mairs later became associated with the Howe brothers and the farm
was increased to 4,000 acres. Captain Noyes, one of the Grandin boat
operators, and a Mr. Reynolds joined forces with Mairs and Howe
and formed one large bonanza near the village of Buffalo.[78] The farm
was later called the Howe farm and was associated with the Dalrymple operations.[79] Noyes and Bond made their first purchase of
4,500 acres in 1880 near the village of Buffalo, then called New Buffalo.[80]

In the following some other less known farms are listed in two
groups; those which have an established history as bonanzas and
those which were probably bonanzas or attempts at bonanzas but
never clearly established themselves as such.[81]

In North Dakota

Cleveland farm ....Richland County
Fingal Enger farm ....Hatton
Garnet brothers farm ....St. Thomas
Glover farms (Samuel Glover & Sons) ....Ellendale and Oakes

Gunderson farm ....Aneta
Johnson Land and Cattle Company ....Oakes
Jones and Brinker farm ....Blanchard
Patterson Land Company ....Burleigh County
Elk Valley farm ....Larimore
Richardson farms ....Wahpeton
Craig farm ....north of Spiritwood
Clifford farm (may be same as Keystone) ...Richland County

In Minnesota

Kilrenny and Argyle farms ....Euclid
Bolman farm ....Georgetown
Elwood S. Corser farm ....Polk County
Donaldson-Ryan farm ....Donaldson
Hancock farm ....Hancock
Humboldt farm, J. J. Hill, owner ....Kittson County
Northcote farm, J. J. Hill, owner ....Northcote
Oakfield and Riverside farms ....Marshall County
Keystone farms ....Marshall County
Lockhardt farm ....Marshall County
Woodward farm ....Warren
G. S. Barnes (Barnes and Tenney) ....Glyndon

Other large farms that possessed 3,000 or more acres but are relatively unknown include the following:

In North Dakota

Buffington farm ....Cass County
Reid farm or Charles M. Reed farm, 14,300 acres..Cass County
George Fowler Farm Company, 4,480 acres ......Cass County
Meadow farm, Colonel Huntington, owner ....Cass County
Houston farm, David Henderson, owner ....Hunter
Treadwell Twitchell farm ....Mapleton
Ely farm, 6 sections ....North of Mayville
Kimmerlee farm, 3,000 acres ....near Fargo
Hague and Brady farm, Willow-Vale farm, John Cudie owner
McRae postoffice, Bottineau
Edgeley farm, F. F. Goodwin, owner,
Glendale farm, 3,000 acres, 150 horses ....Cass County
Ayr farm (may be same as Park farm) ....Ayr
J. W. Pence farm, 85,080 acres, purchased prior to 1880 and 3,000
acres broken that year ....part in Cass County

C. F. Kindred farm ....Valley City
E. C. Sprague ....near Fargo
Wells farm ....near Jamestown
Charles W. Hassler farm, 17,500 acres
Norman H. Galusha farm, 15,300 acres ......Richland County
J. B. Colgate farm, 12,646 acres
Farren, Rhoremier and Company ..12 miles south of Casselton
A. E. Fenton, most of his land absorbed by Amenia and Sharon
                                                    Casselton
George B. Maxwell from Hartford, Conn., purchased large blocks
of land in 1881 and 1882 ....Cass County
J. E. Wisner ....Ransom County
F. E. Sargent farm; Sargent was one time general manager of the
Northern Pacific ....Buffalo
Thomas W. Walker ....on Elm River, Traill County

In Minnesota

Askegaard farms ....Clay County
Comstock farms ....Clay County
Hancock brothers farm ....Hancock
Powell farm ....south of Moorhead

James B. Power: The Father of North Dakota Agriculture

One bonanza, not mentioned in the above list and in some respects not a typical bonanza but one of the most important early forms
of North Dakota history, is J. B. Power's Helendale. If Power had
wanted to establish a big wheat bonanza he could easily have secured
one, but he preferred cattle farming and therefore selected land that
would serve his purpose. Therefore he chose land away from the Red
River Valley so that he would be free to graze cattle and sheep for
many years without having to worry about interference from other
settlers. He settled in an area of light, sandy soil not too far from
what is referred to as the Sand Hills region. It was also in the valley
of the Sheyenne River which served as a water supply.

Power revealed his true understanding of the Sand-Hill country
when he wrote to his brother, Will, whom he was trying to interest
in becoming manager of his farm:

You must on your wife's account remember that as far as society is
concerned, it means isolation, the size of the tract precludes close
neighbors, the immediate surrounding country is not first class for
agricultural purposes, our selection being made so as to give chances
of a large area of grazing lands without having to purchase it and

the few settlers now in that part of the country are Scandinavian, good in one sense, yet not too companious. The farm itself, however, is one of the most beautiful tracts in the N.W.[82]

Power's farm of 6,600 acres was in 21 different sections in Sheyenne and Helendale townships of northwest Richland County near the present-day villages of Leonard, Kindred, and Walcott. All the buildings were located on one quarter section in Helendale Township (N.W. ¼ of Sec. 33, T. 136, R. 52). He also had many other farms spread throughout several counties in Minnesota and North Dakota but he never revealed just how many acres he owned. If he had assembled them all in one location, he might have been one of the largest landholders in the State.[83]

At one time in the early 1880's he held 35 mortgages on 3,100 acres of land which included many 40-, 80-, and 160-acre tracts. In addition, he held a large number of lots in the new towns along the Northern Pacific.[84] In 1886 he listed 8,524 acres of land in Barnes, Stutsman, Griggs, Foster, and Richland counties which he wanted to sell on the time-payment basis. Besides that, he had large tracts of land in Clay, Wilkin, Ottertail, and Becker counties in Minnesota, and Cass, Grand Forks, Welsh, Steele, Pembina, and Ransom counties in North Dakota, including lots in Casselton and Fargo.[85]

A very interesting sidelight in Power's land holdings was given in a letter to J. L. Grandin in Tidoute, Pennsylvania, in which Power thanked Grandin for a gift of a half section of land to the Power twins who were six years old. Power said, "Please accept my acknowledgments for the expression of your appreciation of what you kindly demur my assistance in inauguration of an enterprise that I sincerely hope will prove one of large profit to yourself and benefit to the road." [86]

Helendale was established in May, 1880, and remained in the Power family until 1937 when it was purchased by Gerrit DeVries.[87] Improvements were started at once so that within four years there were seven miles of fence and $20,000 in buildings on the place.[88] There were 14 buildings, including a dwelling, 20 feet by 30 feet, 1-½ stories with a 16 feet by 34 feet annex; an office and dormitory 26 feet by 28 feet; 2 horse barns, one 18 feet by 87 feet, the other 30 feet by 72 feet; 3 cow barns, 18 feet by 50 feet, 30 feet by 72 feet, and 30 feet by 72 feet; a sheep barn 40 feet by 120 feet; and a cattle shed 14 feet by 200 feet, in addition to a milk house, workshop, smoke house, hog barn, and engine shed. The cattle yards were surrounded by solid board fences.[89]

In addition to being the creator of the bonanza idea, Power can rightfully be considered the father of North Dakota agriculture because of his many innovations and his leadership in that field. Power was interested in more than wheat monoculture; he was interested in all phases of farming, in perfecting grains, grasses, and livestock. It is that all-round interest in agriculture and promotion of its many organizations and institutions that made him the great man of early North Dakota farming. He was out to prove that North Dakota was worth something as an all-purpose farm state and disliked the idea that it should be considered fit only for snow birds in the winter and grasshoppers in the summer.

Power was the leader in promoting production of livestock in northern Dakota. He purchased registered cattle for a foundation stock and built up a herd. Power sold most of his increase to local farmers for breeding purposes. In this respect his influence was felt on every livestock farm that purchased or used his cattle. A brief inventory indicates that he possessed a wide array of high-quality livestock. There were 80 horses including one imported registered Norman stallion. The cattle herd consisted of 230 head, including 41 registered Shorthorns and 119 "¾ purebred or better." [90] The pride of the Power herd was Eclipse, a registered Shorthorn bull imported from Scotland at a cost of $800. This bull was secured through his connections with James J. Hill. [91] The Power hog herd numbered 130 head, most of which were purebred Berkshires, although some were Yorkshires. [92] He had 250 sheep, mostly high-grade Cotswolds, including 3 purebred bucks, 6 purebred ewes, and 2 purebred Shropshire bucks. [93] Later Power crossed the Cotswold with the Shropshire, making what he considered a superior animal. In 1881 he purchased one purebred Cotswold buck for $500 which must have been a fabulous price in those days. [94] In the chicken house were 25 highly bred bronze turkeys from a breeder in Ohio who had also supplied him with 25 Plymouth Rock chickens. [95] Also listed were 10 geese, 9 ducks (including 2 Imperial Pekin drakes which were reported to have cost $50), and several dogs. [96] Power planned to expand his livestock operations until he had 200 horses, 750 cattle, 300 sheep, and 500 hogs. [97]

Power had a good market among Dakota farmers for all the livestock produced on the farm. His journals are filled with correspondence from interested buyers and his answers give an interesting insight on his success in this respect. "Our pure bred bull calves are sold as fast as dropped. . . . From our present litter of collie pups . . . we can sell a dog pup when weaned and ready to ship by express . . . at $10." [98] From 1887 on there was considerable correspondence about the sale of horses, cattle, sheep, dogs, hogs, and turkeys.

Power made some changes in his breeding program. Farmers were hard pressed to pay the higher prices that could be asked for registered animals so he bred a large number of high-grade animals which were attractive to Dakota farmers at lower prices.[99] Writing to the *Northwest Agriculturist* magazine, Power asked them to cancel his advertisement in that periodical because "we have sold out our original stock of sheep, dogs, poultry and hogs . . . [and] until next season will not have anything to sell except cattle and horses."[100]

Power was not only interested in raising breeding stock but also in feeding cattle and hogs. He was constantly writing to his manager on the farm, giving instruction how to prepare new rations. He was not afraid to experiment, for he wanted to prove that cattle could be economically and profitably grown in Dakota. In one of his letters he informed the manager how certain feeds should be ground and mixed "so as to experiment in feeding on all the stock, for I am anxious to test results of extra care and feed. I want to show something ahead of anything in the country."[101] His farm was equipped with a scale; cattle were weighed frequently and a close account was kept on gain and feed intake. Entire tables in his journals indicate the results which must have been some of the top performances of that day. His scales, records, and experiments must have made him appear as a freak to his contemporaries.

Power's interest in agriculture did not stop with livestock. He was a leader in adapting new seed varieties and cultivation techniques to his Dakota farm. His need for pasture and hay for livestock feed prompted him to break up the wild hay and pasture lands and seed them to timothy and red-top clover for hay, and blue grass and orchard grass for pasture.[102] Later he was active in promoting Muhlenberg grass which grew wild in his area. He took samples of first and second cuttings of this grass and had the University of Nebraska analyze it. They reported that it was more valuable than blue grass, red-top, timothy, or orchard grass.[103] By 1887 he was growing alfalfa, recording the cutting dates, and writing to the universities to secure feed values at various cutting dates.[104] After he received his reports from the universities and had recorded the results of alfalfa on his cattle, he published some articles in various farm journals describing the value of alfalfa as a crop.[105]

In contrast to the average bonanza farmer, Power was very concerned with soil conservation. His correspondence has considerable mention of crops or the lack of crops during certain years in the Dakotas. In writing to Edwin Willetts, assistant secretary of agriculture of the United States, he explained that poor crops in the late

1880's had been due to the lack of moisture. He added, however, that "there is with us . . . more or less careless farming and some large fields that have been in constant run to wheat for many years would be better for rest or change of tillage." [106] His concern for soil conservation was illustrated by his efforts in sub-soiling. He wrote: "I certainly hope the experiment will develop something that will help our sandy upland fields, for in dry summers every acre planted results in loss and I want if possible to get those fields so they will grow grass for new soil to plow down." [107] To prevent wind erosion, Power secured a press drill which he used in seeding for the first time in the spring of 1888. In June he reported that he did not care to comment on performance until after harvest. He did note that some of the nearby fields had sand drifts six inches deep.

Other agricultural features where Power proved to be an innovator were in the adoption of a windmill, the buckthorn barbed wire fence, and the Oliver chilled-steel plow. Because of his position and the popularity of his farm, he often secured the advantage of an introductory offer when new products were brought into the Dakotas.[108]

In addition to his farm and railroad activities, Power led an active public life. After he left the Land Department of the Northern Pacific Railway he worked in the same position for James J. Hill's railroad, the St. Paul, Minneapolis and Manitoba Railway. He left it in 1885 to become secretary-treasurer of the South St. Paul Union Stockyards Company. Ill health caused him to resign and he lived on his farm until he was appointed by Governor Louis K. Church to become director of the Territorial Board of Agriculture in 1887. He was also president of the North Dakota Dairyman's Association. In 1890 Governor John Miller appointed Power to the Board of Trustees of the North Dakota Agricultural College and also special agent of the State Board of Public Lands. He held those positions until May 9, 1893, when he was named president of the North Dakota Agricultural College and director of the Experiment Station. He remained president until June 29, 1895.[109]

Power wrote many articles for farm journals, promoted agricultural fairs and livestock events, and spoke to many farm groups including the Farmers Institute conducted by the University of Wisconsin. His address at that gathering was on "results and suggestions worked out from the records of a Book farmer." [110] Many of his articles brought him speaking engagements, particularly his information on livestock raising.[111] A speaking opportunity he hoped for but did not receive was one to appear before the Stutsman County Farmers Alliance.

But to him it was "no disappointment, it is in fact a release from what might have been an embarrassing position to me."[112] Power dearly loved the Northern Pacific country, as he preferred to call it. He was a great promoter of the area and as mentioned before was interested in all phases of the State's agriculture.[113]

FOOTNOTES

[1] Coulter, NDSHS, *Collections,* Vol. III, pp. 582-583. Local people were well aware of the demonstration feature of the bonanza. The *Fargo Argus,* other local papers, and distant farm journals carried advertisements selling stereoscopic views of the Dalrymple, Grandin, Elk Valley, and other better known farms. The first of these appeared in 1880. The Northern Pacific carried special excursion trains to the area to show off the bonanzas. Numerous articles carried general descriptions of the bonanza operation. Prominent Americans came to the Valley to see the big bonanzas. In his correspondence, Power indicates that leaders in many fields came to see his farm. Local papers had several articles about easterners who toured the region. Dalrymple had visits from the McCormicks of Chicago and President Rutherford Hayes. John S. Dalrymple commented that he sat between his father, Oliver, and the President as they toured the farm in a buggy. Interview of Leonard Sackett with John S. Dalrymple, August, 1953, Dalrymple Papers, NDIRS, File 549.

[2] Power, letter to editor, *Cultivator and Country Gentleman,* May 10, 1877, NDIRS, File 309.

[3] Poultney Bigelow, "The Bonanza Farms of the West," *The Atlantic Monthly,* Vol. 45 (Jan., 1880), pp. 23-44. This article continued by expressing fears that the small farmer had of this big capitalistic enterprise and that he could not compete against them, not unlike similar stories that are common today against a correspondingly small number of larger than ordinary farms. Alva H. Benton expressed the opinion that many "socialistic writers" felt big farms were "inevitable" in capitalistic agriculture. Benton, *Journal of Land and Public Utility Economics,* Vol. I, p. 411.

[4] William Allen White, "The Business of a Wheat Farm," *Scribners Magazine,* XXII (Nov., 1897), p. 540. This was the seventh in a series of articles entitled "The Conduct of Great Businesses."

[5] Coulter, NDSHS, *Collections,* Vol. III, p. 589.

[6] *Fargo Forum,* Jan. 18, 1927. This was an interview with Walter R. Reed, for many years president of the Amenia and Sharon Land Company.

[7] Most records about the big bonanzas have been destroyed by people who did not appreciate that dramatic and historical epoch of agricultural history. Much of the history of this exciting phase of American agriculture is found in articles written by the more alert members of agricultural journalism. Their stories have to do with the more dramatic aspects but are quite reliable. The editors of the local papers were well aware of the advertising value of the bonanza stories. They wrote tall stories as well as factual accounts. Fortunately, a few of the more progressive-minded members of the bonanza operations retained their records for their historical value. The letters and accounts of James B. Power give much general information on the bonanzas and are an excellent story of the economic conditions of that day. The accounts and records of the Baldwin Corporation are good for a later-day bonanza. But it is the accounts, records, letters, diaries, maps, and all other details furnished by the Amenia and Sharon Land Company that give a most complete and accurate story of the big bonanza farms. (The most complete information regarding bonanzas is found in collections of the North Dakota Institute of Regional Studies in the Library of the North Dakota State University.)

[8] *Fargo Daily Argus,* Sept. 4, 1882 from *Cincinnati Commercial,* Aug. 26, 1882.

[9] *Casselton Reporter,* Aug. 6, 1955, Letter to Editor from R. G. Chase, Milestone, Sask., Canada.

[10] *Fargo Forum,* Jan. 15, 1959 quoted from *Fargo Argus,* Nov. 6, 1881.

[11] W. I. Chamberlain, "Western Notes By The Way," *Cultivator and Country Gentleman*, Vol. 45 (Sept. 23, 1880), p. 611.

[12] *Fargo Daily Argus*, Sept. 2, 1881.

[13] Coulter, NDSHS, *Collections*, Vol. III, pp. 580-581. (There is no intent to imply that this study contains a complete list of all bonanzas that existed. The Minnesota side of the Red River Valley, the area north of Traill County, and any area outside of the Valley were not subjected to close research so most omissions are probably in those areas. This study was concerned primarily with Cass, Richland, and Traill counties of North Dakota. Some of the bonanzas from those counties may not be listed. On the other hand, there will be several mentioned that have not previously been recognized by most bonanza historians.)

[14] White, *Scribner's Magazine*, XXII, 541.

[15] Benton, *Journal of Land and Public Utility Economics*, Vol. I, p. 410.

[16] Power to J. Jennings, Feb. 24, 1899, File 309. Jennings was the superintendent of the Fargo Newspaper Union.

[17] *Fargo Weekly Argus*, June 30, 1880, p. 6.

[18] *Fargo Argus*, Aug. 16, 1883. Information to be listed below will increase the figures for both Grandin and Dalrymple which might have put the Dakota bonanzas in a runaway for first place in all respects. The Grandins actually owned over 75,000 acres.

[19] "Early Bonanza Farms," *The Record*, Vol. I (Dec., 1895).

[20] *Fargo Argus*, June 26, 1883.

[21] *Casselton Reporter*, Jan. 19, 1917.

[22] John S. Dalrymple Interview, NDIRS, File 549.

[23] Coulter, NDSHS, *Collections*, Vol. III, p. 580.

[24] Clippings from the *Moorhead Daily News*, Sept. 12, 1912, Grandin Papers, NDIRS, File 148.

[25] Clipping from *The Goose*, Nov., 1894, Grandin Papers, NDIRS, File 269.

[26] Records of the Amenia and Sharon Land Company, Journal 1, pp. 1, 2. Company Papers, NDIRS, File 134. (Hereafter cited as A & S Papers, File 134.)

[27] Power to Barney, Jan. 11, 1881, NDIRS, File 309.

[28] *Ibid.*

[29] Leonard Sackett correspondence with Mrs. G. E. Dunwell, Spiritwood Farm Papers, NDIRS, File 164.

[30] Interview of Leonard Sackett with Mrs. Sadie Walker, Spiritwood Farm Papers, NDIRS, File 173. Mrs. Walker's father purchased some of the Spiritwood farm.

[31] Power to Barney, Jan. 11, 1881, NDIRS, File 309.

[32] *Cultivator and Country Gentleman*, Vol. 41, p. 340.

[33] *Fargo Argus*, June 27, 1882, p. 2.

[34] *Fargo Argus*, Nov. 24, 1881, p. 2.

[35] *Fargo Argus*, June 26, 1882, p. 3.

[36] Spokesfield, pp. 45-47. In 1882 the Sykes farm had the first dance in Wells County. It was with great difficulty that sixteen women were obtained for the dance.

[37] Power to Barney, Jan. 11, 1881, NDIRS, File 309.

[38] *Ibid.*

[39] *Ibid.*; Fargo Daily Argus, Oct. 8, 1880, p. 4.

[40] Interview of Leonard Sackett with John Walcher, Dwight Farm Papers, NDIRS, File 214.

[41] Interview of Leonard Sackett with E. B. Downing, Downing Farm Papers, NDIRS, File 197, Mr. Bagg lived until about 1953 and as late as the 1930's his farm contained over fourteen sections (9,120 acres).

[42] Interview of Leonard Sackett with Emil Mecklenburg, Keystone Farm Papers, NDIRS, File 607. Mecklenburg was a Keystone employee.

[43] Power, NDSHS, *Collections*, Vol. III, p. 337.

[44] R. D. Crawford notes, Dwight Farm Papers, NDIRS, File 290.

[45] John Miller Papers, NDIRS, File 84.

[46] *Fargo Daily Argus*, April 10, 1880.

⁴⁷ Fargo Argus, Aug. 18, 1880, p. 5.

⁴⁸ John Miller Papers, Dwight Farm Papers, NDIRS, File 84; Horace B. Crandall, *A History of Richland County* (Colfax, North Dakota, 1886), p. 68.

⁴⁹ Dwight, Center, Denton, and Summit townships in Richland County and Norman, Clifton, Bergen, and Highland Townships in Steele County. Records of John Miller estate, H. F. Chaffee correspondence, A & S Papers, File 134.

⁵⁰ Dwight Farms Statement for Jan. 1, 1909, H. F. Chaffee Papers, A & S Papers, File 134.

⁵¹ Benton, *Journal of Land and Public Utility Economics*, Vol. I, p. 409.

⁵² Interview of Leonard Sackett with Emil Trapp, Watson Farm Papers, NDIRS, File 827; A memorial address on "Life and Character of Lewis F. Watson" (Washington: U.S. Government Printing Office, 1891), File 827.

⁵³ *Fargo Argus*, April 15, 1882, p. 4, Dec. 26, 1882, p. 8. Buttsville was not the only town started by the Buttz family. The *Fargo Argus*, April 13, 1882, reported that R. S. Munger and Major Buttz had made a trip to Foster County to lay a plat for the present town of Carrington. Buttz and Munger owned land next to the 34,000-acre farm of Casey and Carrington in Township 135.

⁵⁴ Some early newspaper accounts refer to Addison Leech as Major Leech, apparently the same person. Another reference to A. Leech and Sons indicate that they had 3,800 acres seeded to wheat in 1882. *Cultivator and Country Gentleman*, Vol. 47, p. 571.

⁵⁵ *Fargo Argus*, Nov. 28, 1881.

⁵⁶ *History and Biography of North Dakota* (Chicago, 1900), p. 635.

⁵⁷ *Fargo Argus*, Nov. 28, 1881.

⁵⁸ Interview of Norton Berg with Mrs. Jack Garrett. Mrs. Garrett is the daughter of F. S. Colwell and resides in Moorhead.

⁵⁹ *Fargo Argus*, Sept. 2, 1881, p. 2.

⁶⁰ *Fargo Argus*, Sept. 2, 1881, p. 2, April 22, 1883, April 9, 1884.

⁶¹ *Cultivator and Country Gentleman*, Vol. 47, p. 571.

⁶² Grandin Papers, NDIRS, File 450.

⁶³ Marshall Field had land in this general area. In 1881 he had purchased three sections from John B. Raymond. *Fargo Argus*, Sept. 2, 1881.

⁶⁴ Hilstad interview, Grandin Papers, NDIRS, File 269.

⁶⁵ Power to Barney, Jan. 11, 1881, NDIRS, File 309.

⁶⁶ Benton, *Journal of Land and Public Utility Economics*, Vol. I, p. 411.

⁶⁷ Power to Barney, Jan. 11, 1881, NDIRS, File 309; Power, NDSHS, *Collections*, Vol. III, p. 340.

⁶⁸ Power to Barney, Jan. 11, 1881, NDIRS, File 309.

⁶⁹ *Fargo Argus*, Oct. 12, 1882, p. 8, May 18, 1882, p. 6.

⁷⁰ *Cultivator and Country Gentleman*, Vol. 47, p. 571.

⁷¹ *Fargo Argus*, March 9, 1882, p. 6; Henry J. Winser, *The Great Northwest, A Guide Book and Itinerary* (New York: 1883), p. 134; *Cultivator and Country Gentleman*, Vol. 41, p. 340; Power to Stark, Dec. 12, 1876, File 309.

⁷² *Fargo Argus*, May 12, 1882, p. 8, May 18, 1882, p. 6.

⁷³ *Fargo Weekly Argus*, June 23, 1880, p. 6, July 7, 1880, p. 4.

⁷⁴ *Fargo Weekly Argus*, Feb. 4, 1880, p. 2, March 17, 1880, p. 1, March 31, 1880, p. 7.

⁷⁵ *Fargo Argus*, July 5, 1883.

⁷⁶ *Fargo Argus*, May 18, 1882, p. 6.

⁷⁷ *Fargo Argus*, April 20, 1883; interview with A. R. Byers, an old settler. The von Steinwehr referred to was General von Steinwehr of Civil War fame and a close friend of General Lew Wallace. It is very likely that also included in this farming company was Harry D. Hurley's farm of four sections in Caledonia Township in Traill County.

⁷⁸ *Fargo Argus*, Jan. 18, 1881, p. 4, May 14, 1883, Aug. 8, 1885.

⁷⁹ Lamphere, MHS, *Collections*, X, 21.

⁸⁰ *Fargo Weekly Argus*, Feb. 4, 1880, p. 7.

⁸¹ *Cultivator and Country Gentleman*, Vol. 41, p. 340; Power to Barney, Jan. 11, 1881, NDIRS, File 309; *Fargo Argus*, Sept. 8, 1880, Sept. 22, 1880, Nov. 21, 1881, June 15,

1882, June 27, 1882, July 15, 1882, Aug. 8, 1882, March 26, 1883, Sept. 8, 1883, March 27, 1884. (A compilation of bonanzas by Leonard Sackett is in the files of the NDIRS.)

[82] Power to W. A. Power, March 4, 1880, NDIRS, File 309.

[83] Power to J. A. Pickert, March 20, 1894, NDIRS, File 309; Power to B. W. Benson, April 15, 1885, File 309; Power Letterbook V, 645 diagram of Helendale, File 309. Pickert was the treasurer of Richland County; Benson was an attorney.

[84] Power Letterbook, VI, 179-180, NDIRS, File 309.

[85] Power Letterbook, VIII, 279, NDIRS, File 309.

[86] Power to J. L. Grandin, Jan. 19, 1877, NDIRS, File 309.

[87] Radcliff interview, Helendale Papers, NDIRS, File 254.

[88] *Fargo Argus*, Sept. 1, 1884.

[89] Power Letterbook, VII, 278-281, NDIRS, File 309.

[90] Power to S. S. Lyon, Dec. 10, 1900, NDIRS, File 309. Lyon was a Fargo banker.

[91] Power Letterbook, VIII, 893, File 309.

[92] Power Letterbook, VII, 487, File 309. A speech by Power entitled, "Stock Raising in Dakota."

[93] Power Letterbook, VII, 648, File 309.

[94] Power to Will A. Power, Nov. 14, 1881, File 309.

[95] Power to John J. Maxon, Dec. 18, 1880, File 309. Maxon was an Ohio chicken breeder.

[96] Power to Wm. H. Mills, March 23, 1882, File 309.

[97] Power Letterbook, VII, 648, File 309.

[98] Power to Jeff Sage, Nov. 16, 1888, File 309.

[99] Power to E. N. Hicks, Dec. 14, 1889, File 309.

[100] Power to *N. W. Agriculturist*, Nov. 29, 1890, File 309.

[101] Power to W. A. Power, Dec. 3, 1881, File 309.

[102] Power to W. A. Power, June 27, 1881, File 309.

[103] Power to E. A. Webb, Aug. 26, 1887, File 309. Webb was publisher of the *North Western Farmer* of Fargo, now *The Farmer* of St. Paul.

[104] Power to W. A. Henry, Aug. 12, 1887, File 309. Henry was a professor of agriculture at the University of Wisconsin.

[105] Power to S. M. Owen, July 18, 1887, File 309. Owen was the managing editor of the *Farm Stock and Home* magazine of Minneapolis.

[106] Power to Edwin D. Willetts, April 9, 1890, File 309.

[107] Power to W. W. Hays, Oct. 23, 1895, File 309. Hays was a professor of agriculture at the Agricultural Experiment Station, St. Anthony Park, Minn.

[108] Power to Challenge Wind and Feed Mill Co., March 28, 1888, File 309; Power to Buck Thorn Fence Co., April 9, 1888, File 309; Power to Magill and Co., Aug. 18, 1891, File 309.

[109] Power to Helen G. Putnam, Jan. 5, 1895, File 309. Miss Putnam was the biographer of the New England Society in Fargo.

[110] Power to W. H. Morrison, July 20, 1887, File 309. Morrison was superintendent of the Farmers Institute of the University of Wisconsin.

[111] Power to E. A. Webb, June 8, 1887, File 309.

[112] Power to Chas. W. Blen, March 17, 1887, File 309. Blen was the editor of the *North Dakota Farmer*, Jamestown.

[113] Interview of Leonard Sackett with Robert Reed, Helendale Papers, NDIRS, File 438. Reed was associated with the Amenia and Sharon Land Company and a friend of Power.

CHAPTER IV

Bonanza Farms: General Operations

THE BONANZA farms provide a great drama in American agricultural history. Representing the first factory farms, they were operated like great business enterprises, using professional management in charge of a large labor force. The owners needed good managers to protect their large investment and, if possible, to produce a profit.

The manager in his operation had to start from scratch, breaking the sod, establishing a farmstead, and determining the best system of farming. Thorough accounting methods were necessary to keep the large enterprise under control. Whenever weaknesses in the operation appeared, a quick remedy had to be found for unlike the family farm, the bonanza could continue to exist only if it showed a profit.

The bonanzas succeeded only because they could effectively use a large labor force by adopting large-scale, efficient machinery. The labor force was transient, but the supply was apparently adequate until the 1890's. Labor was not required to be skilled in agriculture as supervisory help did all the technical work which required certain skills. Large machinery not only gave the bonanzas an advantage in low cost of production over the family farm, but the great parades of machines provided much drama to this phase of agriculture.

Professional Management

An outstanding feature of the bonanza farm was the large degree to which it used professional management. Many of the owners were financiers or industrialists who had no farm background but appreciated the need of good management. As men of the business world, the investors realized that if their farms were to be successful, they would have to be large, well financed, and scientifically operated. The owner thought of the farm manager just as he did of the division manager of his railroad or of the branch manager of one of his banks. Business experience taught them that a skilled workman does not always make a good manager. They did not seek out some ex-hired man with a farm background, but sought people with known managerial abilities. The managers were first-class businessmen and many of them became leaders in the State such as John Miller, North Dakota's first governor.[1]

Even a partial list of the better-known farm managers reads like an early North Dakota Who's Who. Among them were: John Miller of the Dwight Farm and Land Company; Charles Cady who succeeded Miller on the Dwight Farms; F. A. Bagg, manager of the Downing farms who became one of the big land owners and prominent citizens of Richland County; the Cooper brothers from Chicago who managed their farm near Cooperstown; Richard Sykes, the Englishman, who operated his own farm and was responsible for developing Sykeston; R. Hadwin who opened up the Wheatland area with his managerial abilities; J. W. McNary, former county agent in Minnesota who ably managed the very extensive holdings of the Baldwin corporation; Moody Watson who did his best to hold the Watson farm together; the Grandins who employed several men of repute on their three separate holdings, among them R. S. Wilson, one of the last agents on the Mayville farm; James McKessich who had managed the Dwight farms and later went to the Grandin farms; W. W. Warren who came from Pennsylvania to superintend the Mayville farm and was very skilled in livestock management; J. R. Hogan who was described by many as the most efficient agent of the Grandins; Alton and William Dalrymple who had a share in the Grandin operations, the Cass-Cheney farm, and their own holdings; E. W. Chaffee, organizer of the Amenia and Sharon Land Company; and Thorwald Thorson, superintendent of the Dalrymple farms from 1894 to 1917.[2]

Three managers who stand above all others in the bonanza story deserve special mention. They are: James B. Power who, although he did not claim to be a farm expert, proved his managing abilities when the going was rough; Oliver Dalrymple, the Minnesota Wheat King, who became the best known of all the bonanza managers (His name is synonymous with bonanza because of the wide publicity about his enterprises); H. F. Chaffee, the real king of the bonanza managers although his life was prematurely ended in his early forties. H. F. Chaffee had not only pyramided his holdings but also built a very sound financial structure under these holdings. His leadership enabled the Amenia and Sharon Land Company to remain in business as a bonanza operation longer than any of the other great farms.

To protect their investment of from $100,000 to $300,000, bonanza owners paid their managers well because after all only the best management could make a profit.[3] The cost of a good manager was only a fraction of the total, and he could easily save his salary in reduced labor expenses. Most of the managers were paid a commission in addition to a straight salary. An exception to this was J. C. McNary of the Baldwin farms who received $6,000 annually for his services.[4] The income of the bonanza manager, wrote William Allen White in *Scribner's*, was the "salary equivalent to that of the superintendent of an important railway division."[5] F. A. Bagg, manager of the Mooreton farm which was the chief unit of the Downing farms, received a salary plus a share in the net profits. As an additional incentive, he was offered a one-fourth interest in all the property if he stayed as manager for twenty years.[6] The highest paid managers appear to be those who worked for the Cass-Cheney, Dalrymple, Grandin, and the Amenia and Sharon bonanzas.

Once Cass and Cheney had secured their land in 1874 they were faced with the problem of what to do with it. One of their objectives was to call attention to the possibilities of settlements in the Northern Pacific country. Power advised Cass:

In one of my letters I spoke of the possibility of the Mennonites taking part of your land and think contracts can be made with some of them for the cultivation of 80 acre lots each, but they are a peculiar people and their primitive way of doing business will require good overseeing to bring profitable results.[7]

He also mentioned that land was cheap and a good offer would have to be made to get tenants. Cass and Cheney turned to Power in an effort to find a good and efficient general manager for their holdings.

Cass inquired of Power about H. S. Back, a prominent realtor and later bonanza farmer and politician of Fargo, as a possible manager. Back was reputed to have the best intimate knowledge of the land within the Valley. But Power replied: "I have no business acquaintance with Mr. Back, but know that he has not a good reputation, being classed among the 'sharps' and is not a man I would recommend as an agent for you." Power himself declined the farm managership by stating:

I should willingly act for you but have had little experience as a farmer and to make the work a success would require more time and close personal attention that it is not possible for me to give without neglect of company business and unless giving the close attention necessary would not want to be held responsible for the results.[8]

Then Cass thought of Oliver Dalrymple, an old acquaintance. He was bankrupt at this time and was waiting for another opportunity to display his managerial skill. Power, who also knew Dalrymple, favorably commented to Cass:

I have your favor relative to arrangements with Dalrymple for cultivation of your lands and am glad the bargain is made for his experience in wheat farming will without doubt make the investment a profitable one for you and his reputation for success in this line is such as to attract others to the same locality—the road over all others interested will secure immediate benefit from the arrangement.[9]

To Cheney he was direct and emphatic. "I have known Mr. Dalrymple since 1857 and have every reason to believe that he is perfectly reliable and a man of excellent judgment in his line of business."[10]

Oliver Dalrymple had become known as the Minnesota wheat king with his large wheat farming operations near Cottage Grove in Washington County, Minnesota. He was associated with the Allegheny College in Pennsylvania and later attended Yale Law School. In 1856 he came to St. Peter, Minnesota, to practice law but soon moved to St. Paul. After the Sioux outbreak in 1862, he was commissioned to go to Washington, D.C. to settle claims for those who had lost property in the Indian attacks. His fee for services rendered was $40,000 which he invested in a 3,000 acre farm.[11] Dalrymple farmed until 1874. He was a very successful wheat farmer but, unfortunately, lost his farming profits by speculating in the grain trade. General George Cass, at that time president of the Northern Pacific, had come to know the "wheat king" while he was operating his Cottage Grove farm. Since Dalrymple was a good farmer who used the latest and most advanced farming techniques, he was hired by Cass to serve as manager on a combined salary plus commission basis.

Oliver Dalrymple received a contract that recognized his great repute as a farm manager. Cass and Cheney were to "furnish everything and pay all expenses" and Dalrymple was to be in complete charge from breaking the land to selling the crop. Cass and Cheney were to be repaid their entire expenses in operations, their investment in the land plus a 7 per cent return on their investment, while Dalrymple was to receive a one-third share in the net profits with which he could purchase one-third of the property at the original cost.[12] This contract eventually enabled Dalrymple to expand his holdings to about 100,000 acres in the late 1890's. In 1896 when a final settlement was made, the farm had paid for itself with interest. At that time Dalrymple had secured 50 per cent of the original bonanza. In 1910 John S. Dalrymple purchased the other half of that farm.[13]

After his primary contract with Cass and Cheney, Dalrymple entered into another with the Grandins that was even more rewarding. His major contract with them, dated May 25, 1876, gave him not only a cash payment, but also an opportunity to purchase an undivided half interest in the 44,980 acres he was to manage for them. Dalrymple was allowed to purchase his half interest for $14,328.15 ($0.65 per acre), the actual cash cost to the Grandins as purchased by Northern Pacific bonds. He was to pay $1,000 down and the balance in five annual payments at 7.5 per cent interest. He was obligated to manage the south Grandin farm for six years.[14] Oliver placed his brother, Alton, in charge of the farm and kept in constant contact with him by telegraph and mail. After he had secured half interest in the Grandin bonanza, Dalrymple continued to buy up a few sections at a time, especially after 1900.[15]

Methods of Bonanza Operation

The bonanza manager was faced with a very challenging task. No text books on how to run a bonanza existed. The manager of the great cotton and sugar plantations of the South could give some advice, but in the South the crops, climate, machinery, and labor force were quite different. The bonanza manager was a true pioneer in directing the first large-scale mechanized farms.

Breaking the prairie sod was the first major task requiring the manager's supervision. This could be done by one of three methods. Men with teams and plows from the nearby smaller farms could be hired for $2.50 an acre and could break an acre or slightly more in one day. There were also some professional "sod busters" in the area. The best known of these was Peter Seims who broke land for most of the bonanza operators, including Dalrymple, Cass, Cheney, the Grandins, and the Amenia and Sharon. Another way of getting the sod broken was to buy the horses and plows and hire a labor force to operate them. This was the most difficult method because horses, plows, and men had to be imported and cared for. Shelters had to be built and all food for men and horses had to be purchased. Dalrymple used all three methods. In 1875, his first year of operation, he broke only two sections of land for crops.[16]

Breaking the sod was a slow and expensive process. In addition to the first breaking, which took place in June and July, the land had to be back-set in September and October. Back-setting was cross-plowing the previously plowed sod so that it was less lumpy for seeding in the spring. The first year's sod breaking expense was at least $3.50 per acre which was much more than the cost of the land. Yet, in spite of the cost and the difficulty of the task, a considerable amount of land was broken in a short period of time. In 1877 Dalrymple had 4,400 acres in crops on the Cass-Cheney-Dalrymple farm and 2,600 acres on the Grandin farm.[17] He planned to break a total of 5,000 acres of prairie sod each year on all the farms he managed. He succeeded, for in 1880 he harvested 22,000 acres of wheat alone from the Cass-Cheney-Dalrymple farm.[18] Most of the bonanzas had a goal of breaking 3,000 to 8,000 acres each year until the entire farm was under cultivation. The Cooper brothers who established a bonanza between Sanborn and Cooperstown in 1880, put 12 plows into operation before a single building was erected and succeeded in breaking 5,000 acres during their first year. On the south Grandin farm which Dalrymple managed, there were 14,000 acres under cultivation by 1892.[19] Breaking a fixed number of acres each year kept the men employed during the summer lull between seeding and harvest. Dalrymple intended to keep on breaking new sod until he had 75,000 acres under cultivation in addition to pasture and hay land.[20]

Establishing the farmsteads was the next great task after improving the land. Because of its location along the main line of the Northern Pacific, the Cass-Cheney-Dalrymple bonanza did not have the problem of securing building materials, equipment, and supplies, a problem that some of the other big farms had. The Cooper brothers, for example, had to haul all their materials and supplies a distance of thirty-two miles by wagon since the Northern Pacific branch line was not constructed to Cooperstown until 1883.[21] They used forty-five of their seventy-five teams to build a wagon road and haul fifteen carloads of lumber and six carloads of oats for horse feed from Sanborn.[22]

The bonanzas were broken into a variety of divisions and subdivisions to suit individual operations. Most had divisions of about 5,000 acres which were made up of stations or subdivisions of 1,200 to 1,800 acres. Under the bonanza manager heading each division was a superintendent, and under him, leading each station or subdivision, was a foreman.[23] This system of divisions and sub-managers was mocked as being somewhat militaristic by the labor force. References to this military type of organization were made by the newspapers to dramatize the size of the labor force on the bonanzas.[24]

The work schedule on the subdivisions had to be flexible. During harvest, which had to be completed within a limited period of time, the entire bonanza labor force worked together. Plowing, however, could be done at a more leisurely pace, and was handled by each subdivision. Accounting, blacksmithing, repair, storage and grain-cleaning were most economically done at bonanza headquarters. In 1877 Power described bonanza management thus: "The management is perfect and [the] most complete system seems to govern. Everything moves forward with the greatest regularity and while there is liberal expenditure yet there is every evidence of careful judicious economy in all pertaining to the work." [25] Such large operations necessarily required a high degree of organization.

The organizational structures of the bonanzas were as numerous and varied as the bonanzas themselves. The Baldwin farms had the largest single operating unit. Much of the farm was rented out to tenants who were supervised by the farm manager, but the remaining land was operated as a single unit. In 1925 the Baldwins still had 6,000 acres in a single unit of operation. [26] This was the exception. The Grandin farms, which contained 75,000 acres, were spread out into at least 10 separate operations. Their land purchased from the railroad was in three widely scattered blocks, each sufficiently large to require subdivision. Oliver Dalrymple managed the south Grandin holdings, centered around the junction of the Elm and Red Rivers. At the same time, W. W. Warren was superintendent of the main Grandin farm, usually called the Mayville farm, located northwest of that village. The third Grandin holding, centered around Blanchard west of Hillsboro, had another manager. The Mayville farm was subdivided into three divisions; Division Number One, or Headquarters farm, with a large and complete set of buildings, and Divisions Number Two and Number Three with similar but less complete sets of buildings. [27] According to James McKessich, who became a Grandin manager at a later date, the Mayville farm was divided into four divisions. An extra division was required when the Grandins increased their livestock operation. [28] The Headquarters Division was, however, the only one that had a full-scale year-round operation.

By 1880 the Cass-Cheney-Dalrymple bonanza had 8,170 acres under cultivation in several divisions with a superintendent and clerk in charge of each. [29] The actual size of the division under a superintendent varied from 3,500 to 5,000 acres. [30] John S. Dalrymple reported that 3,500 acres was the common division size, with each divided into 3 subdivisions of 1,200 acres under the control of a foreman. Each of the subdivisions had basic buildings required for men and animals. [31] The subdivisions were nearly always closed when the fall plowing was complete and everything moved to division headquarters.

In the summer, daily contact between the subdivisions and headquarters was made by horse and buggy. As facilities improved, daily contact was provided by telephone, telegraph, and mail communications. [32] The foremen were instructed to call headquarters each morning and in addition each received a written schedule of operations daily. This was the Dalrymple practice from 1896 to 1917. Each evening the foremen reported the day's progress, the hours for each man, and the request for supplies. All records were kept at the central office after the telephone made daily contact possible.[33] The Grandins had four miles of telephone line connecting the three divisions of the Mayville farm shortly after opening of the headquarters in 1878. Many of the old timers say it was the first practical telephone line west of the Mississippi.[34] In 1883 the telephone line was extended from the depot at Hillsboro to the Grandin farm at Halstad, Minnesota. This system was later purchased by the Community Telephone Company which built an exchange in 1898.[35]

Record Keeping and Profits

One of the most detailed tasks of the bonanza manager was the keeping of records. The bookkeeper was his right-hand man. Adequate office space and a full set of office equipment was provided on each of the big bonanzas, for they were considered as vital as any piece of machinery. The bookkeeper was one of the few full-time employees. The average farmer of that day was interested in feeding his family and getting enough cash to pay the taxes and the mortgage on his farm. His records consisted of a few slips of paper in his hip pocket and some mental notes in the back of his mind. This was not the case of the bonanza owner who employed many people and invested large sums of money. He wanted to be able to look at a balance sheet at the end of the year to determine the success of the operation. The bonanzas were owned by business-minded people and the farms were operated in a business-like manner. Strict accounting caused the bonanzas to change their methods of operation and enterprises more readily than the average farmer because the balance sheet told them what was profitable and what was not.

Because the bonanzas were such big enterprises, it is not surprising that considerable attention was given to the production costs and income. In that respect, some bonanzas were real "bonanzas" in the sense that they produced a great profit, while others were bonanzas in size only. The farmers of that day had many arguments about the most profitable way of farming—the bonanza way or the small-farmer method. Cost figures were freely tossed about to determine the per bushel and per acre cost of raising wheat on the bonanzas.

National magazines carried detailed accounts of costs and profits on the big farms. One of the first such articles, on the Grandins, appeared in the *Cultivator and Country Gentlemen* of February 6, 1879. They figured as their original cost the cost of land, breaking, back-setting, and buildings and fences to average $10 per acre. This figure obviously could not be charged against one year's cost of production, but 7 per cent interest was charged on this amount in addition to their annual operating expense. The cost of raising a crop on the basis of hired teams, hired machinery, and men was $8.50 per acre. This included a $0.30 interest charge per acre on operating capital. The Grandins knew they could operate more cheaply with their own machinery, however, it was not possible to do this all at once. They estimated that they should have an average per acre yield of 16 bushels which would sell for $0.85 per bushel for a gross return of $12 on each acre and a net of $3. Shipping expenses to the higher eastern markets were included in production cost. Yields varied, but the Grandins fared well in their first two years. In 1877 on 2,600 acres the average yield was 24.1 bushels per acre, and in 1878 on 4,000 acres the average was 20 bushels per acre.[36]

Operating costs varied from farm to farm. For example, Dalrymple did not agree with the Grandins about costs. However, he was using farm-owned equipment and power and felt that the total cost was less than $8.50 an acre. The Grandins, having been bankers, were much more aware of such charges as interest and depreciation than Dalrymple who was less interested in details. Accurate bookkeeping was not one of his characteristics.[37] Major Leach, who purchased a farm south of Fargo, said that his total cost per acre for the first year, including $16.50 purchase price, was $26.50. His gross income was $34.50 per acre leaving him a net of $8 per acre profit after the complete return of his money.[38] Dalrymple said that production cost per acre was $6 when company equipment and teams were used with men hired by the month, but that this rose to $8 per acre when custom crews and day labor were used.[39] The owners of the Thompson-Kendall farm declared that their cost per acre was $3.24 using their own equipment and power. Thompson and Kendall operated on a smaller scale and did not charge land cost or their own labor. The latter item was the greatest single expense in the entire operation.[40] The gross profit per acre, disregarding land cost and personal labor, was $10.76 on the Thompson-Kendall farm from a twenty-bushel yield.

The bonanza operators kept records on each task that had to be performed to produce a crop. The Grandins knew that after the first year it cost them $0.65 an acre to plow their land. They quickly learned that if the teams, men, and equipment could do drainage work and road building in their slack season, much of the cost of plowing could be offset by the cash income from those jobs. Normally, the land was harrowed five times for a total cost of $0.85 per acre. This included three harrowings after seeding if they could keep ahead of the grain. Grain was harvested and weighed separately from every field so that once the bookkeeper had all the figures tallied, the manager could tell results produced by a particular seed, new method of tillage, or whether the field needed building up the next year. The cost of harvesting, threshing, and hauling to the elevator was $1.60 per acre. Other costs were taxes, which averaged about $0.20 per acre, insurance, depreciation, the cost of raising hay and oats to feed the horses, interest on investment and operating capital. All expenses were $7.95 per acre. The interest and depreciation were based on a total machinery, land, and building cost of $30 per acre for the year 1879, considerably above its original purchase price. The Grandins averaged an 8 per cent profit in addition to 7 per cent interest for the first seven years of the 1890's.[41]

The Power-Dalrymple Conflict

Record keeping, or the lack of records, served as the basis for a sharp dispute between two of the major figures of the bonanza era. J. B. Power and Oliver Dalrymple were both men of great ability and of sound reputation. Both had good minds which were not easily changed. A little-known conflict arose between Dalrymple and Power over records of the Cass-Cheney bonanza. The dispute, really between the owners and the manager, centered around Power because he was land agent for the Northern Pacific and personal advisor to the road's directors.

Dalrymple was primarily a plunger and speculator. His son, John S. Dalrymple, said that his father was interested in pyramiding his holdings without too much concern about the amortization of the land.[42] Dalrymple counted on time and rising land prices and so proved to be a shrewd prophet of what was to happen in North Dakota agriculture. When he arrived in Dakota in 1876, Dalrymple was penniless, but he made up in experience and proven ability what he lacked in capital. Because of his reputation he was able to do a great deal of marginal financing.

Power, irked to some extent by the rise of Dalrymple, knew his financial situation intimately and did not like the way he handled it. Yet Power, himself, did not have exactly a conservative attitude; he was a great speculator in Dakota lands and a marginal financier also. There was, however, one big difference between the two men. Dalrymple was very careless in keeping accounts while Power was extremely accurate and thorough. It might have been to Dalrymple's advantage to be careless in his accounts; at least Power implied that in his correspondence with Cass and Cheney. Power, Cass, and Cheney, being railroad men, were used to expect very detailed records, while Dalrymple was a farmer and plunger who was not so concerned about them. Power, because he was known and trusted by all concerned, was given the unpleasant task of being the middleman between the owners and the manager.

Power set up a complete system of records, accounts, and vouchers for the Cass-Cheney-Dalrymple operations.[43] Yet the records for 1876 and 1877 were in very poor condition and no accurate results could be derived from them.

After nearly two years of operation, Cass and Cheney, deeply dissatisfied, wanted an accounting and made Power both cashier and accountant in the summer of 1877. When the full railroad accounting system was adopted, Power insisted that Cass and Cheney notify Dalrymple of the new procedure:

To Mr. Dalrymple who has been in the habit of running his business in the usual western way, this will seem like a great deal of unnecessary red tape and at once suggest to his mind an innumerable number of difficulties and objections, but in fact takes from here a great deal of responsibility and after the system is fairly inaugurated will I think be satisfactory to him, unless he has a pride in being the custodian of and handling the funds himself.[44]

Power anticipated the trouble that he was to have with Dalrymple.[45] He wrote to Cheney: "I see it will take some time to educate him [Dalrymple] into our system and during this educational period we do not want to delay payments on account of informalities."[46] Even though Dalrymple objected, he received large quantities of various forms to be made out in triplicate.[47] In addition, Dalrymple had to notify Power whenever he wanted to draw on the Fargo bank accounts of Cass or Cheney.[48]

In the fall of 1877 Cass visited Dakota and with Power reviewed the financial situation.[49] It is no surprise that these men should demand a strict accounting of funds, for neither Cass nor Cheney had expected to expend such large amounts on the bonanza operations. What surprised them most were the unusual requests from Dalrymple for new oat or wheat seed. So the question was raised why the seed wheat always seemed to cost more than the mill-run crops they sold.[50]

The accounts for 1876 and 1877 were not settled until the spring of 1878, but many items were never properly accounted for. Power informed Cass:

Dalrymple has got his accounts for 76/77 and the two farms so completely dovetailed together it will be impossible to make up any balance sheet closing everything for 1877. So far we find a great many irregularities in Dalrymple's accounts . . . all of these items I cannot audit unless his explanations are more lucid than any yet made.[51]

One of the most serious points of dispute was over additional management expenses. Power protested charging room and board expenses for Dalrymple's sons against the farm account as well as $800 for an additional farm foreman as a violation of the contract.[52] He also contended that Dalrymple had no right to charge for a Fargo office because a complete office and equipment were provided on the farm and he was using the Fargo office for his other interests.[53]

After the audit of the records of 1876 and 1877, Cass and Cheney clearly indicated that they "no longer wanted a Dalrymple man" to keep the books. Power advised the need for an outsider in the office on the farm because he felt there were too many of the Dalrymple family involved.[54] Cheney secured the long-sought-for accountant in Boston. It must have been with great relief that Power wrote to Dalrymple in May, 1878:" "Mr. Israel Lombard has been appointed accountant on the Cass-Cheney farms and will take charge at once. He will also be made cashier for payment of laborers and incidental accts. He will have an office, living quarters and transportation." [55]

Dalrymple did not appear to be completely willing to accept the new accountant and frequently by-passed him. Power would not permit this and informed Dalrymple: "This matter of detail I want followed closely. Mr. Lombard is on the farm for the purpose of doing the work it involves, the sooner it is brought to a rigid system the better." [56] Lombard advised Power that there was much "not to his liking with the conduct of business," and things would never be satisfactory as long as Dalrymple had so many other interests.[57] Lombard found his position far from a pleasant one and was in "hot water" with Dalrymple most of the time.[58]

A critical point in the financial affairs of the bonanza was reached in October, 1878, when Dalrymple overdrew his requisitions to Cheney's account by $1,800. Power wrote the bookkeeper that Dalrymple would not explain his overdraft and "when you close the fall work and are ready to pull out, . . . bring your books down here, . . . not in any circumstances [should they] be left on the farm." [59] In December, 1878, Cass and Cheney called Dalrymple east to settle the overdraft. Big operator though he was, Dalrymple lacked money for the trip and Power had to advance him $125.[60] As a result of the conference, Cass sold part interest in his farm to Dalrymple and both he and Cheney drew up new contracts restricting Dalrymple's power as a manager. Much to his gratification, Power was relieved of all responsibility.[61]

The biggest source of provocation to Cass and Cheney was not the irregularities in the accounts, but was Dalrymple's extensive activities beyond the borders of their bonanza. Most of the Power-Dalrymple dispute can be summed up in one letter to George Gray, a Fargo attorney, as follows:

In the study of these [accounts] however, there has been created a very strong impression that the Cass and Cheney farms have been made the vehicle in which to carry outside operations and the basis upon which other enterprises, entirely personal, are to be built; that the interests of the Cass and Cheney farms are but secondary and Mr. D. connection with them are so far as possible made subservient to his own personal advancement, regardless as to the detriment it may be to them.

Engaging in other enterprises, such as the Grandin farm, the Grandin Steamboat Line, their elevator business in Fargo; securing and working other land adjoining the Cass and Cheney farms, through various members of his own family, making constant effort to engage others, like Mr. Billings, in operations similar to that by Messers Cass and Cheney, has required so much of his time as to necessitate the employ and leaving the management of detail on the Cass and Cheney lands to hired superintendents, men apparently equal with himself to carry on the farms and to whom high salaries for such work has to be paid, an expense entirely uncalled for if he had given the work the personal oversight contemplated by the contract.

Now confining myself to the Cheney farm I find that the supt. employed for Mr. Cheney had land of his own adjoining that he was cultivating at the same time he was operating the Cheney farm, thus giving but divided attention to his employers interests. This was known to encouraged and assisted by Mr. D. for stock and utensils from the Cheney farm were used to carry on this outside farm of the supt. as well also other farms nearby worked in the names of different members of the Dalrymple family, all of whom are supposed to be working for and backed by O. Dalrymple. While these people used equipment and horses from Cheney farms he [Cheney] was forced to hire outside extra teams to get work done on his farms.[62]

Land was Dalrymple's chief interest; someone else could handle the records and finances.[63]

Dalrymple's Extensive Operations

Dalrymple's operations were extremely large. He had pyramided his holdings in a short period of time with little cash outlay of his own. Power was the first to be aware of the expansiveness of his operations for he knew who was securing land.[64] Dalrymple obtained twenty-one sections north of Fargo from the Grandins in payment of

his contract with them. In 1877 he acquired six sections near Casselton which became known as the Alton farm. Within 7 years he owned
between 30,000 and 50,000 acres of land which had cost him $0.30 to
$1.40 an acre and by 1883 was worth $10 to $25. At that time he had
an annual income in excess of $100,000 and was reputed to be worth
$750,000.[65] The combined Cass-Cheney, Grandin, and Dalrymple op-
erations, in which he secured an undivided half interest (Dalrymple
operated only half of the Grandin farm), exceeded 100,000 acres, of
which 65,000 acres were under cultivation. When the various partner-
ships were dissolved in 1896, Dalrymple had clear title to over 30,000
acres.[66] Dalrymple played the game well; he had nothing to lose and
was well aware that time and rising prices would make him a wealthy
man. His earlier bankruptcy in the grain market speculation had no
doubt taught him a lesson in practical economics.[67]

Dalrymple's program of personal land acquisition interfered with
his managerial duties and hindered the objectives of the bonanza
owners who employed him. This conflict of interest caused difficulties
between all parties concerned by the second year of bonanza operations. Cass and Cheney were satisfied with the general results of the
bonanza operations, but expressed dislike of Dalrymple's "spreading
out so much." [68] Dalrymple, who was negotiating to establish another
bonanza with Billings, was thwarted in the attempt by Power who
advised Billings: "It is just as well that you 'shook' Dalrymple, he is
a good man but has already exceeded his limit, with too many irons
in the fire some must burn. The interests of those concerned with him
would be better served, if he had but half in hand that he tries to
carry."[69] Dalrymple had misrepresented certain facts regarding profits
to Billings to which Power replied:

I have yours of the 6th enclosing Dalrymple's letter of 26th which
I read with interest and some amusement. I do not think his balance
sheet with Cass and Cheney will quite bear out his statement as to
40 to 100 per ct. profit from his operations, unless under his figures on
the basis of cash capital he has in the enterprise which is represented
by $0.00. His chosen system is practically that of inducing employ-
ment of outside capital, employment of first class men at the expense
of that capital taking ½ net profit if any, if not, losing his time, which
as a rule is usually engaged in working up a scheme. I recommended
Mr. D. to Gen. Cass, to tell the truth privately, I am on some accounts sorry for it, for he is developing traits of character I do not
like and would not want in any business partner.[70]

Because of Dalrymple's excellent job in dramatizing Dakota and
the bonanza farms, the Canadian Pacific offered Dalrymple all the
land he could put under cultivation. This was done with the idea that

he could do as good a job in promoting Canadian wheat lands as he had done the Dakota prairies. Dalrymple declined the offer because he was discouraged by the danger of earlier frost in Canada.[71]

There is no doubt in the minds of most people that the "Mr. Bonanza" of that era was Oliver Dalrymple who had built a great bonanza that existed beyond the real bonanza era. He did all he could to promote that reputation. He probably deserves the distinction because of the fantastic operations which he managed. Power had written to Billings in March, 1876: "I think he is a perfectly reliable man and competent to manage any amount of farm operations."[72] Later Power felt differently, because he realized that Dalrymple had too many conflicting interests.

Cass-Cheney Bonanza Accounts

Because the Cass-Cheney farm was the first Dakota bonanza, its financial success was all-important in the establishment of the bonanza era. An objective analysis of the success of its first years can best be obtained from the records compiled by Power and Israel Lombard up to the close of the first phase of the Cass-Cheney operations, i.e., prior to the partnership contract and purchase by Dalrymple. The accounts of the Cass and Cheney farms were kept separately.

Cheney bonanza accounts	1876	1877
Total operating expenses[73]..	$8,218.97	$20,375.16
Total income	5,913.78	21,345.59
Operating loss	−$2,305.19	Profit $ 970.43
Depreciation	None taken in 1876, added to 1877	
Acres seeded	633.97 wheat	1,217.59 wheat
		134.49 oats
Gross cost per acre ...	$12.96	$15.07
Yield per acre	9.58 bu. wheat	18.10 bu. wheat
		55.40 bu. oats
Cost per bushel	—	$0.65⅝

The balance sheet on the Cheney farm as of January 1, 1878, after two complete years of operation, showed a total capital investment, including land, of $49,971.88 and a loss of $1,334.76. For his management, Dalrymple received a share of the Cheney bonanza equal to $9,517.20 book value. Although Cheney had a minor operating loss in the first two years, he succeeded in paying for a considerable capital investment. It is apparent, however, that Dalrymple was reaping the greater "bonanza," for he had no money invested and the Cheney farm was only a portion of his total operation.[74]

Cass bonanza accounts	1876	1877
Total operating expenses [75]...	$8,745.74	$31,118.38
Total income	7,374.55	57,977.93
Operating loss	−$1,371.19	Profit $26,859.55

No depreciation or interest charged in 1876

Acres seeded	604.93 wheat	2,237.48 wheat
		117.04 oats
Cost per acre........	$14.46	$13.64
Yield per acre	12.54 bu. wheat	25.25 bu. wheat
		59.90 bu. oats
Cost per bushel	—	$0.52

The balance sheet on the Cass farm as of January 1, 1878, after two complete years of operation, showed a profit of $25,488.36 after all expenses, including capital investment. For his management, Dalrymple received $13,947.82 applied toward the purchase of land at the original cost. At this time, Cass had a book value investment of $60,-072.96. Again it is obvious that Dalrymple was reaping the greater bonanza. Prior to the settlement between Dalrymple and Cass in November, 1878, Cass had spent a total of $126,342.24 in operating and capital expenditures during the three years. This included advances to Dalrymple in excess of salary payments. During this period Cass's total income from wheat was $105,333.06, his total inventory at settlement date was $78,297.34, for a gross of $183,630.40, leaving Cass a profit of $57,288.16.[76]

Dalrymple, who had expended only his time, received a net income of $23,465.02 in the first two years of managing the Cass-Cheney bonanza. His operation with the Grandins was even more lucrative. With this income it is no wonder that he became the envy of every citizen of Dakota. The financial outlook for the investors improved and, as Stanley Murray has stated, in a very short time everyone involved was making a small fortune each year. It took men of great courage to make the large capital investment in an untried venture such as the bonanzas. Those with capital were destined to succeed, and some who operated on a shoestring, such as Dalrymple, also became rich.[77]

Capital Requirements

Not all bonanzas were financial successes, however, all had an almost insatiable need for outside funds in their early years. Everyone was curious about their profits. In a letter to *Cultivator and Country Gentleman*, Power wrote: "The result of this enterprise will be looked for with great interest as the proprietors propose to prove that large capital can be engaged as successfully in the cultivation of wheat on an extensive scale as in times past it has been in cotton and sugar." [78] Cass and Cheney, the two proprietors referred to, had a combined expenditure of $233,602.28 in their first three years of operation. The Grandins reported that by the time they had all their land under production, they had $175,000 invested, exclusive of the cost of machinery, buildings, or livestock. [79] Most of this was the expense of breaking the sod which was greater than the purchase price of the land.

Much money was needed for operating expense. It was not uncommon for Power to receive a list of vouchers for one month's expenses as follows:

Cheney Farm for July, 1878

Board for 20 men for 30 days @ $0.50	$ 300
Wages for 20 men for 26 days @ $0.75	390
Eight lumber wagons	480
Five harvesters and binders	1,250
Binding wire	800
One engine, separator, tank, and belt	1,600
1,000 sacks	245
Twelve cross plows	204
	$5,349

The July expenses for the Cass farm were $9,653 making a combined total of $15,002 for that month. [80] The expenses on the Cheney farm were $3,014 for August, $7,430 for September, $2,190 for October, and $300 for November. [81]

Cass and Cheney had adequate capital but others were not so well situated. H. S. Back had a bonanza but quickly ran into difficulty for lack of funds. He ran several advertisements in the *Fargo Weekly Argus* seeking a partner who was willing to invest $10,000 in his 7,000-acre wheat farm. Back managed to get 1,000 acres of sod broken on his Richland County bonanza but then had to stop until he could secure financial help. [82] Others ran into the same trouble. They started farming but were forced to sell due to the lack of funds. The Stephen Gardner farm north of Fargo consisting of 4,130 acres with 1,800 acres broken was sold for $29,000. It would have sold for much more if subdivided. [83] The Williams farm west of Casselton, a large and partly improved operation, was sold for $60,000 down and the balance on contract. [84] Two smaller and lesser known bonanza farmers who attempted to operate on their own capital were John Raymond and R. Hadwin. Raymond's farm was about twelve miles north of Fargo. He was in-

terested in keeping his cost as low as possible. He estimated that his
6,000-acre farm required a total investment of $55,000 before he was
able to secure any return. He was his own manager.[85] R. Hadwin, an
early large-scale farmer who lived near Wheatland, reported to the
editor of the *Fargo Daily Argus* that he had 19,000 bushels of wheat
to sell from his first year's operation of 1,900 acres. He opened his
farm as he secured funds from the profits.[86]

James B. Power found that his big farm, Helendale, in Richland
County, had an endless requirement for funds. An extremely precise
bookkeeper, he revealed that his farm had cost $62,180.63 and that
his total loss for the first three years of operation was $6,266.27.[87] His
farm brought better returns later in the 1880's, but the weather and
low prices from 1888 to the early 1890's caused him to write to his
grocery supply house:

The past two seasons have brought me heavy losses instead of profit
on the farm, outside resources upon which I depended principally
from land contracts, have failed me and it has taken my entire crop
of this year to pay labor bills. Money cannot be collected here from
farmers and banks are slow in putting any out.[88]

Power's farm differed from most bonanza operations in that it had
much more limited financial resources.

Most of the bonanzas were backed by outside capitalists. Some of
these were the directors of the Northern Pacific or easterners such as
Major Leach, a Pennsylvania capitalist, Lewis F. Watson, a congressman, factory owner, and oil man from the same state, and the Grandins. There were also corporations created with a number of stockholders such as the Dwight Farm and Land Company and the Amenia and Sharon Land Company. The Dwight farm, which was capitalized at $125,000, had twelve stockholders at the time of incorpora-
tion with others added later.[89] With such backing, it prospered under
the very capable management of John Miller who later became one
of the principal stockholders. Eventually, its capital stock and surplus
account showed a balance of $404,454.42.[90] Oliver Dalrymple, who had
learned from his Minnesota farm experiences that a bonanza would
take considerable capital, secured a $50,000 operating loan in his ini-
tial contract with the Grandins. For purposes of a more efficient operation, the loan limit for 1878 and after was increased.[91]

Labor on the Bonanza Farms

More than a big money supply was needed to operate the bonanzas.
Power said that the bonanza farm was a unique combination of rich
land, unlimited capital, and cheap labor. Labor costs were a much

more important factor to the operation of the bonanza than they were to the family-operated farm. Even though wages were extremely low, the cost of labor was a major financial problem of the owner. Securing the labor force was a big problem of the manager. Labor was cheap per unit cost, still the total labor bill was the major expense. Labor cost per acre on one year's operation often exceeded the original cost of the land.

Helendale, though not as large as some of the other bonanzas, provides a good illustration of the cost of labor. For example, Power paid an average daily wage of $0.61 per man in 1896, $0.66 in 1897, $0.72 in 1898, $0.83 in 1899, $0.81 in 1900, $0.82 in 1901, and $0.82 in 1902.[92] Very few people were hired by the day. They were hired on a no-work-no-pay basis. Hiring men on a day-laborer basis was common during the acute work periods of harvesting and threshing when a large number of men could be effectively and efficiently employed. In the 1870's and 1880's, the men were paid from $1.50 to $2.50 per day.[93] The lower figure, being the most common, was paid to shockers, spike pitchers, and bundle wagon drivers.

On the big bonanzas there were often several threshing crews. For each crew there was a separator (threshing machine) man who received $2 to $2.50 daily for his services. He often slept under the separator at night for fear of losing his job. On each bonanza there was a chief separator man who received $4 a day.[94] When help was plentiful and conditions were depressed, day labor, even in harvest time, did not receive more than $1 to $1.30 a day. In the slack periods in the summer, men could be secured for from $0.60 to $0.75 per day.[95]

Most of those hired to work on the bonanzas were on a monthly basis. During the crop season from April 1 to November 1 or 15, wages varied from $16 to $25 a month including board, room, and washing. During the winter months, wages were from $10 to $15.[96] Even during the peak work season, however, some farms managed to secure monthly labor for as low as $13.[97] Bonanza operators cooperated to keep wages low. Power advised his farm manager: "Low wages are still the talk. The general expression being that there is no sense in paying farm hands here higher wages than in Iowa, Wisconsin, Southern Minnesota. The employment agent . . . has already engaged men for seeding at $12 per month."[98] In 1888 Power consulted Dalrymple and stated he was considering paying men as follows: April, May, June, $18 per month; July, August, September, $30 per month; October and November $25 per month. This would be $169 per man for the crop season.[99]

Men hired by the year did the livestock chores in the winter and got the machinery in condition for the following year's work. They received $200 to $250 in addition to room, board, and washing.[100] On some bonanzas, men took care of the livestock during the winter for their room and board. It was not uncommon for a bonanza to have at least ten men employed for the winter to take care of livestock and machinery. A daily and much disliked job during these months was hauling hay from the outlying fields to farm headquarters. Great hardships were often suffered when blizzards made sudden appearances.[101] One of the advantages that the bonanza was supposed to possess was that it employed labor only when needed, unlike the small farm which had to absorb the year-round cost of the family labor even though it could not be fully employed.

In addition to field laborers and choremen, there was a non-productive labor force which included the bookkeeper, foreman, superintendent, blacksmith, cooks, and housekeepers. These were the higher paid employees. The foremen commonly received $1,000 if hired by the year. If employed for the crop season, they received $100 per month and could stay on as choremen for the winter for room and board.[102] The bookkeeper received from $600 to $900 per year including room and board. On the Cass-Cheney bonanza Israel Lombard, the bookkeeper, also received transportation. As the farms grew larger, more than one person was needed to keep records. At least one bonanza had five people thus employed in the office. Every bonanza had a blacksmith. The cooks and housekeepers were often the wives of the foremen. The couple was hired on a combined salary including room and board. As many as forty household employees were needed on the big bonanzas.[103] Those who worked throughout the year received $150 to $200 annually, including room, board, and washing. The minimum wage for female employees was $3 per week for those who were hired during the busy season only. Helendale employed three women for cooking and household duties on a year-round basis.[104]

Wages as such were not the sole labor expense; there was the cost of furnishing quarters and board expenses which nearly equalled wages. Power revealed that on his farm the fixtures for the quarters and household expenses for the first two years amounted to $1,071.13 and $4,431.11 respectively. This nearly equalled the cost of labor for that same period and was greater than the purchase cost of all his machinery.[105] In 1885 Power wrote to his manager: "Labor bills for the past 16 months aggregate $5,086 an av. of $10.62 per day. Board bills including your H. H. exp. $3,805 an av. of $7.93 per day—both of these items seem too large."[106] In the early years of the Cass-Cheney bonanza, the average daily board cost per man was $0.50¾ for the Cass farm and $0.51⅜ for the Cheney farm.[107] When Dalrymple requisitioned funds for food supplies, he used a flat $0.50 per day which was equal to about half the daily wage, not including the cost of household help and furnishings. An example of one such requisition read:

October wages ....28 men for 27 days....$	765
October board ....28 men for 31 days....	434
November board and wages...20 men for 10 days....	300
	$1,590 [108]

It often paid the bonanza to have a store incidental to its operation. On the Cass-Cheney farm, the storekeeper had to supply daily the division foreman with the requisitions made the previous day. Separate accounts were kept on each division and later turned in to the manager.[109] The Dwight farm operated a butcher shop, grocery, and clothing store combination to secure supplies for its operations at a reduced cost and also to enable the employees to make purchases.[110] The Keystone farm had an ice house that held ninety tons of ice for the meat cooler on the farm. The Keystone people fed their own cattle and hogs for butchering to insure a steady supply of fresh meat. Chickens were also kept and eggs were plentiful on the tables of the Keystone household. In the threshing season a hog and beef were killed each week to supply the table needs.[111] Consumption of that much meat in one week's time dramatizes the real scope of the bonanza operation. Only the largest feudal estates of Europe or the greatest cotton plantations in the South had anything comparable to the number of men found on the large bonanzas.

The accounts regarding the army of laborers at harvest are staggering when contrasted with the largest farms of today. The largest manpower figures are those reported by Dalrymple about the Cass-Cheney-Dalrymple operation. In 1884 near the peak of his operations, Dalrymple had an army of 1,000 men in the harvest fields operating 200 self-binding reapers pulled by 800 horses. When the harvest was finished, threshing started on the 30,000 acres of wheat with 30 steam-operated separators which produced a total yield of 600,000 bushels.[112]

The manpower requirements grew each year and Power, who was so interested in advertising the bonanza, saw to it that the startling figures were published in leading farm journals. In 1877 the Cass-Cheney-Dalrymple operation had 4,000 acres in wheat which was seeded by 50 men in 3 weeks and harvested by 100 men. That year thirty Wood's self-binding reapers and five steam-powered threshing machines were used.[113] In 1878 there were over 5,000 acres in crops on the part of the Grandin farms managed by Dalrymple. The harvest crew had swelled to 235 plus 25 hired teams and drivers. They used twenty-eight self-binding reapers and six steam-powered threshers.[114] By 1878 the Cass-Cheney-Dalrymple farm had 5,130 acres in wheat which was seeded by 125 men and harvested by a crew of 328 who used 30 seeders to get the crop planted and 45 self-binding harvesters and 8 steam-powered threshers to harvest it.[115]

Under Dalrymple's management the work force continued to grow in 1879. That year 160 men were needed to plant the crop and 400 men were required to harvest it, using 115 harvesters and 21 steam-powered threshers. Each division of the farm then required a larger labor force than the entire farm needed in 1877. The labor force for the slack period after seeding in 1879 was still seventy-five men who were employed for haying and breaking new sod. After the harvest was finished, the crew was stabilized at about 100 men for fall plowing of the crop land and backsetting of the newly broken sod.[116]

In 1879 the labor force on the Grandin farm varied through the season. During seeding from April 1 to May 1, 150 men were needed. From May 1 to July 15 thirty men broke new sod and twenty men made hay. With the start of harvest, the force swelled to 100 men to get the machines in shape and the fields opened. From August 1 a total crew of 250 was on hand until threshing was over about September 15. From then to freeze-up time, seventy-five men were kept busy plowing. During the winter the Grandins hired ten men to care for the livestock. In 1879 they used thirty-two seeders, thirty-four self-binding harvesters, and seven steam-powered threshers.[117]

In 1880 the combined labor force under Dalrymple swelled to 700. That year the Cass-Cheney and Grandin farms under Dalrymple used 135 binders and 24 threshers.[118] Enough new sod was broken and prepared for crops in 1880 so that the labor force was increased to 800 for the heaviest period in 1881.[119] Expansion in the numbers employed slowed down after that date as the machinery became larger and more efficient. When Dalrymple reached the height of his personal ownership and operations in the 1890's, he had a total of 75,000 acres, but because of improved efficiency of machines, he needed a labor force of only 600.[120]

Although the manpower requirements of the Dalrymple operations were the largest, sizeable crews were also used on the smaller bonanzas. The Belle Prairie farm, northwest of Hillsboro, had a harvest crew of forty-two men in addition to the full-time employees.[121] The Antelope farm near Mooreton, like the Belle Prairie farm, had a considerable amount of livestock so its number of full-time employees was equal to that of the largest cash grain bonanzas. This work force was increased to fifty during the harvest season.[122] The Dwight farm in Richland County employed a harvest crew of 200.[123] John B. Raymond's bonanza north of Fargo which contained 10,000 acres employed 10 or 12 full-time men. This number was increased to thirty-five men during seeding and seventy-five men at harvest.[124] Power's Helendale farm required a winter work force of twelve men which was increased to eighteen for spring and early summer work and climaxed in harvest season with thirty men. The great numbers of livestock enabled Power to utilize more full-time help.[125]

There is considerable speculation as to the type and origin of the people who worked on the bonanzas. Although the number of bonanza farms was not great, probably never more than one hundred, a large number of men had to be available for brief periods. They could not all have come from the surrounding area because of the sparse population in northern Dakota at that time. John Dalrymple expressed the view that the difficulty of securing labor during peak work loads was one of the major factors in the destruction of the bonanza operations.[126]

The Northern Pacific helped in advertising for and transporting workers to the grain fields, realizing that the harvest meant a good payload for the railroad. William Allen White said these transients rode from one wheat field to the next throughout the country and never paid fare. According to White, the transient laborers came from two major sources, from the South or from the big cities such as St. Louis, Chicago, Omaha, St. Paul, or Milwaukee. Some men started in the South during the early summer and moved north as the harvest progressed.[127] The *Fargo Daily Argus* referred to these people as professional harvesters who started from Tennessee and worked north. When the harvest was ended, they went to the forests of Minnesota and Wisconsin to work as lumberjacks.[128] John L. Coulter described these men not as bums or tramps, but honest workers out to make a living and credits many of them with becoming farmers in their own right at a later date.[129] He stressed that many of the men traveled between the lumber camps and the wheat fields, thus keeping themselves occupied full time. In 1927 Walter R. Reed of the Amenia and Sharon bonanza, said: "Some of the state's most prominent men of today came to North Dakota originally as farm hands on these great bonanza farms." [130]

As time passed the labor force came largely from neighboring farms. By 1880 the *Fargo Weekly Argus* reported that on some bonanzas as many as nine out of ten workers had their own claims established in the area.[131] Both Dalrymple and the Grandins placed advertisements in the *Fargo Daily Argus* stating that positions were open for harvest hands and threshing engineers in an effort to get help locally.[132] An exception was the Dwight Farm and Land Company which secured its labor supply from New York State during its early years since many of its stockholders were from that area. As many as twenty men at a time would come from New York in answer to a request for help.[133]

Labor Management and the Seasonal Routine

The labor problem was more than securing help and paying them. Such large armies of men had to be strictly controlled or trouble was bound to occur. Many of these men were not trained for farming so it was necessary to have strict control to see that the machines were properly operated to prevent damage to them or loss of the crop from faulty operation. Horses had to be protected from men who had very little understanding of the animal's limitations. Work had to be organized to keep this army moving systematically.

The manager relied on the foremen or superintendents to handle the field operations. Each had frequent contact with the general manager. The number of men under a foreman varied from ten to twenty-five, depending upon the task involved. The men under a foreman usually operated as a single crew, all working on the same task such as seeding, haying, harvesting, or plowing. This enabled one foreman to keep track of his entire labor force.[134] Sometimes the work was not done strictly according to the subdivision. For example, if the wheat ripened more quickly on one subdivision than another, the entire labor force might be diverted to a single field. The Watson farm was divided into 3 divisions of about 7,000 acres, each under a superintendent. All major decisions were made by the general manager.[135] The foreman was often one of the full-time employees who did chores and repaired machinery in the winter. When the cropping season came, he was put in charge of a crew of men. Some farms hired men in the spring as foremen. The Mayville farm of the Grandins had one foreman in winter and hired three additional ones each spring.[136] To gain uniformity of operations like that in large factories, supervisory help was responsible for all adjustments and settings of the machinery. Men were forbidden to tamper with the machinery.

A foreman, or binder boss, followed the binders around the field in a buggy. The binder operator was instructed that if something went wrong he was to pull out of line and call the binder boss by raising his hat on a pole.[187] When the repairs were made, the binder was allowed to rejoin the procession by falling in at the rear. The binder boss also kept a sharp eye for any horses that might be panting too hard. If this happened, the binder operator pulled out of line and rested his horses or took fresh ones. The binder operator was not even allowed to knot the twine or thread the needle; this was done by the binder boss. The number of binders under a single boss varied. On the Keystone farm, he was in charge of twenty-eight binders.[188] The Fairview farm which had thirty-five binders in the same field under one boss had the rule that a binder driver was not allowed to have a wrench or pair of pliers. All repairs were done by the binder boss or a repairman.[189]

The large shocking crews were supervised by a shocking boss who rode around the field in a buggy. His task was two-fold; first, he had to keep an eye on the shockers so there was no loafing; second, he got around the field about once each hour with the water barrel.[140] The shocking boss did not necessarily have to drive the men as the labor requirements were quite standardized at two shockers for every binder in heavy grain, or three shockers for two binders in light grain. The ratio of workers to machines was not "too wearing on the man." As William Allen White said: "Death from natural causes up on the big farms seldom occurs." [141] Shocking, which was introduced in the Valley by Dalrymple, became the accepted practice on the bonanzas. Previously, the harvested grain was hauled to the farm yard and stacked to be threshed later in the season. This was impractical on a large-scale operation.

Threshing was started as soon as all the grain was shocked. There was very little delay because by the time all the harvest was finished, the first grain had ample time to be cured. There was much less damage from moisture when grain was shocked as it was cut, which meant that most wheat from the bonanzas was No. 1 hard and brought a premium of five cents a bushel or more.[142] Threshing took slightly longer than harvesting, usually from four to six weeks. By 1897 it still required one and one-fourth days to thresh one day's harvest.

A threshing crew commonly consisted of thirty men and had from six to ten bundle teams and wagons to haul the shocked grain to the separator. Helping the bundle haulers were from four to six spike pitchers who stayed in the field and assisted in loading the wagons. The crew around the separator was made up of one separator man who greased and tended it. He was aided by a man with a team and bucking pole to pull the straw from the separator. Some of this straw was fed into the fuel box of the engine by a fireman. There was also an engineer. Receiving the bundles were two band cutters whose job it was to cut the wire or twine around each bundle; then they put the grain into the separator. Alongside it were three men who measured and sacked the grain as it came from the separator. Two men with teams hauled the grain to storage. Water for the steam engine and crew was supplied by a man and team with a water wagon. He also hauled lunch to the crew. Back on the farm yard was the stable man who took care of the horses. The crew used twenty-two to thirty horses but there always were several spares. The thirtieth man on the crew was a foreman who also served as timekeeper.[143]

If there was a rainy spell during harvest and threshing season, the crew was diverted to other jobs. Some began the fall plowing and others did road work which was jointly sponsored by the townships and the bonanzas to provide not only roads, but also drainage. Others helped on the place getting things ready for winter. For some years there were buildings to erect and others to paint. Some men helped the blacksmith. If the rainy season lasted too long and all the odd jobs were completed, the men just had to wait until they could get back to harvest.[144] As soon as threshing was over, most of the crew was discharged. Those who were left completed the fall plowing.

Laborers preferred working on the bonanzas rather than on the small farms. They did so because there was less pressure on them and living conditions were better.[145] On the big farms each man was given a job for the day. He did not have to repair machinery, take care of livestock, pump water, or do garden work as on the small farms. The lumberjacks thought that working on the bonanzas was easier than that of either in the woods or on the small farms.[146]

The bonanza manager realized that the best way to keep his men under control was to work them hard and feed them well. The diet on the big farms has been described as "quite good" to "very good." Skimping on food was not a practice of the bonanza operators. This accounts for the fact that, next to wages, it was the big expense on the bonanza. There were strikes because of poor food on farms in certain sections of the country but they were unheard of on the Dakota bonanzas. A bookkeeper said that when the men first appeared, their appetites were generally one-third larger than they were after about two weeks.

The quantity and quality of the food were as good as "agricultural generosity" could provide. A sample menu on the Grandin farm for one midday meal during harvest read as follows: corned beef and salt pork, boiled potatoes and baked beans, stewed turnips and pickles, coffee, tea, milk, and white sugar, hot or cold bread with syrup, cookies, doughnuts, and a choice of two kinds of pie.[147] Beef, pork, and eggs were always in plentiful supply, as well as an adequate supply of vegetables.[148] Breakfast and supper were served indoors, but the two lunches and dinner were served in the field during harvest and threshing. The lunches were necessary because it was a long time between the regular meals. The men were called at 4:00 A.M.; breakfast was ready at five. Dinner was usually a full hour, starting at twelve noon. The full-hour break was found most feasible; furthermore, the horses needed the rest. The machines ran until 7:00 P.M. and supper was served at 7:30 P.M.

The work day during harvest and threshing was thirteen hours; during seeding, haying, and plowing it was reduced to ten hours.[149] After six days of thirteen hours each, the managers did not require Sunday work. Best results were obtained from rest on Sunday, unless time was lost during the week due to inclement weather. Some bonanza managers were exceedingly strict about Sabbath enforcement.

If it was sound economics to invest in good quality food, the manager reasoned the same would be true for lodging. It did not take long, after some experiences at outdoor cooking and sleeping, for the bonanza operator to realize that this was more expensive than adequate housing. Sick men cost money to care for and were not very helpful with the harvest. A good table and good rooms were sound investments. William Allen White, who personally visited on some of the big farms, said each division of the Grandin farm had a large white-washed dining hall and dormitory. The dormitory had a smoking and loafing room in the front and "the beds are clean . . . better than those in the average American farm house."[150] There was more variation in sleeping quarters than there was in the quality of the food. The bunkhouses were big and sometimes not kept as clean as they might have been. A reference to the Keystone farm said that the bunkhouse held forty men and was "verminous," while there were no bugs in the barns because they were cleaned once and sometimes twice daily. During the busy season many additional men were required and rather than crowd into the bunkhouse, they preferred to sleep on straw outdoors or in the haylofts.[151] The Grandin cook house, as it was called, contained a large dining room, pantry, kitchen, waiting room, girls' bedroom, and sitting room on the first floor. The second floor was a large, single room with twenty-four double beds. A second, less pretentious, bunkhouse was supplied for the extra help needed at harvest, but not all could comfortably sleep in the quarters provided. The Grandins and many of the other big farms had big boilers which supplied plenty of hot water for baths. This was a special treat for farm employees of that day.[152] The Spiritwood bonanza had the largest known bunkhouse built in 1880 with bunks for 102 persons.[153]

Men employed on the bonanzas were not always busy at work. So many people working and living together naturally caused some discipline problems and general discontent. Therefore, the rules governing the men, similar on all the farms, had to be strict. Typical of the rules were those posted by Datus C. Smith of the Cloverlea bonanza:

We desire to treat everybody well and fairly. If you have any complaints to make or fault to find, go see the man who employed you.

Bringing or using intoxicating liquor on the farm is positively forbidden.

When men work they require rest. Therefore all lights must be out by 9 in the evening, except Saturday evening when they may burn until 10, but not later.

No fire arms to be used on the farm without permission of superintendent or the owners.

Dancing or scuffling are all right in their places, but the place is out of the house.

It is the duty of everyone to be of proper speech and cleanly habits at all times.[154]

John Peterson, a Grandin employee, stated that he was never aware of any big card games on that farm, however, "there was a little penny ante."[155] There is some dispute regarding mealtime regulations. Some have said that if a man talked at the table he was fired, others denied it.[156] One night the entire crew of easterners working for the Dwight farm got into a "big jamboree" and then disappeared. Such incidents were probably a not uncommon occurrence.[157] But generally speaking, there was not a great deal of trouble with help on the bonanzas. The management was quite strict and the workers well behaved.[158] But the female employees had to be well guarded. Separate quarters were provided, but there were no bars on the windows and locks were meant to be picked.

There was not, of course, the close tie between the men and owners as on the small farms. In fact, the farm hands sometimes felt that the managers and owners were "living too grand, living another kind of life than theirs." Guests from eastern cities, domestic servants, high living, and long vacation trips added to their resentment. But Thomas Radcliffe, a boss around the farm yard at Helendale, reported that "almost everybody about here worked sometime for the Powers." Radcliffe said that even the domestic servants, once they became acquainted with the Powers, felt that they "were wonderful people, with no airs, no feeling of superiority." Lars Anderson, a choreman at Helendale, said: "It was a good place to work."[159]

The Use of Machinery

The bonanzas were instrumental in introducing large-scale machinery to American agriculture. It must have been a machinery salesman's dream to receive an exclusive order from a bonanza. Power, who was responsible for one of the first nation-wide articles on bonanza farms in *Cultivator and Country Gentleman,* reported that in the second year of operation of the Cass-Cheney farm, the following equipment handled 4,000 acres of wheat: 80 horses, 30 wagons, 26 breaking plows, 40 cross plows, 21 seeders, 30 Woods self-binding harvesters, 60 harrows, and 5 steam-powered threshing machines.[160] In 1878 the farm expanded its line to 126 horses, 84 plows, 81 harrows, 67 wagons, 30 seeders, 8 threshing machines, and 45 binders.[161] The entire line of machinery was purchased directly from the manufacturer which represented a saving of 33⅓ per cent of retail price. The cash savings on the five threshing machines alone was $2,000. In 1878 a visitor on the Grandin farm counted "79 plows, 55 harrows, 24 seeders, 28 binders, 6 threshers, 40 wagons." [162]

The bonanza operators liked to amass a great number of machines in one field. The Downing farm had 96 binders and 480 horses and mules in action at one time. The Downings possessed only thirty-six binders but Adams, of the Fairview bonanza, came over with his sixty binders to help finish harvest.[163] In 1883 when special visitors from Europe were at the Cass-Cheney-Dalrymple farm as well as an eastern party headed by Henry Villard, Dalrymple exhibited 130 binders in operation in one field. That year the farm had 28,000 acres in wheat.[164]

Even the smaller bonanzas used a large amount of machinery. The Cloverlea farm had a picture of plowing in its advertising brochure which showed twelve, gang plows pulled by five horses each.[165] The G. S. Barnes bonanza, on the Minnesota side of the Red River, operated twenty-two Walter A. Woods binders in the 1880's. This farm contained 10 sections at that time, which was small by Dakota standards, but it still required 200 horses to handle all the work load.[166]

Plowing provided a severe test to the early Dakota farmer. The prairie sod was tough but, fortunately, the steel plow had been perfected and it scoured well even in the heavy, fertile soil. During the first year or two when a twelve-inch walking plow was used, a good team could break from one to two acres daily. The sulky, which had either a single fourteen- or sixteen-inch plow and carried the driver, was used after the initial breaking. The power required for a sulky was provided either by three good horses or two yoke of oxen. By 1879 the double gang replaced the single sixteen-inch sulky; it could turn a thirty-two inch furrow and was pulled by five horses. These plows could turn over five acres per day or ten plows could turn a section in two weeks. There was at least one month's plowing each fall for ten plows on each subdivision.[167] In 1879 the Cass-Cheney farm had 8,170 acres under cultivation which was plowed in 51 days using 32 gang plows. Plowing usually started as soon as threshing was finished and seldom stopped before freeze-up.[168] Sulky plows cost $65 each and gangs were $100, so each plow had to be used as much as possible to keep the per acre charge low.[169]

After the gang plow, steam power made the next big change in plowing. Thomas W. Hunt, who owned six sections west of Blanchard, hired J. G. Allen, a custom plower, to steam plow all of his land. Allen demonstrated his outfit on the Dalrymple farm in May, 1882, and boasted that his rig traveled three miles an hour and turned over an acre per mile or three acres per hour. A crew working around the clock could plow seventy-two acres, equivalent to fifteen horse plows.[170] Yet steam plowing did not become too popular in the bonanza operation. It was not until the gasoline tractor was perfected near the end of the bonanza era that large plowing operations became practical.

Harrowing, the next step in field preparation, was considerably faster and less expensive than plowing. Land was broken up by the harrows before seeding. Prior to 1879, two-section harrows pulled by two horses were used; after that date four-section harrows using four horses became the standard. The four-section harrow was twenty feet wide and covered forty acres in a day. In 1880 the Cass-Cheney farm had 114 harrows. In spite of their great capacity, many harrows were necessary for three reasons: the quicker land could be prepared in the spring after the frost was out, the quicker it could be seeded; harrowing the land became necessary to reduce wind erosion and it had to be worked quickly in serious wind storms; the three harrowings after seeding had to be done in a very short period of time to prevent damage to the new crop.[171]

The common seeding equipment until the late 1880's was the eight-foot broadcast seeder pulled by two horses. If properly supplied with grain, one man could seed an average of eighteen acres daily. In 1879 the Cass-Cheney farm had 40 seeders for 8,170 acres. The seeding period had to be short to avoid a difference in the maturity date of the crop and to stay within the optimum seeding period. The entire spring planting operation normally lasted one month for small grains. If weather permitted, all small grain was planted by May 1.[172]

After seeding was finished, the time was spent cutting and stacking wild hay. This lasted at least three weeks during late June and early July. The Grandins owned six hay mowers. A larger number was not necessary because hay could be cut over a longer season without too much damage to the crop. About 600 to 800 tons of hay were put up on that farm.[173]

Harvesting and threshing were the big rush of the year. Depending on the season, the oats harvest started between July 15 and August 1. Oats, barley, and wheat were normally harvested in that order. Wheat, of course, was harvested when it was ready, and other crops might be delayed to make sure the wheat was not lost. One self-tying binder could harvest from ten to twelve acres daily, depending on the thickness of the grain. The Cass-Cheney farm averaged eleven acres a day per binder in 1878 and 1879. In 1878, 5,130 acres of wheat were harvested by 45 binders in 11 days. In 1879, 55 harvesters on 8,170 acres finished in 13 days.[174] The highest daily average harvested per binder was seventeen acres reported in 1882 on the C. F. Kindred farm near Valley City.[175] Sufficient machines to take care of the entire crop in ten to fifteen days were necessary to avoid any great losses due to over-ripe grain or inclement weather. To keep machine cost per acre low, 250 acres was the planned acreage per binder.[176] In some years Dalrymple was able to cut as much as 415 acres with one binder, but in others he was limited to 175 acres.[177] These binders were big users of twine. The Grandins used more than a carload of twine in a single harvest.[178]

After harvest came threshing, which was no less spectacular. The same crews were used. A virtual flood of golden grain was produced when the bonanzas started threshing. The daily carloadings of the Northern Pacific skyrocketed. Oats could be threshed at a greater volume than wheat. One big thresher on E. C. Sprague's farm near Fargo was reported to have threshed 740 bushels in four hours. There were three other threshers operating on this farm, which was a small bonanza.[179] By 1877 the total daily capacity of the five steam threshers on the Cass-Cheney farm was 5,000 bushels.[180] A separator, or threshing machine, was found economically feasible for each 1,200 or 1,300 acres of grain.[181] The capacity of the machines increased through the years so that by 1880 the threshing machines on the Cass-Cheney and Grandin farms averaged 1,700 bushels daily. In 10 work days 640,000 bushels were threshed from 32,000 acres by 36 machines.[182] In 1881 Dalrymple threshed enough wheat each day so that three trainloads totaling 30,000 bushels of wheat were shipped out daily.[183] By 1897 the capacity of the threshing machine had increased so it could handle 2,500 to 3,500 acres and the daily output increased to between 2,000 and 3,000 bushels.[184] In that year Dalrymple's own operation threshed 25,000 bushels daily with only 12 machines, enough wheat for 2 trains of 25 cars each.[185] The average separator cost about $600 and the 16 horsepower steam engine another $800.[186]

Buildings on the Bonanza Farms

In addition to machinery, a tremendous investment in buildings was necessary. It was difficult to operate in the early years until the buildings were erected. In 1876 the Cass-Cheney farms received sufficient material to build living quarters for twenty-four men and other buildings for horses and grain.[187]

From that small beginning the buildings of each bonanza increased so that when William Allen White visited the region he noted that the fixed improvements (chiefly buildings) on the Cass-Cheney farm were valued at $35,000. This farm had 2 elevators of 40,000- and 60,-000-bushel capacities. There was a central office and supply building; the bookkeeper had a modest home and a much more substantial one was provided for the manager. On each of the farm's divisions a combination dining hall and dormitory served all of the employees. Machine sheds held the more valuable equipment but were never intended to hold all the machinery needed on the bonanza. Machinery was used so extensively that most pieces lasted only a few years. Under such practice the resulting loss from unshedded machinery was not enough to make machine housing economically feasible.[188] The houses on each of the divisions were thirty-two feet by thirty-two feet and were two stories high. But so many men were housed that even such sizeable buildings could not be considered roomy. The division stables were 56 feet by 64 feet but were not overly adequate for the 100 horses put in them.[189]

The Grandins operated on a similar basis. By 1878 headquarters on Division No. 1, commonly called the Mayville farm, consisted of the following buildings: a 1½-story house, 32 feet by 32 feet; a 1-story office and storehouse, 25 feet by 50 feet; a 2½-story, 50,000-bushel granary, 56 feet by 60 feet; a 2-story blacksmith shop, 16 feet by 26 feet; a stable, 50 feet by 60 feet with 20 foot posts which provided a hay loft above the horses; a stable wing, 28 feet by 60 feet along one side of the stable; a 2-story feed and mill room, 16 feet by 40 feet; a feed-mill annex, 18 feet by 26 feet, attached to the feed building; a 2-story, 9,000-bushel wheat elevator, 18 feet by 40 feet; a machine shed, 18 feet by 75 feet, for steam engines and threshers.

Division No. 2 contained the following buildings; a 1½-story house,

32 feet by 32 feet; a 2-story stable, 56 feet by 60 feet; a 2½-story, 50,000-bushel granary, 56 feet by 60 feet; a 2-story, 10,000-bushel wheat elevator, 20 feet by 40 feet.

Division No. 3 had these structures: a 1½-story house, 32 feet by 32 feet; a 2-story stable, 30 feet by 60 feet.

There was stable capacity for 190 horses and storage space for over 100,000 bushels of grain.[190] After the railroad was constructed in 1882, more farmsteads were erected and elevators built along the track. The Grandins also maintained a store for company and employee needs.[191] The main buildings of each division were supplied with piped water, a novelty for rural Dakota of the 1880's.[192] Water was forced into the buildings from a water tank fifteen feet in diameter that was located either up on the windmill tower or the upper story of the barns. Galvanized pipe was used in the system.[193]

In 1882 the Grandins made news by building a large round elevator which held 75,000 bushels of grain. They constructed a sheep shed which measured 32 feet by 100 feet, plus a cattle barn 28 feet by 80 feet which was 1½-stories high with a lean-to of 14 by 80 feet. Two additional farmsteads were erected that year to enable the Grandins to operate more efficiently the 4,000 acres of newly broken sod.[194] The famous round elevator was destroyed by fire in the early 1890's.

Only two bonanzas exceeded the Grandins in the overall number and size of buildings. Helendale had a very elaborate, well-kept set of buildings, and the Amenia and Sharon Land Company, in addition to its great number of farmsteads, owned and operated the towns of Amenia and Chaffee and a line of elevators. Mooreton, the headquarters of the Downing farm, had 32 buildings including 3 large horse barns and an 80,000-bushel elevator.[195] The Keystone farm, which was not an exceedingly large bonanza, had 3 horse barns which housed 170 work horses and 55 driving horses and a cattle barn for 75 beef and milk cattle. Keystone also had a ninety-ton ice house with a six-foot by eight-foot meat cooler.[196] The Dwight farm had a dining hall which was a separate building and a dormitory which was a ten-room, two-story building, plus a butcher shop and general store for the farm. Nearly all of its buildings were on the headquarters farm. The division called the South Ranch had a few storage buildings, and the other, called the East Ranch, had no buildings.[197] One of the largest buildings on any bonanza was the barn on the Fairview or Adams farm which measured 84 feet by 176 feet.[198]

The buildings on the bonanzas were costly for lumber had to be shipped in. Although much lumber came from the Detroit Lakes region in Minnesota, it still involved shipping and loading expenses. President E. P. Wells of the James National Bank in Jamestown, reported that five sets of buildings on his farms had cost him $26,217.04 which was more than the land had cost.[199] Elevators at the tracks, such as the 45,000-bushel affair that the Buttz brothers erected at Buttzville, were a tribute to men not afraid to invest for the future.[200] The assessor knew the cost and value of these big buildings. He assessed the Dalrymple elevators at Arthur and at Alton, the Dalrymple headquarters farm, at $4,000 each. The elevators alone on the Cass-Cheney farm had an assessed value of $18,000.[201]

The story of investment, labor, machinery, and buildings on the bonanzas illustrates the great magnitude of their operation. No less dramatic, however, is the story of the great number of livestock, horses, and mules, acreage involved and certain characteristics that were peculiar to the bonanzas.

FOOTNOTES

[1] John Miller, Dwight Farm Papers, NDIRS, File 84.

[2] William Guy, governor of North Dakota in the early 1960's, is the son of a manager of some of the land of the Amenia and Sharon Land Company. His opponent in the 1962 gubernatorial campaign, Mark Andrews, later elected to Congress, farms part of one of the old bonanzas.

[3] Coulter, NDSHS, *Collections*, Vol. III, pp. 608-611.

[4] Benton, *The Journal of Land and Public Utility Economics*, Vol. I, p. 408.

[5] White, *Scribner's Magazine*, XXII, 540.

[6] F. B. Downing Papers, Downing Farm, NDIRS, File 197.

[7] Power to Cass, Nov. 16, 1875, NDIRS, File 309.

[8] Power to Cass, Nov. 16, 1875, File 309.

[9] Power to Cass, Feb. 17, 1876, File 309.

[10] Power to Cheney, Aug. 9, 1876, File 309.

[11] Dalrymple interview, Dalrymple Papers, NDIRS, File 549.

[12] *Fargo Daily Argus*, Oct. 10, 1883.

[13] John S. Dalrymple interview, NDIRS, File 549.

[14] Grandin Papers, NDIRS, File 760. Dalrymple-Grandin contract, May 25, 1876, recorded in Traill County, Nov. 4, 1878, Book A of Misc., p. 199.

[15] John S. Dalrymple interview, NDIRS, File 549.

[16] Power to Billings, April 25, 1876, NDIRS, File 309. In 1876 after 1,280 acres were seeded, some farm buildings were built. The first two houses built along the Northern Pacific main line between Fargo and Bismarck were erected at Dalrymple siding, one on the Cass farm and the other on the Cheney farm. John S. Dalrymple interview, NDIRS, File 549.

[17] Coulter, NDSHS, Collections, Vol. III, p. 575.

[18] *Fargo Daily Argus*, Jan. 15, 1881, p. 4.

[19] *Fargo Daily Argus*, Nov. 11, 1880; Grandin Papers, NDIRS, File 450.

[20] *Fargo Daily Argus*, Jan. 15, 1881, p. 4.

[21] *Fargo Daily Argus*, Oct. 8, 1880, p. 4.

[22] *Fargo Daily Argus*, Nov. 15, 1880.

[23] Power to *Cultivator and Country Gentleman*, May 10, 1877, NDIRS, File 309; Coulter, NDSHS, *Collections*, Vol. III, p. 575

[24] The military touch is portrayed well in an article from the *Fargo Argus*, Septem-

ber 1, 1881, entitled "A Golden Sketch." The 30,000 acres were divided into 5,000 or 6,000 acre tracts under superintendents. Each regiment was divided into batallions with a foreman or major, who controlled 2,000 acres. Under him were three companies each with a captain, cultivating a section. "Dalrymple oversees it all and superintendents have charge of their part and report to him. Rivalry amongst them to produce the biggest crop. For plowing men go out in gangs, 640 acres each. A foreman goes along on horseback. All in military style. All drawn up before starting and inspected. At the close of day all is again inspected."

[25] Power to *Cultivator and Country Gentleman*, May 10, 1877, File 309.

[26] Benton, *Journal of Land and Public Utility Economics*, Vol. I, p. 409.

[27] "The Grandin Farm in Dakota," *Cultivator and Country Gentleman*, Vol. 44, (Feb. 6, 1879), p. 83.

[28] Interview of Leonard Sackett with James McKessich, Dwight Farm Papers, NDIRS, File 138.

[29] "Grain Farms in the Northwest," *Cultivator and Country Gentleman*, Vol. 45 (Jan. 8, 1880), p. 19.

[30] Coulter, NDSHS, *Collections*, Vol. III, p. 577. He uses 5,000 acres as the division size.

[31] *Cultivator and Country Gentleman*, Vol. 42 (May 17, 1877), p. 317. This was an untitled news article.

[32] *Fargo Daily Argus*, March 15, 1866.

[33] John S. Dalrymple interview, NDIRS, File 549.

[34] Louis Dussere of the *Fargo Forum* staff has contacted Northwestern Bell Telephone Company headquarters on the truth of this statement. The Bell Company reported that there may be some dispute here and a large farm manager in Iowa may have been earlier. John S. Dalrymple said, "The Grandins had a smart little bookkeeper . . . who rigged it up."

[35] Hilsted interview, NDIRS, File 269.

[36] *Cultivator and Country Gentleman*, Vol. 44, p. 83.

[37] The popularity of information about bonanzas is well illustrated by the fact that the July, 1879, edition of *The Nineteenth Century Magazine* of London carried a lengthy article entitled, "Our New Wheat Fields in the Northwest." The article carried a full account of figures from Dalrymple as to size of operation, cost and income per acre and net profits. From that article, it is no wonder that some Britons would be interested in investing in bonanzas.

[38] *Fargo Argus*, Nov. 28, 1881, "Caanan."

[39] *Fargo Argus*, Sept. 1, 1881, p. 2.

[40] Bigelow, *Atlantic Monthly*, Vol. 45, p. 30.

[41] White, *Scribner's Magazine*, XXII, 540.

[42] John S. Dalrymple interview, NDIRS, File 549. John S. Dalrymple presented another interesting aspect about his father. Dalrymple never carried a fire insurance policy. He lost heavily in two burnings of the main Cass-Cheney elevator. After the second fire, John S. and William Dalrymple secretly insured the rebuilt elevator and collected on the third fire. John Dalrymple stated at this same time that he paid the mortgages on his father's farms about 1900. John S. Dalrymple interview, File 549.

[43] Power to Cass, July 22, 1875, NDIRS, File 309.

[44] Power to Cheney, June 4, 1877, File 309.

[45] Power to Dalrymple, Sept. 6, 1877, File 309.

[46] Power to Cheney, Sept. 6, 1877, File 309.

[47] Power to Dalrymple, Sept. 17, 1877, File 309.

[48] Power to Cheney, Sept. 27, 1877; Power to Shelby, Sept. 27, 1877, File 309.

[49] Power to Cheney, Oct. 13, 1877, File 309.

[50] Power to Shelby, March 28, 1878, File 309. Dalrymple irked Cass and Cheney when he sold their wheat on the market and then sold seed to them for above market price from his personal operations. Power noted that seed wheat could have been pur-

chased locally for from $0.80 to $0.90, but Dalrymple charged $1.05. Power to Cheney
Dec. 16, 1878, File 309.

[51] Power to Cass, May 13, 1878, File 309.

[52] Power to Dalrymple, April 25, 1878, File 309

[53] Power to Cass, May 13, 1878, File 309.

[54] Power to Cheney, April 25, 1878, File 309.

[55] Power to Dalrymple, May 7, 1878, File 309.

[56] Power to Dalrymple, May 11, 1878, File 309.

[57] Power to Cheney, July 2, 1878, File 309.

[58] Power to Cheney, June 19, 1878, File 309; Power to Shelby, July 4, 1878, File 309.

[59] Power to Lombard, Oct. 16, 1878, File 309.

[60] Power to Cheney, Dec. 16, 1878, File 309.

[61] Power to Cass, Dec. 1, 1877, File 309; Power to Lombard, Jan. 7, 1879, Jan. 9, 1879,
File 309.

[62] Power to George Gray, Dec. 10, 1878, File 309.

[63] Power to Cheney, April 25, 1878, File 309.

[64] John S. Dalrymple interview, NDIRS, File 549. John S. Dalrymple reported that
he never really knew what their largest acreage was. In his original contract with the
Grandins, Dalrymple was to secure approximately thirty-five sections in payment of
his managerial services. Grandin Papers, NDIRS, File 760.

[65] *Fargo Daily Argus*, Oct. 10, 1883. For example, Dalrymple reported that the harvest from the bonanzas he managed in 1880 enabled him to ship 500,000 bushels of wheat
to Buffalo where it sold for $1.25 per bushel. He estimated that production cost that year
had been $0.50 per bushel and transportation to Buffalo was $0.20, leaving a net of $0.55
per bushel after all expenses. Dalrymple was entitled to half the profits. *Fargo Daily
Argus*, Jan. 15, 1881, p. 4.

[66] Benton, *Journal of Land and Public Utility Economics*. Vol. 1, p. 4.

[67] The actual Dalrymple records were not available for this study. However Dalrymple
was very publicity-conscious and kept the newspapers well informed as to the size
of his operations. The *Fargo Argus* of August 16, 1883, credits a farm in California of
60,000 acres as being the largest known farm in existence in contrast to the Grandins,
who had over 50,000 acres under their control, but the same article credits Dalrymple
as having the largest farm under cultivation, 28,000 acres. *Fargo Argus*, Aug. 16, 1883.
The following year Dalrymple was credited with being two-thirds owner of 75,000 acres
of land. Of that amount 30,000 acres were in wheat. It is said that he accumulated all
this in the brief period of eight years. *Cultivator and Country Gentleman*, Vol. 49 (Oct.
9, 1884). p. 839.

[68] Power to Cheney, Oct. 13, 1877, NDIRS, File 309.

[69] Power to Billings, May 8, 1877, File 309; Power to Billings, Dec. 17, 1877, File 309.

[70] Power to Billings, Jan. 11, 1878, File 309. Of particular irritation to Power, Cass,
and Cheney was Dalrymple's attitude of self promotion. The bonanzas attracted much
attention and Dalrymple saw that he got his share of the publicity. Power sent to
Cheney a clipping from the St. Paul *Pioneer Press* about an article entitled, "The Dakota
Harvest" which was a story of the big "Dalrymple" bonanza. Power commented, "an
illustration of unmitigated cheek in blowing ones own horn." In the same paper there
was an advertisement of "Mr. Dalrymple" regarding bids on wheat, which was so worded
that no reference was made of the bonanza owners. Power to Cheney, Aug. 13, 1878, File
309. A second letter about the same subject to Mr. Cheney began: "Where are the Cass
and Cheney farms? Has the little 10,000 acre lot become so absorbed in larger operations
as to be lost sight of? Such however is the usual fate of pioneers." The letter referred
to a Dalrymple article in *Frank Leslie's Illustrated*. Power to Cheney, Oct. 14, 1878,
File 309. Dalrymple used his connection with Northern Pacific officials to good advantage. He brokered or sold his advice on land in the area. Congressman L. F. Watson
of Pennsylvania was dealing with Dalrymple on land and had asked him to make some
examinations and give opinions on certain Dakota land. When Watson did not hear
from Dalrymple he contacted Power asking for the reasons of delay. Power informed

him that Dalrymple had too many other business matters pressing him and also paying Dalrymple to give an opinion was a waste of money because "Dalrymple's selections are governed as much by our surveyor's reports as by personal examination, unless it may be that his examination proves so conclusively the correctness of our notes that copies of them express the facts better than Dalrymple can state them." Power to Congressman L. F. Watson, Oct. 27, 1877, Nov. 26, 1877, File 309.

[71] John S. Dalrymple interview, File NDIRS, 549.

[72] Power to Billings, March 10, 1876, NDIRS, File 309.

[73] Included are 1876 and 1877 cost of 21 per cent of total depreciation charge on buildings, livestock, and machinery $3,001.84; 66.6 per cent depreciation on household fixtures $178.76; 7 per cent annual interest on gross investment $3,327.75.

[74] Power Letterbook, IV, 88, 91, 109, NDIRS, File 309.

[75] Included are 1876 and 1877 costs of 21 per cent depreciation charged on buildings, livestock and machinery $4,521.35; 66.6 per cent depreciation on household fixturess $374.39; 7 per cent annual interest on gross investment $2,772.82.

[76] Power Letterbook, IV, 102, 103, 105, 270, File 309; Power to Lombard, Jan. 9, 1879, File 309.

[77] Murray, *Agricultural History*, XXXI, 57.

[78] Power to *Cultivator and Country Gentleman*, May 10, 1877, File 309.

[79] White, Scribner's Magazine, XXII, 542.

[80] Power to Lombard, July 18, 1878, File 309.

[81] Power to Cheney, Aug. 17, 1878, File 309.

[82] *Fargo Weekly Argus*, Feb. 4, 1880, p. 5.

[83] *Fargo Daily Argus*, Jan. 18, 1881, p. 4.

[84] *Fargo Argus*, March 9, 1882, p. 6.

[85] *Fargo Argus*, Sept. 2, 1881, p. 2.

[86] *Fargo Daily Argus*, March 7, 1881, p. 4.

[87] J. B. Power to W. A. Power, Feb. 2, 1884, File 309. W. A. Power was James B. Power's brother and manager of Helendale until he disappeared when conditions became critical in the Dakotas in the late 1880's.

[88] Power to Allen, Moon, and Company, St. Paul, Minn., Jan. 13, 1891, File 309.

[89] Interview of Leonard Sackett with J. Carlson, Dwight Farm Papers, File NDIRS, 257. Carlson was an employee on the Dwight farm.

[90] Annual Statement, Dwight Farm and Land Company, Jan. 1, 1910, H. F. Chaffee Papers, NDIRS, File 134. Chaffee was the administrator of the Miller estate and had these papers in his personal file.

[91] Dalrymple contract, Jan. 4, 1878, Grandin Papers, NDIRS, File 760.

[92] Power Letterbook, XIV, 678, NDIRS, File 309.

[93] Coulter, NDSHS, *Collections*, Vol. 111, pp. 577-579.

[94] Interview of Leonard Sackett with S. G. Downing. Downing Farm Papers, NDIRS, File 166, Downing was manager of the farm for many years.

[95] Power to John Manz, Merrill, Iowa, Feb. 23, 1899, NDIRS, File 309.

[96] Coulter, NDSHS, *Collections*, Vol. III, pp. 577-579.

[97] S. G. Downing interview, Downing Farm Papers, NDIRS, File 166.

[98] J. B. Power to Alley Power, March 10, 1894, NDIRS, File 309. Alley was J. B. Power's son who managed the farm for several years.

[99] Power to Dalrymple, March 28, 1888, File 309.

[100] Power to J. H. Worst, Oct. 11, 1891, File 309.

[101] Torgerson interview, G. S. Barnes Papers , NDIRS, File 867.

[102] *Fargo Daily Argus*, Jan. 15, 1881, p. 4.

[103] That many cooks and dishwashers were required to feed the large harvest crews because the food was brought to them in the field for some of the meals. This meant transporting food and utensils from the farmstead. Also, three big meals and two lunches were the common practice in the long days during the harvest season. *Fargo Argus*, Sept. 1, 1881, p. 2.

[104] Power to J. H. Worst, Oct. 11, 1891, NDIRS, File 309; Power to H. B. Starkey, Feb. 19, 1892, File 309.

[105] Power to W. A. Power, Feb. 2, 1884, File 309.

[106] Power to W. A. Power, June 10, 1885, File 309.

[107] Power to Cass, July 3, 1878, File 309; Power to Cheney, July 2, 1878, File 309.

[108] Power to Cheney, Oct. 17, 1878, File 309. In 1878 the monthly labor bill for the Cass-Cheney farm was consistently over $1,000. For June, 1878, it was $1,150 for the Cass and $560 for the Cheney operation, a total of $1,710. Power to Lombard, July 5, 1878, File 309.

[109] *Fargo Argus*, Sept. 1, 1881, p. 2.

[110] Carlson interview, Dwight Farm Papers, NDIRS, File 257

[111] Mecklenburg interview, Keystone Farm Papers, NDIRS, File 607

[112] *Cultivator and Country Gentleman*, Vol. 49 (Oct. 9, 1884). p. 839.

[113] Power to editor, *Cultivator and Country Gentleman*, Vol. 42 (May 10, 1877); *Cultivator and Country Gentleman*, Vol. 42 (May 17, 1877), p. 317.

[114] Coulter, NDSHS, *Collections*, Vol. 111, p. 575.

[115] *Cultivator and Country Gentleman*, Vol. 44 (Jan. 2, 1879), p. 9. An untitled news article.

[116] Coulter, NDSHS, *Collections*, Vol. 111, p. 577.

[117] Bigelow, *Atlantic Monthly*, Vol. 45, p. 40. In late March the bonanza labor force was increased by eight to ten men to get the seed cleaned and the machinery ready before the big field crew was hired. Coulter, NDSHS, *Collections*, Vol. 111, p. 577.

[118] *Fargo Weekly Argus*, Jan. 28, 1880, p. 1, Feb. 4, 1880, p. 2.

[119] *Fargo Argus*, Sept. 1, 1881, p. 2.

[120] "Bonanza Farming in the Northwest," *The Farmer*, XXV (Dec. 1, 1907), 770.

[121] Hilstad interview, Grandin Papers, NDIRS, File 269.

[122] *Fargo Daily Argus*, Dec. 1, 1884.

[123] Interview of Leonard Sackett with Ward, Dwight Farm Papers, NDIRS, File 258, NDIRS. No first name was used.

[124] *Fargo Argus*, April 9, 1884, p. 2.

[125] Power to J. H. Worst, Oct. 11, 1891, NDIRS, File 309; Power to Louis Hatop, May 20, 1892, File 309.

[126] John S. Dalrymple interview, NDIRS, File 549.

[127] White, *Scribner's Magazine*, XXII, 534.

[128] *Fargo Daily Argus*, April 9, 1884, p. 2.

[129] Coulter, NDSHS, *Collections*, Vol. 111, pp. 577–579. Working conditions were satisfactory and the duties proceeded systematically and harmoniously. Very few men had to be fired because of refusal to work or rough behavior. Employees who did not desire to stay were free to draw their pay and leave at any time. Coulter expressed the view that contemporaries of the bonanza era felt that labor was well controlled, cared for, and behaved for such large numbers. Coulter, NDSHS, *Collections*, Vol. 111, pp. 578–579.

[130] *Fargo Forum*, Jan. 18, 1927, interview with Walter R. Reed.

[131] *Fargo Weekly Argus*, Jan. 28, 1880, p. 1.

[132] *Fargo Daily Argus*, Sept. 3, 1880, Aug. 14, 1881, p. 4.

[133] *Fargo Argus*, April 10, 1890.

[134] Coulter, NDSHS, *Collections*, Vol. 111, pp. 577–579.

[135] Interview of Leonard Sackett with Emil Trapp, Watson Farm Papers, NDIRS, File 827. Trapp was the son of a long-time employee of the Watson farm.

[136] McKessich interview, Dwight Farm Papers, NDIRS, File 138.

[137] Every binder had a bamboo fish pole on it which was used to encourage the horses; sometimes it enabled the operator to clear the sickle without having to get off the seat.

[138] Keystone Papers, NDIRS, File 607.

[139] Ward interview, Dwight Farm papers, NDIRS, File 258.

[140] Keystone Papers, File 607; S. G. Downing interview, Downing Farm Papers, NDIRS, File 166.

[141] White, *Scribner's Magazine*, XXII, 534. Coulter mentioned that two men following a Marsh-type harvester was the common practice. This machine was a self-tying binder which used wire until 1879 when twine was introduced. It had a six and one-half foot cutting bar and was pulled by three horses. The greatest handicap to the shocker was that the bundle carrier was still not in use which meant that bundles were scattered throughout the field and required excessive walking. Coulter, NDSHS, *Collections*, Vol. III, pp. 572-573. As a boy of twelve, the writer helped his aunt shock heavy grain following an eight-foot binder which, of course, had a bundle carrier. At a steady pace they could keep up with a binder drawn by four horses.

[142] John S. Dalrymple interview, NDIRS, File 549; *Fargo Argus*, Sept. 29, 1881.

[143] Coulter, NDSHS, *Collections*, Vol. III, pp. 573-574.

[144] White, *Scribner's Magazine*, XXII, 535.

[145] Keystone Papers, NDIRS, File 607.

[146] Interview of Leonard Sackett with John Peterson, Grandin Papers, NDIRS, File 308. Peterson served as a lumberjack in the winter and Grandin employee in the summer.

[147] White, *Scribner's Magazine*, XXII, 536.

[148] Mecklenburg interview, Keystone Farm Papers, NDIRS, File 607.

[149] Coulter, NDSHS, *Collections*, Vol. III, p. 579.

[150] White, *Scribner's Magazine*, XXII, 536.

[151] Keystone Farm Papers, NDIRS, File 607.

[152] Hilsted interview, Grandin Papers, File NDIRS, File 269; John Peterson interview, Grandin Papers, NDIRS, File 308.

[153] Walker interview, Spiritwood Farm Papers, NDIRS, File 173.

[154] House Regulations, D. C. Smith Papers, Cloverlea Farm, NDIRS, File 159.

[155] John Peterson interview, Grandin Papers, NDIRS, File 308.

[156] Interview of Leonard Sackett with Herman Deike, Dwight Farm Papers, NDIRS, File 259.

[157] John Miller Papers, Dwight Farm, NDIRS, File 84.

[158] Carlson interview, Dwight Farm Papers, NDIRS, File 158.

[159] Interview of Leonard Sackett with Ella Bratland, Helendale Farm Papers, NDIRS, File 254. Hereafter cited as Radcliffe interview. Ella Bratland was the daughter of Thomas Radcliffe.

[160] Power to Editor, *Cultivator and Country Gentleman*, May 10, 1877, File 309.

[161] This included seventeen gang plows which had just been invented.

[162] Coulter, NDSHS, *Collections*, Vol. III, pp. 575-577; *Cultivator and Country Gentleman*, Vol. 44, p. 2.

[163] F. B. Downing interview, Downing Papers, NDIRS, File 167. There is a picture of this event showing forty-nine binders all in action.

[164] *Fargo Argus*, Aug. 29, 1883, Oct. 10, 1883.

[165] Scrapbook of Cloverlea, D. C. Smith Papers, Cloverlea Farm, NDIRS, File 159, Cloverlea farms specialized in developing and producing for sale high quality and new varieties of seed for Dakota agriculture.

[166] Torgerson interview, G. S. Barnes Papers, NDIRS, File 867.

[167] Coulter, NDSHS, *Collections*, Vol. III, pp. 571-572.

[168] *Cultivator and Country Gentleman*, Vol. 45, p. 70.

[169] *Fargo Weekly Argus*, March 31, 1890, p. 1.

[170] *Fargo Argus*, May 11, 1882, p. 4, May 18, 1882, p. 6.

[171] Coulter, NDSHS, *Collections*, Vol. III, pp. 572-573; *Cultivator and Country Gentleman*, Vol. 46 (Oct. 26, 1881), p. 841.

[172] Coulter, NDSHS, *Collections*, Vol. III, pp. 572-573.

[173] Bigelow, *Atlantic Monthly*, Vol. 45, p. 30.

[174] *Cultivator and Country Gentleman*, Vol. 44, p. 2; Vol. 45, p. 19.

[175] *Fargo Argus*, Aug. 21, 1882, p. 1.

[176] White, *Scribner's Magazine*, XXII, 534.

[177] *Fargo Argus*, Aug. 14, 1880, p. 4, Aug. 18, 1880, p. 7.

[178] White, *Scribner's Magazine*, XXII, 536.

[179] *Fargo Argus*, Sept. 4, 1883.

[180] *Cultivator and Country Gentleman*, Vol. 42, p. 317. The early Northern Pacific cars held 400 bushels of wheat so this meant 75 train cars. The early trains often were not over twenty-five cars in length, so, fantastic as it seems, three trainloads of wheat could be produced in one day by a single bonanza threshing operation. File 513; *Fargo Daily Argus*, March 15, 1886.

[182] *Fargo Argus*, Aug. 14, 1880, p. 4, Aug. 18, 1880, p. 7.

[183] *Fargo Argus*, Sept. 1, 1881, p. 2.

[184] White, *Scribner's Magazine*, XXII, 536.

[185] *The Farmer*, XXV, 770.

[186] Coulter, NDSHS, *Collections*, Vol. III, pp. 573-574.

[187] *Cultivator and Country Gentleman*, Vol. 41, p. 340.

[188] White, *Scribner's Magazine*, XXII, 537.

[189] *Cultivator and Country Gentleman*, Vol. 42, p. 317.

[190] *Ibid.*, Vol. 44, p. 83.

[191] Grandin Papers, NDIRS, File 148.

[192] Coulter, NDSHS, *Collections*, Vol. III, pp. 575-576.

[193] *Fargo Daily Argus*, March 15, 1886.

[194] *Fargo Argus*, June 9, 1882.

[195] F. B. Downing interview, Downing Farm Papers, NDIRS, File 197. These buildings are now (1962) part of the Bagg farm about one mile from the village of Mooreton. They are in poor repair but are dramatic examples of the bonanza era.

[196] Mecklenburg interview, Keystone Farm Papers, NDIRS, File 607.

[197] Carlson interview, Dwight Farm Papers, NDIRS, File 257.

[198] Walcher interview, Dwight Farm Papers, NDIRS, File 241.

[199] *Fargo Argus*, Jan. 26, 1883, p. 4.

[200] *Fargo Argus*, Dec. 26, 1882, p. 2

[201] *Fargo Argus*, July 16, 1883.

CHAPTER V

Crops and Livestock on the Bonanza Farms

Aᴌᴛʜᴏᴜɢʜ ᴛʜᴇ machinery parades, army of laborers, and production techniques were important and dramatic in the life and picture of the bonanza farms, it was income that determined how long a bonanza could remain in existence. Assembly-line and mass-production techniques were adapted to agriculture by the bonanzas when they concentrated on the large-scale production of a single crop. In the sub-humid Red River Valley wheat proved to be the most profitable crop. Many bonanzas grew only wheat, but as time passed and the land lost some of its fertility or became too weedy, other crops had to be introduced. Most bonanzas shifted to other crops only to enable them to supply feed for their great horse herds and feed grain to the livestock that was needed to supply the tables of the farm. Only a few bonanzas produced livestock for commercial production. Diversification tended to reduce the efficiency of the bonanza.

Concentration on Wheat

What in the main provided the income to keep these agricultural enterprises operating? The bonanzas had perhaps two sources: grain and livestock. In the final end wheat proved to provide the most profitable income and so bonanza farming meant wheat farming. For a one-crop system was necessary for the most efficient use of machinery. In the earlier period of the bonanzas wheat definitely dominated as a crop, however, in the 1890's there was a gradual shift away from it to other crops and livestock.

So wheat was of primary interest to the bonanza farmer. Walter R. Reed of Amenia and Sharon fame stated it in this way: "At first these farms were almost invariably straight wheat farms. They did not even raise oats for their horses, figuring that they could buy oats cheaper than they could raise them." [1] The *Fargo Daily Argus* in commenting on wheat monoculture wrote in 1883:

[The] absence of familiar vegetables will strike most travelers, for

131

everybody rushes into wheat culture and pays high prices for food
on the table. You would fancy that a man could at least spare an
acre for potatoes, lettuce, parsnips, turnips, cabbage, and other garden truck but no, except for a few corn patches, you see nothing but
wheat.[2]

Fantastic as it may appear, the statement was not a newspaper exaggeration. There seemed to have been a general aversion to other
crops. Some bonanzas turned to fallowing when the need arose rather
than rotate wheat with other crops. James B. Power informed E. B.
Chambers of Chicago that the Cass-Cheney farm had 3,692 acres in
crops for 1877 of which 3,415 acres were wheat and 277 acres were
oats. At the same time the Grandin farm had 2,600 acres in wheat
and 140 acres in oats.[3] In 1878 the Cass farm alone had 3,526 acres
in crops of which 3,213 acres were in wheat, 158 in oats, and 155 in
barley.[4] Similar proportions were true of all the bonanzas. In 1878
all bonanzas had 244,240 acres under cultivation of which 185,430 were
devoted to wheat.[5] The acres of land under cultivation increased each
year so that by 1880, when the farms under Dalrymple contained 75,-
000 acres, 25,000 were in wheat with just enough oats and barley
for horses and other livestock. The rest of the land was still not
broken.[6] In 1879 the part of the Grandin farms under Dalrymple's
management had 5,316 acres under cultivation, of which 4,855 acres
were in wheat, 303 acres in oats, and 158 acres in barley. On the Cass-
Cheney farm 8-170 acres were cultivated. Of that amount 7,515 acres
were in wheat which produced 139,822 bushels and 389 acres of oats
yielded 15,867 bushels, while 266 acres of barley raised 6,449 bushels.
In 1879 the three farms contained 13,486 acres of which 12,320, or
91 per cent, were in wheat. In 1879 the average yield on the Cass-
Cheney bonanza was 18.6 bushels per acre while Grandins had a
22.2-bushel yield. This wheat sold for $0.95 per bushel on the track.
In 1882 the Dalrymples were said to have 50,000 acres under cultivation of which 45,000 were in wheat.[7] The Kimmerlee farm, a small
bonanza of only 3,000 acres, had 2,700 acres seeded to wheat, the same
90 per cent ratio as established by the larger farms.[8] In 1883 W. F.
Dalrymple reported that of the 30,000 acres under his management,
28,000 were in wheat and the other 2,000 in oats and barley.[9]

As seen above most of the bonanza leaders preferred wheat monoculture, however, it was obvious to the few who understood good soil
management that such a concentration on one crop could not go on
indefinitely, even on the fertile soil of the Red River Valley. The
Grandin farms had an average yield from 1883 to 1893 of one pound
less than 17 bushels per acre on an acreage that varied from 8,995

to 11,222 acres. In 1891 they produced their largest wheat crop of 257,369 bushels.[10] In 1883 Dalrymple reported that much of the land under his supervision had been in wheat for five straight years and some for the eighth year. His top yield up to that time was twenty-three bushels per acre and his seven-year average about eighteen.[11] In 1885 Dalrymple secured a yield of sixteen bushels per acre on land which had been in wheat for nine successive years. In 1886 after 10 consecutive years of cropping his plan was to fallow 3,000 acres each year until the entire farm had been rested and cultivated for weeds.[12] He felt that such a one-crop system would not "run out the land" and that it would be an easy matter to let it go back to pasture if production dropped. He intended to continue with wheat and break new land until he had 75,000 acres under cultivation.[13] At the time of the Dalrymple farm sale in 1917 one of Oliver Dalrymple's sons said that "for 25 consecutive years nothing but wheat was raised." [14]

To the soil-depleting aspect of the one-crop system was added the wasteful practice of burning most of the straw. Straw piles were only in the way until they were decomposed if not burned at once. There was no apparent practical use for such a massive volume of straw for not all could be used as bedding for horses or as fuel for the threshing engines. So, wasteful as it was, burning was the logical way to dispose of it. The small farmer who threshed stacks in his yard saved the straw for his livestock enterprise. But for practical and economical reasons it would not have been feasible to disperse the straw piles on the bonanzas by plowing the straw under. And it was not until the adoption of the combine that the straw could be economically returned to the land for decomposition.

Diversification of Crops

Some of the bonanza owners, such as the Grandins and Amenia and Sharon, promoted a gradual shift away from wheat monoculture. The Grandins were opposed to continuous wheat cropping from the start and expressed a desire for livestock and other crops. Even as early as 1878 the Mayville farm, although very heavily oriented toward wheat, produced 14,025 bushels of oats, 5,701 bushels of barley, 3,000 bushels of turnips, 2,000 bushels of potatoes, and 2,000 tons of hay in addition to 8 acres of beans. Most of the produce was for the cattle and hogs, although the potatoes and beans were table crops.[15]

Because of their livestock interests, the Grandins added feed-grain crops at an early date. By the late 1880's they were seeding 1,000 acres of corn, several hundred acres each of oats and barley for grain,

and millet which was cut for hay.[16] Although not the first to raise
corn, the Grandins became one of the greatest corn growers of the
bonanza operators. They did it because they were progressive farmers
and doubted the advisability of continuous wheat, and they were very
interested in a livestock operation which necessitated the growing of
corn. The Grandins reported that in 1894 they planted 175 acres of
corn on one farm and of that amount 140 acres was husked and a
total yield of 11,500 bushels was produced.[17] The other 35 acres were
cut green and yielded 105 tons of silage. In addition, the Grandins
took 295 tons of shreddings from the field which they husked. They
used steam-powered mechanical pickers.[18] The reported profit from
those 175 acres was $3,400 or $19 per acre which appears exceedingly
high.[19]

The Baldwin bonanza, which was established in the 1890's, went
directly into diversified agriculture and had a large acreage of corn
and alfalfa with practically no wheat. J. W. McNary was the manager
of this successful operation which secured the major portion of its
income from cattle, wool, cream, and hogs.[20] In the early 1880's the
Upson Farming Company used flax as its major crop. No account of
returns are known but it is likely that flax on the weed-free and newly
broken sod was a very successful crop.[21]

After 1890 even Dalrymple, the propagator of wheat monoculture,
had to change his system although he still raised wheat on some land
for twenty-five consecutive years. Gradually, however, he made shift
to a rotation which included flax, barley, oats, millet, corn, rye, and
other crops.[22] Dalrymple gave two reasons for this shift. First, he
felt corn, rye, barley, and other crops in rotation helped to keep
the soil in better condition. By 1906 he was growing 1,200 acres of
corn and at least 1,000 acres of each of the other crops, wheat still
being the major crop. Second, the labor scarcity required diversification, for by raising crops which could be planted and harvested at
different dates a much smaller labor force could handle the same number of acres as previously.[23]

In spite of their preference for the one-crop system, the bonanza
managers were early alerted to the need for a shift to a crop rotation
program. They were the most advanced scientific farmers of their
day and were probably called "book farmers" by their less progressive contemporaries. They were open to innovations and by being under constant economic pressures they were more receptive to new
ideas. Records were a novelty to the average farmer, but they were
the backbone of the bonanza for they told the manager what part
of his operation was profitable and what part needed a change. The

yields were checked regularly from each section. Any section that clearly showed a loss in productive capacity was either fallowed or seeded to Hungarian grass or some hay crop to build up the fertility.[24]

To handle such crops, some bonanzas developed features of integrated agriculture. For example, Hugh Moore of Mooreton, owner of the Antelope farm, had a grist mill with a daily capacity of seventy-four barrels of flour. When the wheat market was low, the wheat was ground into flour, enabling the bonanza to increase the income from the original product as well as to use the by-products for feeding the animals on the farm.[25] John C. Betz of Philadelphia who owned 23,000 acres raised barley for his brewery. He intended to raise malting barley and do some of the preliminary processing in malting before shipping it to Philadelphia. Betz hoped he could assure himself of at least 500,000 bushels of barley a year from his farm.[26]

Leaders in another progressive agricultural feature were the Grandins who planned to plant trees around sixty-three sections of land in an effort to reduce wind erosion and aid in moisture retention on their land. On one division alone more than twelve miles of trees were planted and references to the tree lanes on the Grandin farms were frequent.[27]

Livestock on the Bonanza Farms

Diversification was forced upon the bonanzas, in some respects, because of the large amount of feed crops necessary for the horses and mules. The bonanzas consumed more of these crops than the local market could provide and they became too expensive to ship in.

In the early period of bonanza farming the internal combustion engine had not been fully developed, therefore, the bonanzas needed a great amount of animal power. Horses and mules were the chief source of power, although some of the early "sod busters" used oxen. No oxen were used on the bonanzas for cultivation and harvesting once full-scale operations had commenced. Big shipments of horses and mules into the Red River Valley clearly illustrate the great number of those animals necessary for this type of farming. Horses and their upkeep ranked second only to wages and board of the men in the great expenses of the bonanza.[28] It was not only the original expense of securing the horses, but the need for constant replacement in addition to feed, labor, and housing that made the cost of animal power a great factor in the financing of the bonanzas.

To what extent mules or horses were used was based on two factors, the preference of the manager and their availability. St. Louis was the greatest source of animal power. Its geographical association might indicate that mules had the upper hand. Two daily newspaper reports from March, 1881, reported that 165 mules and 9 horses arrived in Fargo from St. Louis for the Grandin, Cheney, Alton, and Hauge and Brady farms, in addition to 10 cars of other stock for the Grandins.[29] It was just 3 days later that another shipment of 100 mules arrived from St. Louis for the Dalrymple farms.[30]

Each year as more acres were cultivated, the animal power requirements increased. The Cass-Cheney farm used 158 mules to produce the crop of 1879.[31] Dalrymple's total farming operation was said to have required 400 "work animals" for the year 1879. If that figure is correct, one must assume that there were at least 50 horses on the Cass-Cheney farm in addition to the 158 mules and an equal number of work animals on the Grandin farm. That year Dalrymple used 115 harvesters which required 3 horses each or a total of 345 which reliably indicates that there were 400 animals on the combined farms in 1879.[32] Dalrymple reported that at the beginning of the 1881 season there were 400 horses in his operation.[33] He expressed doubt at that time that steam could replace horses because steam plowing was still not practical in his opinion. He added that he would let the manufacturer experiment to prove otherwise.[34] The Dalrymple and Grandin farms, two of the larger bonanzas, used at least 800 work animals each at their peak of operation in 1884 and 1885.

Even the smaller bonanzas had large horse herds. The Keystone farm had 225 horses of which 170 were work horses and the others were buggy horses or young stock.[35] The Fairview farm located near Keystone had an equal number. Fairview had as many as thirty-five binders, requiring four horses each, in the field at one time. This meant 140 horses in addition to the spares and buggy horses that were necessary in normal operations.[36] The Mooreton farm in Richland County, owned by the Downings, had 200 horses at work during the peak of the harvest season.[37] The Belle Prairie farm of Traill County, one of the smaller bonanzas, used seventy-two horses and mules for its operation. It is interesting to note that its peak manpower requirement was only forty-two.[38] The Raymond farm north of Fargo used only fifty mules and horses, but had forty-five men employed during the peak season, clearly indicating that it is difficult to establish any ratio between manpower and work animals required for bonanza operations. Raymond was one of those bonanza farmers who had a business agreement with the lumbering interests regarding his mules and horses. His animals were sent to the woods each winter for a six-month period. He reported that he received $12.50 a month for each animal while they were in the lumber camp.³⁹ The Dalrymples and Grandins did not send their horses to the lumber camps but many of the smaller bonanzas apparently rented their horses out for the winter.⁴⁰

Another variation of how horses were used on the bonanza arose relative to the Leech farm which was purchased by James Kennedy in 1893. Kennedy, a large Fargo contractor, purchased the farm as a subsidiary to his construction business. The farm provided feed and housing for the horses needed in his construction work. The barn was reputed to have been the largest in the state in its day, 120 feet by 120 feet and had a capacity of 180 horses.⁴¹

Just as animal power requirements were partly responsible for diversification to feed grains, so manpower requirements necessitated the raising of animals for food. Some farms raised livestock because this was what the operators preferred, while others had them because they fitted in well with sound operation of the farm. The meat requirements for the large, hard-working crews were great. The Keystone farm butchered a beef and a hog each week during the busy seasons of seeding and harvesting.⁴² It had 75 head of cattle compared to its 225 horses. The cattle were only an incidental activity. August Trapp, the gardener and choreman on the No. 1 Watson farm, took care of the 25 cattle and 100 hogs which were normally kept for consumption on the farm.⁴³ At least one bonanza, Helendale, butchered animals on the farm for sale to retail outlets in Fargo. Hogs, sheep, and cattle were dressed on the farm and transported to the city. In the late 1870's and early 1880's many cattle were shipped into Fargo from Iowa and were butchered by the local meat markets indicating a lack of livestock production in the Valley.

While many bonanzas did not raise animals for their own consumption, others became interested in commercial livestock production and had large-scale operations. By 1878 the Barnes-Tenney farm on the east side of the Red River had a large cattle feeding operation. Tollef Torgerson, employed on that farm, reported that hauling hay in the winter to feed the 200 horses and 600 beef cattle was a steady job.⁴⁴

The first big cattle bonanza west of the Red River was the Mayville farm of the Grandins. This was in no way connected with the South Grandin farm managed by Dalrymple. The Mayville farm, which was designated as a cattle farm from the first, was an ideal choice, for it was well supplied with water from the headwaters of the Elm and Goose rivers. By 1878 the Grandins had 151 head of cattle, including 2 purebred Shorthorn bulls which were valued at $3,500 each. There were also 73 purebred Cotswold sheep and 100

Berkshire and Poland-China hogs. A farm-journal writer commented: "This is an entirely new departure in utilizing our Dakota prairies, and the result will be watched with more than ordinary interest."[45] By the summer of 1880 the farm had increased its cattle numbers to 300 including young stock. A fabulous twenty-two pound fleece was sheared from one sheep that spring.[46] James McKessich, manager of the Grandin stock farm at a later date, stated that 300 sows farrowed yearly, producing 1,500 pigs. In the spring of 1884, 250 sheep were sheared. Large numbers of cattle and hogs explain the Grandin interest in corn production.[47] As total livestock numbers crew, the Grandins stressed quality in their purebred Shorthorn cattle, Berkshire hogs, and Cotswold sheep.[48]

The Grandin interest in livestock influenced Datus C. Smith of the nearby Belle Prairie farm. Smith's farm had a complete assortment of livestock. In addition to the 72 horses and mules, it had 15 colts, 12 milk cows, 40 young stock, 25 hogs, 200 chickens, and 500 sheep. Sheep obviously were the only livestock in sufficient numbers to really be considered a commercial operation, although not all the other livestock products could be consumed on the farm.[49]

The Grandins, in their crop-payment plan, very definitely encouraged livestock production in that area of the Valley by giving preference to land buyers who were engaged or interested in a livestock enterprise. The same was true of the Amenia and Sharon Land Company.

Spiritwood, the bonanza of Russell and Adams located near Jamestown, had livestock from its beginnings. Sheep was their major livestock interest but how many they had is not clear. At least 159 sheep were sheared in 1880.[50] Fairview farm, in the southern part of the Valley, had an intensive sheep raising operation. The nine sections that it had under cultivation were all fenced with woven wire so that sheep could graze after the crop was removed. In addition, Fairview had three sections that were specifically for sheep pasture and another three sections for hay land for winter feeding. The farm had 3 sheep sheds 76 feet by 240 feet each and at one time there were 10,000 sheep on the place.[51]

The above information is adequate proof that some bonanzas were not strictly wheat operations. Horses and livestock were a necessary part of the operation. Livestock was maintained either because it was necessary for economics of operation relative to supplying necessary food or diversification to livestock stabilized and improved the financial aspect of the bonanza. Only the Amenia and Sharon bonanza developed livestock to such a great extent that it produced a major portion of its income.

FOOTNOTES

[1] *Fargo Forum*, Jan. 18, 1927.

[2] *Fargo Daily Argus*, Aug. 23, 1883.

[3] Power to E. B. Chambers, Oct. 10, 1877, NDIRS, File 309. Chambers was a map maker for Rand and McNally.

[4] Power to Cass, Oct. 14, 1878, File 309.

[5] *Cultivator and Country Gentleman*, Vol. 45, p. 611.

[6] Chamberlain, *Cultivator and Country Gentleman*, Vol. 45, p. 611.

[7] *Fargo Daily Argus*, July 15, 1882. This is probably an exaggeration of the number of acres under Dalrymple's management but the ratio of wheat acres to the total is very likely correct. There were several Dalrymples in Dakota at the time and this may have been the total of all their operations.

[8] *Fargo Daily Argus*, July 15, 1882. ,

[9] *Fargo Argus*, June 26. 1883.

[10] Clipping from *Moorhead Daily News*, May 8, 1893, NDIRS, Grandin Papers, File 148; *Fargo Forum*, May 5, 1893.

[11] *Fargo Argus*, Jan. 31, 1883.

[12] Lewis F. Crawford, *History of North Dakota* (Chicago, 1931), Vol. I, pp. 478-483.

[13] *Fargo Daily Argus*, Jan. 15, 1881, p. 4.

[14] *Casselton Reporter*, Jan. 19, 1917. A feature article about the Dalrymple farm sale.

[15] *Cultivator and Country Gentleman*, Vol. 44, p. 83.

[16] McKessich interview, Dwight Farm Papers, NDIRS, File 138.

[17] Grandin Papers, NDIRS, File 269. This yield seems very large considering that the Carrington Experimental Station produced only an eighty-five bushel yield in 1960 on irrigated land. It is probable, however, that if this was husked and the husks and stems left on the ears that the bushel volume could actually have been eighty-two bushels per acre. With husks and stems removed the volume would be reduced by half, making the figure more probable.

[18] What they mean is not clear but these were probably stationary corn shredders.

[19] Clipping from *The Goose*, Grandin Papers, NDIRS, File 269.

[20] Benton, *Journal of Land and Public Utility Economics*, Vol. I, p. 409.

[21] *Fargo Argus*, Feb. 13, 1882, p. 6.

[22] *Casselton Reporter*, Jan. 19, 1917.

[23] *The Farmer*, XXV, 770.

[24] White, *Scribner's Magazine*, XXII, 538. The two top wheat yields reported on bonanzas for fairly large acreages came from the Leech farm which is reputed to have had a 25 bushel average from 4,000 acres. *Fargo Daily Argus*, Aug. 31, 1883. The Elk Valley farm at Larimore had a 32 bushel average from the first 100 acres cut in 1883. *Fargo Daily Argus*, Sept. 12, 1883. The above are still below the famous forty bushel per acre crop produced along the Sheyenne River in 1873.

[25] *Fargo Daily Argus*, Dec. 1, 1884.

[26] *Fargo Argus*, June 27, 1882, p. 3.

[27] *Cultivator and Country Gentleman*, Vol. 45, p. 19. Another novel feature of Grandin Farm No. 1 was its race track. The Grandins liked horse racing and the farm offered them an opportunity to develop the hobby. Hilstad interview, Grandin Papers, NDIRS, File 269.

[28] Coulter, NDSHS, *Collections*, Vol. III, p. 577.

[29] *Fargo Daily Argus*, March 28, 1881, p. 4.

[30] *Fargo Daily Argus*, March 31, 1881, p. 4. At least one bonanza farmer, T. M. Elliot of Ransom County, raised blooded horses for his farm use and for sale. *Fargo Argus*, May 1, 1882, p. 4.

[31] *Cultivator and Country Gentleman*, Vol. 45, p. 19.

[32] Coulter, NDSHS, *Collections*, Vol. III, p. 577.

[33] The term "horses" here clearly indicates a work animal and does not distinguish between horses and mules.

[34] *Fargo Daily Argus*, Jan. 15, 1881, p. 4.

[35] Mecklenburg interview, Keystone Farm Papers, NDIRS, File 607.

[36] Ward interview, Dwight Farm Papers, NDIRS, File 258.

[37] S. G. Downing interview, Downing Farm Papers, NDIRS, File 166.

[38] Hilstad interview, Grandin Papers, NDIRS, File 269.

[39] *Fargo Argus*, Sept. 2, 1881, p. 2. The figure $12.50 seems quite high considering that top men during the peak season did not get more than $25 a month but probably it was cheaper for the lumber interests to pay a good rate for rented animals on a six-month basis rather than to have and care for their own animals for twelve months. The only other reference that stated the pay for these animals in the lumber camps used the figure $6.50 a month and up.

[40] Peterson interview, Grandin Papers, NDIRS, File 308

[41] Interview of Norton Berg with William Berg, Nov., 1960. These notes are of the author. William Berg's father was harness maker on the Leech farm.

[42] Mecklenburg interview, Keystone Farm Papers, NDIRS, File 607.

[43] Trapp interview, Watson Farm Papers, NDIRS, File 827.

[44] Torgerson interview, G. S. Barnes Papers, NDIRS, File 867.

[45] *Cultivator and Country Gentleman*, Vol. 44, p. 83.

[46] *Fargo Weekly Argus*, July 7, 1880, p. 2.

[47] McKessich interview, Dwight Farm Papers, NDIRS, File 138.

[48] Letters from Golden Latitudes, p. 33, Bonanza Farm Papers, NDIRS, File 71. This is a long, typed account of a visit to the Grandin farm, May and June, 1885. No author is given.

[49] Hilstad interview, Grandin Papers, NDIRS, File 269.

[50] Dunwell interview, Spiritwood Farm Papers, NDIRS, File 164.

[51] Walcher interview, NDIRS, File 214

CHAPTER VI

The Amenia and Sharon Land Company: Formation, Land Policy, and Operation

THE RECORDS of the Amenia and Sharon Land Company provide the most complete information regarding the detailed operation of a bonanza. While not the best known bonanza, the Amenia and Sharon in many respects was the greatest of them all. Its success was due to a great extent to the father-son team of E. W. and H. F. Chaffee. Their progressive, forward-looking policies created a multi-million-dollar organization.

The Chaffees, who had great faith in the soil of Dakota, built a bonanza in spite of the opposition of many of the stockholders of the company. After a bitter internal struggle over how to operate the land and over the building of a railroad, the company split into two organizations in 1893. After the split, H. F. Chaffee, though still in his early twenties, assumed control of the remnants of the original group. The managing genius of the bonanzas, he created a highly integrated farm with a tenant system of operation, a complex system of land companies, and an experimental farm, all of which blended themselves into a progressive, rapidly growing organization.

The Origin of the Company

Between September 1873, and September 1875, the Northern Pacific Land Department offered millions of acres for sale and sold 483,-141 acres of which 304,165 acres went to eastern buyers. The remainder was sold in small purchases. The most unusual sale was to a group of forty bond-holders who pooled their stock of Northern Pacific holdings in order to purchase a large tract of land in Cass County. They were middle-class New Englanders who could not afford to lose the money they had invested. They had invested in Northern Pacific bonds for several reasons. First, many leading citizens from New England were promoting this railroad. Second, the proposed route was in harmony with New England's expansion ideas. Third, Jay Cooke and Company had carried on an extensive advertising campaign among them pointing out the large return, for these bonds paid 7.3 per cent interest. Finally, railroads seemed a safe investment. So it was not surprising that these thrifty New Englanders should have bought Northern Pacific bonds.[1]

The original group lived in the communities of Amenia, New York, and Sharon, Connecticut. The Amenia and Sharon Land Company was incorporated on July 14, 1875, and domiciled at Sharon, Litchfield County, Connecticut.[2] The original twenty-seven stockholders grew to forty shortly before any land was purchased. Each received shares in the new corporation in proportion to his railroad holdings. In all, there were 926 shares in the company. They were quite evenly divided with two exceptions, Mrs. A. Flint possessed 80 and Eben W. Chaffee, the largest stockholder, had 82. The company was capitalized under the laws of Connecticut for $125,000, although the total paid-in capital never exceeded $92,600.[3]

The articles of incorporation state that the company was formed for the

conversion of bonds of the Northern Pacific Railroad Company into lands of said Co.—The improvement and occupancy of the same by mining for coal, iron, or other materials in said land; by erecting all necessary buildings and by farming said land and generally to do all things necessary and convenient for the prosecution of said business, together with the purchase and sale of Real Estate in the State and elsewhere.[4]

Eben W. Chaffee, a director in the company, was sent to Dakota to select the land and handle the company's operations. On July 30, 1875, the company secured 27,831.66 acres of land, all in Cass County, for $104,009.81 or an average price of $3.75 per acre.[5]

Eben W. Chaffee Assumes Leadership, 1876–1893

E. W. Chaffee was to become a big man in the early Dakotas, not as well known as Dalrymple or Power, but just as powerful. On July 23, 1875, he took over the reins of the company. On his first visit to Dakota in order to select land he became convinced of its great fertility and decided, contrary to the intent of the stockholders, that it should be held and operated. He was not satisfied to develop and sell, reaping only a minor windfall. Without fully informing the stockholders back East of his actions, Chaffee hired Peter Seims, a professional sodbuster, who broke the first land in 1876. The following year R. Gallup, a Casselton liveryman, was hired as foreman to put in the first crop.[6] An excellent prospective wheat crop was partially ruined by a hail storm, but a fifteen-bushel yield and the news of great success by Cass-Cheney-Dalrymple prompted E. W. Chaffee to enlarge the company operations.

The farm was operated as a single unit from 1876 to 1893, that is, throughout the life of E. W. Chaffee. In 1877 there were 640 acres seeded to wheat and the following year 2,200 acres were under cultivation.[7] In 1877 the company paid Chaffee $750 which was raised to $1,000 in 1878, to $1,200 in 1879, and to $1,500 in 1880. It was this salary in addition to his share of the company profits that enabled Chaffee to acquire personal holdings and build a sizeable fortune.[8] The company furnished the teams, equipment, capital, and hired labor to do the farming. At first, it was one big unit but as it grew, divisions of three or four sections were created, and the farm continued to be operated in this manner until 1893. There was some exception to this as share leasing of half sections or sections gradually started in 1889 and increased rapidly after 1893.[9]

Cautious management was needed in the early years. In 1877 the directors allowed E. W. Chaffee to execute a mortgage against the land to meet operating expenses. That right had to be renewed several times in the following years. In 1878 an assessment was levied against each stockholder for 25 per cent of the par value of his stock. This was not sufficient so increased borrowing power was granted to the president.[10] No other assessment was ever necessary.

Dakota was blessed with favorable rains from 1877 to 1883, and income became adequate to pay expenses and dividends. By 1878 the gross income was $14,934.62, the bulk of which came from wheat though some came from the newly opened blacksmith shop. In 1879 it rose to $18,866.90 and soared to $33,785.78 in 1880. In 1881 it was $38,330.10. A dividend of $5,964 was paid in 1880 and also in 1881. This amounted to 6 per cent each year on the paid-in capital. Chaffee's faith in the soil of Dakota was justified. Income rose steadily each year and in 1883 two dividends totaling 16 per cent, or $15,905, were paid. Section 35 produced a gross income of $9,340.80 and a net profit of $2,198.11 or $3.50 per acre. Such returns spoiled the stockholders, but the returns in 1886 exicted them beyond all expectations when they received $42,245, nearly 50 per cent of the paid-in capital. This was followed in 1887 with a 10 per cent dividend of $9,940. After 1888, however, lack of rain made operations a nip-and-tuck affair. In 1889 Herbert F. Chaffee wrote to his father, E. W. Chaffee, that the rains "have improved the crop outlook. If we can get eight or ten bushels to acre and $1 per bushel we shall be pretty well fixed." [11]

Early growth of operations can be easily pictured from the size of the labor force involved. In 1878, the first year of large-scale operation, the total labor bill was $6,833.34 which was paid to 63 men, representing about one-third of all expenses. The highest paid men in 1878 were the foremen, R. Gallup who received $279.94, and F. W. Mucky who received $297.12. In 1879, $6,914.91 was paid to 74 men, and in 1880 wages totaled $10,960.61. That year the first husband-wife combination was hired for $348.78.[12] In 1881, 104 men were employed at a cost of $14,210.83. By 1891 the wage schedule provided for a range of $300 to $400 annually for foremen, $25 per month for regular hands, and $1.75 to $2 daily for harvest and threshing help. The blacksmith, who was the highest paid man outside of the officers, received $40 per month. By 1903 the blacksmith's salary was increased to $55 per month but he was required to pay $5 a month rent for a company house. Even after the farms were leased out, the total labor bill remained very high because of the great many subsidiary activities conducted by the company.[13]

The first big investment exclusive of land was made in March, 1877, when E. W. Chaffee spent $2,783.50 for 25 horses, plus $665.19 for harness, blankets, and horse equipment, and $2,065.24 for machinery. The machinery included six wagons, thirteen plows, five harrows, four seeders, and four harvesters.[14] From this modest beginning steam engines and separators and other machinery were added each year until the peak was reached in 1892 when the annual inventory revealed 171 horses and mules, 36 seeders, 36 plows, 34 wagons, 15 harrows, and 40 harvesters, worth $30,000.[15]

It was only logical that a large farm operation such as the Amenia and Sharon Land Company should become involved in subsidiary enterprises. In 1878 the blacksmith shop was built, chiefly for the repair of equipment used on the farms, but outsiders were soon utilizing its services. Each year the blacksmith shop contributed to the net income of the company. In 1879 the directors authorized E. W. Chaffee to deal with the Northern Pacific Railway Company for a right-of-way and a depot location near the company farms. On July 15, 1880, the agreement was completed for the construction and maintenance of a side track and depot on the N. W. ¼, Sec. 25, T. 141, R. 52 Cass County. This was the beginning of Amenia, the first of two company towns. The location selected for the Amenia depot became the center of the farming operations. As soon as the depot was finished, E. W. Chaffee built a store which was intended as a general supply post and office for the farm operations but it also served the public. In 1881 the directors empowered Chaffee to build an elevator for the company interests. The elevator was the beginning of a quite large chain and is today the largest independently owned elevator in North Dakota.[16] A town grew up around the elevator and depot. It was a company town from the beginning, and E. W. Chaffee "held the village property closely in order to keep out undesirable people or business." [17] In 1893 the second town, Chaffee, was built around an elevator to handle company business for its lands in the southwestern part of Cass County.

After 1884 it was obvious that more than a mere farming enterprise was under operation. That year out of a total income of $82,839.92, wheat produced $63,910.64 and the other came from interest income, elevator, and blacksmith earnings.[18]

An interesting event was portrayed in a picture of plowing on the Chaffee farm which was used on a United States postage stamp in connection with the Omaha Exposition of 1898. This picture was taken in 1888 at the height of the single-unit operation. H. L. Chaffee explained the picture in this way:

Large crews of men, horses, and machinery, operating in groups of fifteen to twenty units, were commonly used in field work. The picture was taken . . . when one of these crews, working eighteen units, was in the field plowing down a wheat crop that had been hailed out. The usual size of the fields worked was one mile square, 640 acres, and a workman and his horses were generally understood to have put in his miles whenever he had crossed the field twenty times.[19]

E. W. Chaffee's Personal Life

As the farm increased in size, Chaffee became more involved in its management. At first he spent only the summers in Dakota, but by 1886 things had progressed sufficiently so that Mrs. Chaffee (Amanda) came to establish a permanent home in Amenia. She brought out her grandson, Robert B. Reed, who later became active in the company.[20] From a small farm background in Connecticut, Chaffee became a first-class farm manager. In addition to his farm duties he became active in local affairs and in 1889 served as a member of the North Dakota Constitutional Convention in Bismarck.[21]

A very strict Congregationalist, E. W. Chaffee helped in the formation of a Congregational Church in North Dakota with the establishment of a congregation at Amenia on August 15, 1886. He served as its treasurer and guiding light until his death. A church building was erected under his guidance and was dedicated July 14, 1887. John Reed was a deacon and H. F. Chaffee the secretary of that congregation.[22] E. W. Chaffee's last will and testament portrayed his devotion, for he left a house to serve as the parsonage for the Amenia parish and $1,000 to the Congregational Ecclesiastical Society of Ellsworth at Sharon, Connecticut.[23] Chaffee practiced his religion and allowed no work on the Sabbath. Robert Reed, his grandson, said, "He would not have harvested a field on Sunday if he had certain knowledge that a hail storm would thresh the grain Sunday night."[24] He stopped ball playing several times on Sunday and refused to let any of his men hunt on that day. He was considered very strict by his men who were "a little in awe of him."[25]

He showed his faith in Dakota soil by his purchase of several farms. He instilled this faith into others so that even in the seriously depressed years of American agriculture in the late 1880's they were willing to stick with him and the land. James S. Chaffee, a nephew, wrote in 1889:

Some of our stockholders could not stand an assessment and I fear would have to make a partial sacrifice of their holdings. Yet a total failure this year would not impair the value of the property to me.... We must take the bitter with the sweet yet it is hard to have our realization of expectations deferred and some of our stockholders now wish to sell something besides the elevators.[26]

E. W. Chaffee purchased small single tracts as soon as he had the money. By 1888 he owned 12 farms containing 3,493 acres.[27] Some of this land was not cheap, considering the availability and cost of land in those early days. For example, in 1886 he purchased 800 acres from the company together with a share of the personal property, stock, and machinery for $25,000. This was at least $25 an acre for the land.[28] Not all of his offers or purchases were at that high a price. In 1888 his offer to buy 4,200 acres from the company at $12.50 was declined. At the time he personally owned 3,500 acres.[29] His final offer to the company was on May 27, 1892, when he proposed to buy the entire property for $298,200. This offer was made by letter to a company meeting at which it was tabled unanimously.[30] Had he succeeded, he would have become the largest individual land owner in North Dakota.

Although not successful in securing absolute ownership of the company, he did have virtual control of it. At the time of his death he held 528¼ of the 994 outstanding shares and was in a position to acquire more. In addition to owning five-ninths of the stock of a company which was very conservatively valued at over $400,000, he owned personally 4,570 acres of land. His other assets, including cash on hand, wheat, retail stock in stores, livestock and notes receivable, amounted to $125,463.61. At his death his gross estate was conservatively estimated at $312,836.65, nearly all of which was acquired after he moved to Dakota.[31]

The Company's Real Estate Policy, 1876 to 1893

The original intent of the company was to improve the land and "form a nucleus for a community, and to sell in parcels to settlers." This seemed very logical to the stockholders who remained in the East and had no desire to farm the land. It was also logical in the light of contemporary events. The land along the Northern Pacific was attracting a large number of immigrants, and land prices were rising rapidly. In its early years the company did not realize any "extravagant profits," so there was no reason for the stockholders to change their minds about developing for immediate sale.[32] In 1877 the company even had to mortgage some of its land to meet operating expenses. At this time this event encouraged the stockholders to push for liquidation. In order to expedite the sale of land the annual meeting February 8, 1879, passed a resolution making all deeds conveying land valid when signed by the president and secretary. Later on to hasten the sale of land by contract-for-deed, all such conveyances were made valid on the signature of the secretary alone.[33] In 1880 E. W. Chaffee placed an advertisement in the *Fargo Weekly Argus* offering 25,000 acres of wheat land for sale.[34] During the next five years he sold thirty-five farms on contracts, twelve sales in 1879, one in 1880, two in 1881, eight in 1882, five in 1883, and seven in 1884. Sales ranged in size from 160 to 640 acres.[35] The company's terms on its land sales were lenient, but many farms had to be repossessed because they were not profitable on account of dry weather, inadequate capital and the small size of operation of many purchasers.[36]

The company became involved in financing farms and tenants by methods other than the sale of its own land. Because it had a cash surplus after a few years of operation, many people sought, quite naturally, to borrow money. In the mid- and late 1880's, the company loaned a large amount of money on non-company land mortgages, chattel mortgages, and a great many personal notes. The company even purchased notes from the local banks to help renters or contract buyers. Such purchases gave the company better control over the finances of certain individuals. Many times the local farmers asked the company to co-sign notes or let them charge in the company name at implement dealers.[37]

The company store, blacksmith shop, and elevator did business on the credit basis. Many times when it could not collect on bad accounts, the company acquired pieces of property in return for the

obligation owed to it. Some lands that had never previously belonged
to the company were secured because people placed mortgages with
them and could not repay.[38] E. W. Chaffee reasoned that it would be
to the advantage of all to keep the debtors on the land and keep it in
cultivation. It not only gave them a chance to redeem themselves but
also saved the company the headache of having to take over operation of the land. One of the debtors wrote to E. W. Chaffee: "I will
need some repairs for my binders. . . . I am also badly in need of plow
shares . . . send me an order for them for what I need if you feel disposed. . . . I certainly feel very grateful to you for your many kind-
nesses to me and interest in my behalf and will bend every energy in
my power to recompense you." [39] At one time the company had over-
extended its credit to tenants and contract buyers so that it was a
concern of some of the management whether or not they would be
able to collect "enough of our back bills . . . so that we may not be
obliged to raise any more money from outside sources." [40]

Many people who rented and later purchased land from the company started out as day laborers. They were steady workers and when
it came time for them to go into business on their own, the company
"financed them and set them up." The company actually "carried
renters and contract purchasers." A regular draft form was used which
served to enable the company to pay for operating, labor, and other
expenses for the renters direct from headquarters in Amenia. In the
fall the renters or contract buyers came in by appointment and a settlement was made. The renter or buyer received all that was left after
expenses were deducted from his grain sales. The company had security in that the grain had to be sold to its elevators located in the area.
Some of the renters never did get on their own. Many times the farm
managers, particularly A. I. Cure, had to go out to these farmers and
take an inventory of all they owned to see if the company could extend more credit to them.[41]

Financing renters and contract buyers was big business for the company. The interest income and contract payments greatly increased
the net income and resultant surplus. Repossession of land and its resale at higher prices proved profitable. Table 8 indicates the scope of
the financing carried on by the company.

The contracts issued to land purchasers were very reasonable and
closely tied to the ability of the land to produce. John Pagel of Winona County, Minnesota, made the first purchase from the company
by contract-for-deed on April 8, 1879. He purchased 320 acres for
$3,200, no payment due until December 1, 1880, at which time $400
had to be paid. The company carried the entire contract at 10 per

Mr. and Mrs. J. B. Power on their golden wedding anniversary in 1907.

John Miller, first governor of North Dakota

Jerome Francis Downing, owner of the Downing farms.

Rollin C. Cooper

Oliver Dalrymple

John S. Dalrymple, Sr.

John S. Jr. and Mary Dalrymple in a field of
flax on Dalrymple No. 1 about 1960.

Front porch of Dalrymple home in 1906.
Left to right: unknown, Mrs. John Pollock
(Dorothy Dalrymple), John S. Dalrymple,
Sr., and Mrs. Oliver Dalrymple.

Eben Whitney Chaffee.

H. F. Chaffee

H. L. Chaffee with prize
pronghorn antelope.

Robert B. Reed, (First student to
enroll at N.D.A.C. and a member
of its first graduating class in
1895).

Advertising lands and appealing
to settlers for the Northern
Pacific country.

The Northern Pacific Grant.

The grant of lands to the Northern Pacific Railroad by the United States, to aid in its construction, extends from Montreal River, on the eastern boundary of the State of Wisconsin, to Puget Sound, in Washington Territory, a distance of about 2,000 miles, and embraces an area of about 42,000,000 acres. It confers upon the Company the odd-numbered sections (each section being one square mile and containing 640 acres) for a distance of 40 miles on each side of the road in the Territories and for 20 miles in the States. This great landed estate equals in its aggregate nearly the whole area of the State of Minnesota. Within this broad belt across the continent every variety of land may be found, suited to the wants of all classes of settlers. Workers in every department of human industry may find scope for their energy and enterprise and profitable occupation on the rich wheat lands of Northern Minnesota, Dakota, Montana, Idaho, Washington and Oregon; in raising cattle and sheep on the unsurpassed grazing lands all along the Northern Pacific Railroad; in the extensive forests of the unsurpassed timber in Montana and Idaho, and by developing the rich deposits of gold, silver and other minerals found in all the Mountain Districts traversed by this line.

The extent and variety of the resources of the Northern Pacific country are, as yet, inadequately comprehended, and those who have the sagacity to perceive and the energy to seize upon the advantages of this country will soon find their reward in ample fortunes and happy homes. When completed, by midsummer of 1883, the Company will operate over 2,500 miles of main line and branches, and will open to the settler on its line the markets of the world. The outlet by the great lakes from Duluth and Superior City, on Lake Superior, insures the cheapest means of reaching the sea-board.

The building of the road into Montana from the East, and also from the West, leaving a gap of only about 250 miles, and the vigor with which the gap is being closed, insuring a great through line at an early day, is directing public attention as never before to this great enterprise, and exciting fresh interest in the development of *the Northern Pacific country, the most productive portion of the United States.*

The Country Along the Line.

MINNESOTA.

The Northern Pacific Railroad starts from St. Paul, the head of navigation on the Mississippi River; also from Minneapolis, at the Falls of St. Anthony, the greatest water power in the world, and at Brainerd, 136 miles from St. Paul, forms a junction with that part of the line extending from Duluth and Superior City, at the head of Lake Superior, and passes through Minnesota, Dakota, Montana, Idaho, Washington and Oregon—THE GREAT NORTHERN PACIFIC COUNTRY—FROM THE GREAT LAKES TO THE PACIFIC OCEAN.

From Duluth west for 150 miles the road passes through a densely timbered country, the growth consisting principally of pine of different varieties, with oak, maple, birch, ash, linden, elm, etc., much the same as is found in Maine, Northern New York, Canada, Michigan and Wisconsin. These forests extend a few miles south and a great distance north of the railroad, and furnish an unlimited supply of cheap lumber and fuel for the western prairies. Large quantities of pine lumber is manufactured at various points on the line and furnished to settlers at reasonable prices. These lumbering interests give employment to thousands of men, especially during the winter. Many of the settlers on the prairies find occupation for themselves and their teams, at the season of the year when they are not employed on their farms, in logging, and in getting out wood and ties for the railroad company in these timbered regions.

The surface of the country in Northern Minnesota is level or gently undulating, well watered by running streams and innumerable lakes, and interspersed with meadows, whose natural production is a rich growth of red top, blue joint and native meadow grasses, yielding from one to two tons per acre and making excellent hay.

The soil is a dark loamy mould, with a good retentive subsoil, and, when cleared, makes good farms for agricultural purposes and grazing.

The settlers who occupy these lands west of Brainerd raise excellent crops, and have a ready market for all their products. The forests are filled with game and the lakes with game fish.

From Verndale to Muscoda, 81 miles, the country is more open, about two-thirds timbered, the growth being of the same varieties as east of the Mississippi River. Interspersed with the timber are open glades of clean prairie and meadow, the surface gently undulating, the soil being a rich, dark, loamy mould with a subsoil of clay, with slight admixture of sand, well adapted to general agricultural purposes, producing fine crops of wheat, oats, barley, corn, and extremely fine vegetables.

This section of the country is well watered by numerous streams of clear running water and sylvan lakes, which, with the prairies and meadows, offer fine inducements for dairy and stock farming. For about 50 miles of this distance the road runs through what is known as the "Lake Park Region," a beautifully diversified rolling country with groves of forest trees, fertile prairies bordered by timber, and handsome lakes with wooded shores. This is one of the best regions for general farming on the line of the railroad. The soil is a rich black loam, from two to six feet deep, with a clay subsoil, producing prolific crops of all of the smaller grains, corn and potatoes, and garden vegetables of great size and in large quantity. The wheat crop is always large in this section. Detroit and other points in Lake Park Region are fine Summer Resorts, with excellent hunting and fishing. Lake Park and Audubon are largely settled by Scandinavians.

Between Muscoda and Moorhead, a distance of 22 miles, the Northern Pacific Railroad enters the Red River Valley, which it traverses for a distance of about 50 miles, crossing the river at the latter place. The surface is level, the soil is alluvial black mould, resting on a tenacious clay subsoil, and produces excellent crops of wheat, oats, barley, buckwheat, rye, potatoes and garden vegetables.

The distance from St. Paul to Fargo, on the west bank of the Red River of the North, is 274 miles, and from Duluth 253 miles. Thriving towns have sprung up along the railway throughout Minnesota.

DAKOTA, EAST OF THE MISSOURI RIVER.

From Fargo, on the Red River, to Bismarck, on the Missouri River, a distance of 195 miles, in Dakota, the road pursues an almost direct line west across a great prairie country, which is level in some parts and rolling in others. It is, for most of the distance, a vast fertile field covered, except where cultivated, with nutritious grasses. The same general qualities of soil and climate characterize this whole region, which embraces the best wheat-producing, general farming and stock-raising lands in America.

From Fargo to Wheatland, 27 miles, the road runs across the flat and fertile lands of the Red River Valley in Cass County, large areas of which are under cultivation. Here the great bonanza farms are located, the most famous one being the Cass-Cheney-Dalrymple farm, near *Casselton.* It was on this farm that the first experiment in wheat growing on the Dakota plains was made, which demonstrated their wonderful fertility and their capacity to produce the best spring wheat in the world. The development of this county, and Traill on the north and Richland on the south, have been phenomenal, and the influx of settlers and investors is constantly increasing, attracted by the profits of wheat-farming. The railroad land in Cass County is nearly all taken up, and settlers are occupying the equally productive lands farther west. There are millions of acres of government lands, and thousands of acres of choice tracts in this country owned by non-residents, that can be purchased on liberal terms, both as to price and time of payment. This region is watered by the *Red, Sheyenne, Maple, Elm, Goose* and *Rush Rivers.*

From Wheatland, the western limit of the Valley, through the counties of Barnes, Stutsman, Kidder and Burleigh, a distance of 168 miles, the country presents the same general characteristics; but these higher undulating lands are proving to be even more productive than the flat lands in the Red River Valley, lying as they do in a fine upland prairie country, with gently rolling surface, and watered by the *Sheyenne and James Rivers, The Pipestone, Beaver, Long Lake Creek, Turtle and other streams,* their tributaries, and numerous sparkling lakes. The soil is a rich black loam, with a clay subsoil, and contains all the ingredients necessary to the production of superb wheat and all species of grain and root crops, as has been abundantly demonstrated by thousands of settlers. The Sheyenne River traverses Barnes County—one of the largest and richest in Dakota—from north to south, and is lined with settlers. Large areas are already under cultivation, and its upland, rolling surface is attracting great numbers of settlers.

Stutsman County embraces the beautiful, wide and fertile valley through which the James River runs. Settlers are pouring into this county rapidly, attracted hither by its productive soil and railroad facilities. In Stutsman County the railroad has large quantities of excellent land for sale.

The Jamestown Branch Railroad, now under construction northwest from Jamestown, in Stutsman County, to the Devil's Lake, Mouse River and Turtle Mountain regions, will open to settlement an attractive section of country. English capitalists have purchased large tracts of land from the Railroad Company on this Branch, which they are putting under the plow and subdividing into small farms.

West of Jamestown, in Stutsman, Kidder and Burleigh counties, settlers are availing themselves of the opportunity to make selections of railroad and government lands near the railroad track. Among the numerous other farms along the Northern Pacific in this section, the Troy farm and Steele farm in Kidder County, and the Clark farm in Burleigh County, are noted for having successfully demonstrated the adaptation of the land for wheat raising and general farming. Stock growers are utilizing the uplands of Kidder and Burleigh Counties for sheep raising, recognizing in the nutritious grasses, abundance of water, ready market and a plentiful supply of hay, which can be had for the cutting, conditions altogether favorable for that industry.

Burleigh County, of which Bismarck is the county seat, has a gently rolling surface, and the soil is of the same fertile character as that of the prairies farther east. The great Northwestern Exposition, held at Minneapolis in September, 1882, offered a premium to the county in all the Northwestern States and Territories which should exhibit the finest samples of agricultural products, and the prize banner was awarded to Burleigh County, Dakota. The military posts along and west of the Missouri River furnish a ready market at good prices. The demand for railroad and government lands is rapidly increasing in this region, and an immense number of farms are being opened. At *Painted Woods,* north of Bismarck, there are several large and thriving Scandinavian settlements. There is an abundance of fine timber along the Missouri River, and settlers find profitable occupation during the winter chopping wood for the supply of steamboats on the river in the summer.

DAKOTA, WEST OF THE MISSOURI RIVER.

The magnificent Northern Pacific iron railway bridge over the Missouri River (costing $1,000,000) connects Bismarck on the east bank with Mandan on the west shore. Both towns are growing very rapidly, and are shipping points for Missouri River steamboats in connection with the Northern Pacific Railroad. With the exception of about 28 miles—the famous PYRAMID PARK, an excellent grazing range and tourists' and sportsmen's resort—the railroad runs west through a section unsurpassed for general farming and stock raising for 200 miles. The surface is rolling, varied and picturesque. The soil is very fertile and abundantly watered by rivers, streams and living springs, among which are the *Big Heart (150 miles long), Square Butte, Buck, Sweet Briar, Whitefish, Muddy, Curlew, North and South Forks of the Cannonball (each 175 miles long), Dogsteeth, Big Knife (125 miles long), Green, Little Missouri (350 miles long), Andrews, Box Elder, Buffalo, Butte, and the Beaver,* near the western boundary of Dakota. These, with their tributaries, parallel and cross the fertile lands of the Northern Pacific in every direction. This country possesses many advantages. There are fine opportunities now for settlers to secure good railroad and government lands *lying immediately along the track* and near to towns such as Blue Grass, Kurtz, Eagle's Nest, Antelope, Green River, Dickinson, Houston, Little Missouri, Sentinel Butte, Keith, and other new settlements which are springing up along the line in Dakota.

FUEL.—The forests of Minnesota, and the lignite coal found in Dakota west of the Missouri River, furnish an unlimited supply of fuel for settlements in Dakota. *The whole country west of the Missouri River, as far as Bozeman, Montana, is underlaid with lignite coal of good quality.* Mines are now being successfully worked at Bly's, Little Missouri, Glendive, Miles City, and other points on the road, affording an abundant supply of coal all through Dakota at reasonable prices. THE SETTLER WEST OF THE MISSOURI RIVER CAN MINE HIS COAL ON HIS OWN LAND. The extension of the Jamestown Branch to the Mouse River coal-fields will furnish all Eastern Dakota with additional facilities for obtaining good coal at cheap rates.

WATER.—The country is watered by numerous streams

Copy of a brochure describing
the Northern Pacific land grant.

Time table of the Northern Pacific, July, 1879.

Magazine advertisement, September, 1879.

Claim shanty built in Clay County, Minnesota, 1870.

Settlers, with their ox teams, hauling supplies from the Northern Pacific station at Mandan, Dakota Territory. In the late 1870's.

Excursion train of the Northern Pacific in the bonanza country.

Railroad bridge across ice on the Missouri River between Bismarck and Mandan. From 1879 to 1882 trains operated on the ice in winter and by ferry in the summer.

Northern Pacific depot at Casselton, 1881.

Northern Pacific Colonists' Reception House, Glyndon, Minnesota, 1876.

Jay Cooke House, Moorhead, Minnesota, 1881.

An early NP train around 1875 at Moorhead.

Transient farm laborers waiting for transportation at Casselton. Reproduction from Harper's Weekly, 1890.

The first house between Fargo and Bismarck. Built by Oliver Dalrymple in 1876.

Oliver Dalrymple home built in 1880's. Still in use in 1964.

Dalrymple home after remodeling in the 1890's.

Dalrymple headquarters farm. From left to right office, Oliver Dalrymple's home, and foreman's home. These buildings were still in use in 1964.

The original Dalrymple elevator east of Casselton.

The Potter home on a branch of the Dalrymple farm.

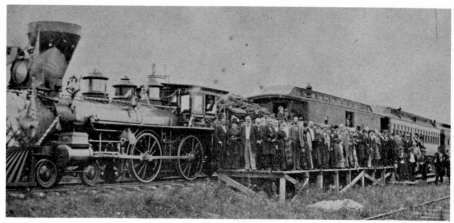

Presidential party with train on the Dalrymple farm, Sept. 6, 1878. President Hayes fourth from left holding top hat.

Dalrymple farm No. 5. Part of the 800-head horse herd.

Mule teams on the John Dalrymple farm east of Casselton.

Bundle teams on the Dalrymple farm.

Shocks of wheat on Dalrymple farm. Dalrymple introduced shocking to this area.

Fourteen 8 ft. seeders on the Dalrymple farm.

Casselton in 1881.

Amenia, North Dakota in the 1880's. Small building in upper right is E. W. Chaffee claim shanty.

Amenia and Sharon blacksmith shop, built in the 1880's, still standing in 1964.

Elevator at Amenia with sheep fattening pens in background.

Amenia in the early 1880's. Office and store building at the right.

Sheep sheds and corn crib on Amenia and Sharon farms.

Store and Headquarters building of the Amenia and Sharon Land Company. Amenia about 1890.

H. F. Chaffee house in Amenia. Demolished after his death.

Elevators with 300,000 bushel capacity in Amenia. The company had 7 other elevators on its farms at this time, 1912.

Chaffee-Miller Company, Casselton.

Walter Reed, president of the Amenia and Sharon Land Co. after the death of H. F. Chaffee. Note pictures of E. W. and H. F. Chaffee on wall.

Sweet clover plow-down on the Amenia and Sharon farms.

Eighteen gang plows turning under a hailed-out field of wheat on the Amenia and Sharon farms. The famous "postage stamp" picture.

This postage stamp was made to commemorate the Omaha Exposition of 1898.

Breaking sod on the Cooper Brothers' farm in the early 1880's.

Harvest scene on Cooper Brothers' farm. Cooperstown in background.

Boarding house and barn built in 1881 on Cooper Brothers' farm.

Barns and mules at Ranch 7 of the Cooper Brothers' farm.

Barn on the Cooper Brothers' farm built in 1881 and used until 1953. Lumber hauled 30 miles by wagon teams from the Northern Pacific tracks.

Cook house on Cooper Brothers' farm. Note outside stairs to sleeping quarters and bell on roof.

Harvesting on Cooper Brothers' farm 1882 before the days of the bundle carrier. R. C. Cooper in helmet hat.

Grandin farm between Hillsboro and Halstad now owned by D. Viker. Note Buckthorn hedge and trees. It was customary for visitors to bring a seedling from their area to the Grandin home to be planted around the house.

Buildings on Grandin farm at Halstad, Minnesota.

Grandin elevator on the banks of the Red in 1878. J. L. Grandin steamer and barges in foreground.

Threshing scene on the McKessick farm. Note straw bucker in center rear.

Threshing scene on Belle Prairie farm. Note straw bucking left.

Barns on the Downing farm — 40 ft. x 128 ft.

A Downing farm branch located in La Moure County, 1897.

Plowing on the Downing farm, 1895, Alfred Egenes, crew boss.

1884 view of Helendale farm. W. A. Power standing, T. W. Radcliffe seated.

Sheep herd
at Helendale farm.

Guest house
on Helendale farm.

The Glover farm, Dickey County, 1915.

James J. Hill's Humboldt farm in Minnesota, 1899.

M. J. Gummers threshing crew near Mayville about 1889.

Threshing rig illustrating straw cart to fire engine.

Threshing crew on Keystone farm, Richland County, N.D.

Jack Anderson custom threshing crew and cook house, 1915.

George Jacobson's threshing crew and cook car.

David Askegaard home, Comstock, Minnesota about 1900.

Barn on the David Askegaard farm, Comstock, Minnesota.

Horse teams on the David Askegaard farm, Comstock, Minnesota.

Auction bill for Aske-
gaard bonanza estate,
1920.

AUCTION
SALE

WED., OCTOBER 27, 1920

⁘ and ⁘

THURSDAY, OCTOBER 28, 1920

⁘ on the ⁘

DAVID ASKEGAARD FARM
in the Village o
Comstock, Minn

We will sell to the highest bidder, at Public Sale, all the Personal Property belonging to the
David Askegaard Estate, including Horses, Cattle and all Farm Machinery used
on the Askegaard farm at Comstock, Minnesota

80 HORSES 80		

80 HORSES 80
17 Horses under four years old
28 Horses four to eight years old
14 Horses eight to twelve years old
20 Horses twelve years old and over
1 Registered Black Percheron Stallion
List VI, sired by the famous List No. 17304 by
Coeu by Jean LeBlanc.

Sale Starts at 10 a.m. Each Day

Free Lunch Served At Noon

51 Head   CATTLE   51 Head
50 Cows, heifers and calves
1 Registered Shorthorn Bull, two years old
Silver Choice
No. 76624b
HOGS
100 Hogs, Sows and Shoats
1 Full blooded Hampshire Boar

50 TONS ALFALFA HAY   50 TONS PRAIRIE HAY   800 BU. OATS

MACHINERY

FIVE   TRACTORS   FIVE
One 40-80 Minneapolis Tractor
Two 35-20 Minneapolis Tractors
Two Nilson Tractors
One 300 Gallon Gasoline Tank with Truck
SEPARATORS
One Minneapolis 36-56, new, run only 26 days
One Aultman-Taylor 36-56, good as new
Two Stewart Shock Loaders
Three Ten-Bottom Engine Gangs
One Four-Bottom Engine Plow

19   BINDERS   19
14-8 ft. McCormick Binders   5 8-ft. John Deere Binders
All in good running order
3 Corn Binders   11 Drills   16 Cultivators   19 Wagons
4 Potato Diggers   5 Potato Planters   2 Weeders
1 Ensilage Cutter   1 Corn Shredder   5 Grain Tanks
3 Hay Rakes   4 Mowers   15 Hay Racks
5 Manure Spreaders   3 Bob Sleighs   1 Bob Cutter
3 Discs   4 Potato Sprayers, two wet and two dry

One Carriage
Two Buggies, single
One Double Buggy
Blacksmith Tools
One Feed Mill
One Corn Planter
Two Four-section Spring Tooth Harrows
One Fairbanks-Morse Gasoline Engine
One Ford Truck
One Glide Seven Passenger Touring Car
Other Articles too numerous to mention

Terms: All sums of $10.00 and less, cash. On sums over that amount time will be given until fall of 1921 on bankable paper. H. E
Roberts, Cashier of the Moorhead National Bank, will take the paper at this sale. Credit arrangements may be made with
the Bank by correspondence or in person prior to the sale. Delivery of articles purchased will be made upon order from the Clerk.

A. H. MILLER
Auctioneer

EUGENE ASKEGAARD
ARTHUR D. ASKEGAARD
OLE NILSON
Administrators

One of the first ga
engines in Cass
County on the L. A.
Barnes farm.

Manure hauling on Downing farm, 1904. J. F. Downing on horse.

One of the first Buffalo-Pitts steam engines on the Grandin farm No. 1, about 1908. Note the cart carrying wood.

Peerless steam-lift plow, 1909, on the first horseless farm in North Dakota, Highland farm, Fullerton, North Dakota.

A Pazandak farm harvest scene, 1910.

Steam plowing.

Rear view of steamer pulling 14, 14-inch plows powered by tandem compound 45 h.p. Minneapolis engine, 1910.

Threshing scene at Casselton in 1880's. Note straw elevator.

Straw burning engine around 1904. Thresher requiring bandcutters. Straw elevator with swinging stacker attachment.

Lunch time at Dalrymple farm No. 1 east of Casselton. Foreman, Thorvald Thorson, standing second from right.

Bunk house and crew at the Downing farm in 1907.

Partial view of
dining room,
Downing farm,
1911. Four tables
with 25 places
each.

Baking bread at
the Downing
farm, 1911.

Kitchen at the
Downing farm,
1911.

Harvest scene at the Cooper Brothers' farm.

Harvest scene on the Dalrymple farm. Note the mules.

Threshing scene in Richland County.

Fairview farm. Adams home extreme left, mess house, bunk house, 125-head horse barn, and office building at extreme right.

960 acre wheat field on Fairview farm.

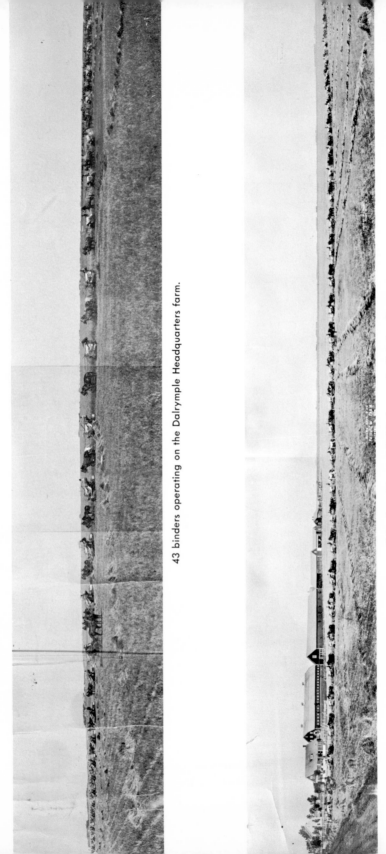

43 binders operating on the Dalrymple Headquarters farm.

Thirty-four 4-horse 8 ft. binders on the Fairview farm.

TABLE 8ᵃ. Financing of Contract for Deed Purchases by the Amenia and Sharon Land Company, 1880-1923

Year	No. of Contracts	Value of Land Contracts	Payment on Contracts Received	Interest Received
1880	..	....	....	$ 605.00
1882	..	$ 23,419.60	$ 3,069.88	....
1883	..	39,306.44	4,477.61	....
1884	..	103,073.40	3,917.87	....
1885	..	246,735.65	21,299.96ᵇ	....
1886	22	365,248.40	25,000.00	....
1887	29	260,056.14	18,709.20ᶜ	....
1888	..	301,605.91	8,425.09	....
1889	..	200,236.04	3,771.02	....
1890	28	114,506.79	24,649.70ᶜ	....
1891	20	100,097.71	8,516.45	....
1892	15	69,704.35	2,859.06	....
1893	16	73,255.05	5,048.37	....
1894	..	63,960.34	4,596.84	....
1895	12	52,197.99	3,711.55	....
1896	..	24,952.18	1,183.96	....
1897	9	35,338.70	1,845.06	....
1898	9	34,566.40	4,964.61	....
1899	12	52,927.53	5,695.10	....
1900	14	79,450.03	....	....
1901	14	61,608.44	31,687.10	3,306.62
1902	10	37,227.96	5,046.33	2,307.21
1903	9	34,488.84	8,054.15	2,236.37
1904	10	39,687.06	11,927.75	1,659.55
1905	9	33,618.86	3,482.39	2,065.40
1906	9	37,601.87	15,653.23	2,132.48
1907	8	24,081.12	4,722.33	1,541.99
1908	7	20,900.78	4,785.47	1,243.50
1909	6	17,358.81	5,230.21	1,157.26
1910	5	13,285.86	918.17	862.42
1911	6	21,491.66	1,610.65	1,106.14
1912	6	20,987.15	11,421.43	925.51
1913	5	10,491.23	671.57	726.23
1914	5	10,599.89	1,102.53	713.71
1915	5	10,211.07	4,354.06	548.06
1916	3	6,405.07	1,602.20	418.20
1917	2	5,221.07	1,508.77	349.28
1918	..	40,621.07	....	....
1919	..	35,500.00	....	....
1920	..	31,000.00	....	....
1921	..	80,000.00	....	....
1922	..	79,000.00	....	....
1923	..	79,000.00	....	....

ᵃ Annual report for each year, also summary of land contracts, 1901–1917, A & S Papers, NDIRS, File 134.

ᵇ Includes interest received.

ᶜ Includes payments received on notes.

cent interest, the normal rate at that time. The annual payment after 1880 was $200 plus interest. The contract did not require any money for two years but it did demand that Pagel build a good house on the land in 1879 and that seventy acres of sod be prepared so crops could be harvested on that acreage in 1880. It further stated that an additional seventy acres be broken during the 1880 season. The deed would be delivered to Pagel after five year's payment of principal and interest had been made.[42] With such financing an individual had to have funds to build his own house, purchase machinery, horses, seed, and enough to live on until the crop was produced in the second year. Contract-for-deed purchases were subject to the whims of the weather. Those who had good crops in their early years paid for their farms quickly; the others generally lost them.

Most of the contracts written were similar to that of John Pagel's. If a person bought 160 acres, the sod-breaking requirement was 20 acres per year until it was all broken and the annual principal payment was $100. On a 640-acre farm, 100 acres was the annual standard requirement for sod-breaking and $1,000 the principal payment. The standard price for all unimproved land regardless of the size of acreage purchased was $10 per acre from 1879 through 1880. In 1881 it was $14 per acre, in 1882, $12.50, in 1883, $15 with one 2,080-acre farm including personal property being sold for $25 per acre. The interest rate stayed at 10 per cent until 1883 when it dropped to 7 per cent where it remained until the turn of the century.

Some contracts used the Grandin plan whereby each year the purchaser had to put a specific number of acres into wheat which was to be applied to principal and interest payments. This was a benefit for the purchaser because no payment was due in case of crop failure. One contract specified that the entire farm be in wheat and half the total crop be used as payment.[43]

After World War I the land-sale policy of the company changed slightly due to the greatly inflated prices and the belief that a greater down payment was necessary as a hedge against any decline in land values. After its decision to sell large holdings in 1920, the company informed Murray Brothers and Ward Land Company that it wanted $1,000 down per section and 30 per cent additional when possession was granted. The company would carry a 40 per cent first mortgage for ten years and a 30 per cent second mortgage for five years, both at 6 per cent interest. Land averaged about $105 per acre at that time, and as the stockholders correctly foretold, that was more than could be justified, hence the stiff terms.[44]

The Company Splits

Most of the stockholders of the Amenia and Sharon Land Company were not interested in farming. They were concerned only with improving the land for a quick sale. From the beginning E. W. Chaffee, who appreciated the fertility of the Red River Valley land, had failed to operate the farms in accordance with the original intent. Even though he had built a substantial fortune for himself and had brought good returns to the other stockholders, he still had not convinced them of the feasibility of bonanza farming.

Because he had not complied with the original intent of the corporation, formal action was brought against E. W. Chaffee at a company meeting on May 27, 1892.

The President and General Agent of the Company, Mr. J. S. Chaffee, reported substantially that he had been unable to carry out his instructions: that the Treasurer obstructed him in every way possible. That he was refused access to the Company's books and accounts. That he could not learn anything about the amount of wheat or any other personal property owned by the Company and that he was informed by the Treasurer of the Company that the Company's accounts and those of Mr. E. W. Chaffee were internally mixed and that it would take an expert six weeks or more to unravel them. And further that the company's affairs had been run in the interest of E. W. Chaffee and not in the interest of the stockholders and further that if E. W. Chaffee ever got control of a majority of the stock that the other stockholders would probably never get anything for their property.[45]

As a result of this, legal action was brought against the company, in a summons delivered by the sheriff of Litchfield County, Connecticut, to appear in Superior Court June 1, 1893, to answer charges from seventeen stockholders. These charges were:

(1) After seventeen years of operation the company still possessed 19,000 acres of land including $6,000 of additional purchases,

(2) E. W. Chaffee had persuaded the directors to sell him 800 acres at less than half its value,

(3) In 1888 the management had borrowed $74,461.05 to speculate in wheat and other grains and this has continued to the present,

(4) Although land has steadily increased in value the net inventory of the company has reduced from $514,035.41 in 1886 to $416,405.85 in 1893 and no dividends were paid in that period.

(5) Officers have extended and enlarged its farming business beyond the company's original scope and intent,

(6) The Corporation is financially embarrassed and certain officers were proposing an assessment of stockholders or mortgaging the company's property,

(7) The account books have been in possession of the treasurer in North Dakota and have been inaccessible to the plaintiffs,

(8) The accounts have been hopelessly mixed with the accounts of E. W. Chaffee,

(9) In February 14, 1893, the officers decided to spend $70,000 to purchase additional lands for the purpose of constructing a company railroad,

(10) Frank Lynch with one share was made director and president and combined with other officers to secure plaintiff's stock at a price greatly below its value, and

(11) Since 1884 E. W. Chaffee has been in control of a majority of stock and the plaintiffs wanted to appoint a receiver and dissolve the corporation.

The plaintiffs represented 366¼ shares out of the total of 994 and were unhappy with the company's operation. With no interest in farming, they wanted to sell the lands and divide the proceeds among the stockholders as quickly as possible.[46] This legal action was one of the causes of division of company property.

E. W. Chaffee controlled or had the favor of twenty-one other stockholders as opposed to seventeen who were contrary to his management. As long as he was alive he maintained the operation of the company land as a single unit, but on his passing it was divided into many farms. There was no question as to his leadership, but a "big readjustment period came upon his death," said H. L. Chaffee when questioned about the change of operation in 1893.[47]

On March 4, 1892, E. W. Chaffee submitted his resignation as treasurer and general manager because physical disabilities prevented him from performing the duties of those offices. He was replaced by his son, Herbert F. Chaffee, who had been acting as his assistant since 1888, and by a nephew, James S. Chaffee.[48] They were also executors of E. W. Chaffee's estate and were to have exclusive control of all 528¼ shares of his family's stock in the company for a ten-year period "to enable them to make and unite the vote belonging to all of said stock as they think most for the interest of the owners thereof." [49]

E. W. Chaffee died October 19, 1892, while returning from a business trip to Casselton. He had been active to the last.[50]

In 1892 the company was involved in a legal struggle regarding E. W. Chaffee's management. The stockholders who were interested in liquidating the farm all lived in the east and were called the eastern faction. Those who came west, primarily of the Chaffee family, were interested in developing a bonanza farm and became known as the western faction. E. W. Chaffee clearly dominated the western group. The easterners, paradoxically, would never consider selling their stock to the westerners. After E. W. Chaffee's resignation, the stockholders were at a loss for leadership. The easterners sent James S. Chaffee west with the idea of selling the property. While in the west, Herbert F. Chaffee convinced James S. Chaffee not to sell and then began a drive for leadership in the company. On May 27, 1892, E. W. Chaffee attempted to satisfy his son's ambition by offering to purchase the entire property of the other stockholders for $298,200. His offer was unanimously tabled and from that day until January 5, 1895, the company was involved in a bitter internal struggle.[51] After his resignation in 1892, E. W. Chaffee went after the shares from individuals and by paying as much as $300 per share, he was able to secure 528¼ shares before his death late that year. His enlarged holdings gave him majority control of the 994 shares in the company. At least another 100 shares were in the hands of friendly relatives.

A third party introduced into the internal dispute after E. W. Chaffee's offer to buy the company was Frank Lynch, a large Casselton implement dealer and local financier. Lynch secured the consent of George B. Chapman, leader of the easterners, to sell all their stock to H. F. Chaffee for $300 per share, but for unknown reasons the sale was never consummated. Lynch had been working closely with both E. W. and H. F Chaffee to secure the remaining company stock because the three intended to build a railroad through much of the company lands near Chaffee. On June 22, 1892, a contractual agreement between E. W. Chaffee and Frank Lynch stated that the two "have agreed and do hereby mutually covenant and agree to cooperate with and assist each other in securing joint control of and purchasing that portion of stock . . . not now owned by said first party . . . [until] each of said parties shall own a half interest in the whole stock of said company."[52]

After the death of E. W. Chaffee, the agreement continued between H. F. Chaffee and Lynch. Lynch had a keen business sense and knew how to make his way in financial circles. He was close to the Grandins and if the eastern group had sold, the Grandins would have financed Chaffee and Lynch.[53]

Lynch and H. F. Chaffee began to push their plans for a railroad with elevators along the road. Lynch secured one share of stock and at the February 14, 1893, meeting was elected president of the company. Reluctant to make any further financial investment, the eastern faction opposed his aggressive expansion policy which, in part, was the cause of the court action of June 1, 1893. Lynch was forced to resign on October 13, 1893.[54] During his short administration con-

siderable headway was made toward the eventual construction of
the Red River Valley and Western Railroad. This railroad was to
run from Addison Station to Sec. 10, T. 138, R. 53, the town-site for
Chaffee, a distance of twelve miles. The Amenia and Sharon Land
Company would profit much from a railroad into Chaffee, for all
grain had to be hauled by wagon to Casselton, a long and expensive
drive with type of equipment available. Frank Lynch was in a personal position to gain because he had a large amount of property in
Maple River Township which lay along the proposed railroad. The
station at Lynchburg was established in the midst of his land.

Lynch and H. F. Chaffee had attempted to secure a railroad branch
from both the Northern Pacific and Great Northern Railway companies. The Northern Pacific refused to build a branch. The Great
Northern was prevented from doing so by an agreement that it would
build no lines parallel to the Northern Pacific main route.[55] In spite
of the agreement between the Northern Pacific and Great Northern,
President James J. Hill negotiated with Lynch and H. F. Chaffee
and encouraged them to secure a right-of-way and organize a railroad.
Lynch and Chaffee were able to get most of the farmers concerned
to donate land for the right-of-way and to buy railroad stock. The
total cost of securing twelve miles of right-of-way was $3,500.37. The
corporation fees and other organizing expenses were $862.00. The Red
River Valley and Western Railroad Company was incorporated June
2, 1893, with a capital stock of $100,000. Its first board of directors
were Frank Lynch, H. F. Chaffee, Walter R. Reed, James C. Gill,
and Samuel Bullard, all but one connected with the Amenia and
Sharon Land Company.[56]

James J. Hill kept in close contact with the new railroad. Lynch
wrote to H. F. Chaffee:

I shall not take any steps in the R. R. matters until I hear from
you or until you hear or confer with President Hill as soon as he
arrives home you better go down and see him personally. Unless we
can arrange to buy the Eastern stock [it would not] be of any advantage to us. They might advance the stock so it would cost more
than we would make by building the road. I am inclined to believe
it would be much to our advantage to secure all the stock first even
if we did not build the road for another year.[57]

Money was not exactly plentiful in 1893. Lynch had difficulty raising the money to purchase some the right-of-way, but he was not
sidetracked from his objective. His comments to Chaffee indicate
that he was both a bit of a prophet and also one to take advantage
of a given situation. In June he wrote: "If money matters keep grow-

ing tighter President Hill may go back on his proposition. It looks to me that the country is on the eve of a financial crash. It would take but little to start it." [58] Two days later he wrote that he would see Oliver Dalrymple about borrowing some graders and scrapers to commence work at once but "we should have about $2,000 cash for outlay for right-of-way and grading and so far as I know there is no money here to be had. There never was a time before that I could not get $5,000 to $20,000. Elevator men can hardly get money to buy wheat with." [59] Lack of funds to build the railroad did not prevent him from giving the following advice to H. F. Chaffee: "You better give your attention immediately to construction of the elevators, etc." He further advised Chaffee to submit plans to as many lumber dealers and contractors as possible because "by doing this we can make money and take advantage of the hard times, cheap labor, etc. There is no building going on. No sale for lumber and labor is cheap." [60]

The eastern faction opposed every angle of the railroad construction and disliked the big promotional campaign carried on by Lynch and H. F. Chaffee. Lynch informed the easterners that railroad was essential to economical operation of the farm property around Chaffee:

I had a long interview with President Hill of the G. N. R. R. . . . in regard to putting in a railroad to the south property We can build a road for about $70,000 and own it, or bond the town of Chaffee for $50,000 and give it as a bonus. The better way is to build it and own half until paid for, then turn it over to the Railroad Company. You . . . know . . . that the R. R. is an absolute necessity and I am determined to push it through either one way or the other so if you or any of your friends object to our management you had better sell out [or] take land for your stock, or stand by the management, and I will either push it to victory or defeat. I have a much larger interest in the company [Amenia and Sharon] than you think . . . You know that you have no grounds for a receiver, however, if such a step is undertaken I will be in it to the end. And if ever started it will I presume be a war of extermination on both sides.[61]

The eastern faction refused to cooperate or back down, so after Lynch and H. F. Chaffee were assured of financial support from the Grandins, they forced a legal battle. The tactics of Lynch and H. F. Chaffee were to entangle the eastern group in so much legal argument that they would get disgusted and back down.[62] After a year of litigation the eastern faction decided that it wanted to withdraw property equal to the proportion of its stock and form a separate company. A. H. Burke and John Miller were called in as appraisers and James B. Power as referee. Joseph R. Guernsey was made trustee of the seceding group which represented 367 shares of the 994 in the company. The Guernsey trustee group received 7,360 acres of land, elevators, buildings, personal property, and land contracts valued at $175,912.92. The Chaffee faction, which retained the name of the company, representing 627 shares, received 14,331 acres plus several elevators, other buildings, personal property, and land contracts valued at $301,590.19.[63] The decision to split was made at a special meeting on January 5, 1895. The actual division of property took place on March 27, 1895. The capital stock of the Amenia and Sharon Land Company was reduced from $99,400.00 to $62,700.00. The railroad was completed and purchased by the Great Northern Railroad Company in 1895. The purpose of the Red River Valley and Western Railroad Company was only to promote a railroad and not to operate one. Because it was a local organization it could secure right-of-way much more reasonably than could such a large railroad as the Great Northern. It is now a branch of the main line from Wahpeton to Devils Lake.[64]

H. F. Chaffee, "Managing Genius of the Bonanzas"

The title, "Managing Genius of the Bonanzas," more properly fits H. F. Chaffee than any of the great bonanza managers—Oliver Dalrymple, James B. Power, John Miller, or the leaders of the Grandin, Spiritwood, and other farms. Dalrymple's story has been well told; he was a great manager, a plunger, and an opportunist who made good more times than he missed and ended with a substantial fortune.

Herbert F. Chaffee was a very exacting man. He was a far more capable administrator than Dalrymple who had a reputation for not being interested in details. Although he knew how to delegate authority, he was not one to overlook even the smallest details. Chaffee learned to handle the details of finances early in life. Personal letters and files among the company records have lists of expenditures made as a youth on train trips to his academy in Connecticut and even have day-to-day accounting of all money that he spent, down to the penny for candy. Throughout his life he carried an account book on his person. It was not even forgotten on his honeymoon trip to Hawaii in the late 1880's. From 1893 to 1912 he built the Amenia and Sharon Land Company into a million-dollar organization when other bonanzas were liquidating rapidly. The net assets of the company far exceeded those of any of the other bonanzas. Chaffee was the man most responsible for building a great and durable financial empire.

Chaffee had a good teacher in his father, E. W. Chaffee, who delegated many duties to him at an early age and who impressed upon him a realization of the great opportunity that lay before them on the fertile prairies of North Dakota. E. W. Chaffee had to be absent from Amenia often, and H. F. Chaffee was always left in charge. In 1884 when the elevator business was just getting under way and the senior Chaffee was east on a business trip, H. F. Chaffee had sole responsibility for buying and selling grain.[65] When H. F. Chaffee was not more than eighteen or nineteen years of age, he sold nine carloads of wheat; later in that day the market dropped three cents per bushel. He was happy over his early sale. When E. W. Chaffee attended the State Constitutional Convention in the summer of 1889, his son ran the complete farm operation and the elevators. He made decisions as to hiring men, harvesting, credit to tenants and outsiders, and even selling grain on the futures market, all tasks which required a considerable degree of maturity for one in his late teens.[66] His responsibilities were greatly increased when on July 13, 1892, some four months after E. W. Chaffee's resignation, James S. Chaffee, who was acting as general manager of the company, made H. F. Chaffee superintendent, conferring upon him "the same powers and authority exercised by me [James S. Chaffee]."[67] James S. Chaffee preferred to stay in the East and after the split in the company, H. F. Chaffee became general manager.[68] Chaffee deserves the title of managing genius of the bonanzas.

H. F. Chaffee was one of those fortunate few who not only inherited talent but also a sizeable fortune. Like his father, he had considerable personal holdings which grew along with his company interests. E. W. Chaffee had acquired 528¼ shares of stock in the company prior to his death. Of that amount H. F. Chaffee received 176½ shares in addition to the 83½ shares he already held.[69] These stocks represented an original investment in 1872 of $26,000. By 1907 their value increased to $203,000. Besides the stocks, he inherited a sizeable personal acreage held by his father plus $102,400 from his mother. By 1907 he had earned a gross personal estate of $325,600. His net estate, inherited and earned, was valued at $568,400 at that time. Under his leadership the stock of the company continued to increase in value so that by 1910 his inherited estate had increased to $430,000. His leadership and investments in the Chaffee-Miller Land Company, in the Miller-Chaffee-Reed Company, in the John Miller Company, and in private farms made his earned personal estate grow even more rapidly to a net of $388,920, making his combined fortune $818,920.[70]

A $100 share of stock in the Amenia and Sharon Land Company was then worth $1,400.

After Chaffee's untimely death in the sinking of the *Titanic* in 1912 at the age of 46, appraisers valued his estate at $1,228,118.15. To keep that large block of property together so as not to upset the financial status of the Amenia and Sharon Land Company, his estate was formed into a holding company, the H. F. Chaffee Company, on July 28, 1913. It possessed 313 shares of the 627 shares of the Amenia and Sharon Land Company. Its officers were his wife, Carrie T. Chaffee, his son, H. L. Chaffee, his daughter, Dorothy Chaffee Stroud, and her husband, P. E. Stroud.[71] In 1912 Walter R. Reed was elected president and general manager of the parent company replacing the deceased, and Carrie T. Chaffee was made vice-president at a special meeting held August 31, 1912.[72]

Real Estate Policy, 1893 to 1912

From the first controversial purchase of land for $6,000 in 1891, the company stepped out to become one of the big land buyers in North Dakota. It was buying, selling, and trading land constantly from that date to its dissolution in 1925. Some of the land that the company secured was in return for unfulfilled obligations by debtors. For example, on September 1, 1901, B. M. Brown and L. L. Butterfield borrowed $8,168.15, pledging 320 acres of lands as security. When Brown and Butterfield could not repay, the company foreclosed.[73] The company's purpose in buying land was to secure a more solid block, especially in the Amenia, Hunter, and Mapleton areas. Many of the farms it purchased were obviously too small for efficient farming units. These were quarter and half sections, and the company was in a position where it could pay more for the land than the nearby small farmers. A striking feature of its land purchases was that very few of them were for cash. The company bought on a contract-for-deed, realizing full well that it could pay a major portion of the land's annual income on the contracts.[74]

For better financing of additional land purchases and also to enlarge the financial capacity of the company, a series of subsidiary companies was formed. These companies had some of the same stockholders as the Amenia and Sharon Land Company which acted as the parent holding company. The Amenia and Sharon Land Company's assets were often used as the basis for the newly created companies. The four chief land companies were the Red River Valley Land and Investment Company, the Miller-Chaffee-Reed Company, the Chaffee-Miller Land Company, and the Wanotan Land Company.

These new subsidiary companies appeared in the financial statement to the parent holding company. To give the new organization capital, money or credit was extended to the subsidiary by the Amenia and Sharon Land Company. For example, the 1899 annual report of the parent company listed $18,817.77 in inventory as a book account to the Red River Valley Land and Investment Company. In the 1910 annual report the parent company listed $360,475.51 as accounts receivable on open accounts. This amount was divided as follows: $211,475.51 by the several stockholders who were using some of this money in the new organizations, $15,000 to the John Miller Company, $114,000 to the Chaffee-Miller Milling Company, and $20,000 by the Red River Valley Land and Investment Company. At the same time the parent company owed $40,000 which it had borrowed from two subsidiaries, $13,500 from the Miller-Chaffee-Reed Company and $26,500 from the Chaffee-Miller Land Company. This was not marginal financing, for at that time the total assets of the parent company were $859,606.84 and the surplus account was $664,-192.15, a very healthy financial position for a company with a paid-in capital stock of $62,700.[75] The subsidiaries often started on very limited capital, but because of the superior financial strength of the parent company, all eventually proved successful.

The Red River Valley Land and Investment Company, was incorporated on July 30, 1895, with $110,000 capital stock. Its stockholders were H. F. Chaffee with ninety-seven shares, his wife, Carrie T. Chaffee, and his nephews, Walter R. and Robert B. Reed, all with one share each, and James B. Vail of Chaffee with ten shares.[76] The purpose of the Red River Valley Land and Investment Company was to secure control of the lands held by the J. R. Guernsey trustee. These lands, 7,360 acres and other property that had split off from the Amenia and Sharon Land Company in 1895, represented 367 of the original 994 shares that formed the parent company. The factional group had liquidated most of the personal property and surplus which they received in the split and now desired to sell the land. H. F. Chaffee created the new company for the purpose of buying the land for $110,000. On August 2, 1895, the deal was completed with a $20,000 down payment and the balance in nine annual payments at 5 per cent interest. Thus, by 1895 most of the land originally owned by the Amenia and Sharon Land Company was really a family farm in the hands of the son and grandsons of E. W. Chaffee.[77] From 1895 to 1911 the Red River Valley Land and Investment Company, the estate of E. W. Chaffee, and the Amenia and Sharon Land Company were all operated as separate organizations with H. F. Chaffee in charge of all three.[78]

The Red River Valley Land and Investment Company proved to be another in a series of profitable ventures for H. F. Chaffee. Dividends of 6.5 per cent were declared each year from 1902 to 1908 when it was absorbed by the Chaffee-Miller Land Company. In addition to the dividends paid, the surplus increased annually so that by 1908 it was $60,790.96. This means that in addition to $56,000 paid in dividends, there was $60,790.96 in surplus and $110,000 paid up capital, a total of $226,000 assets acquired in thirteen years on $32,000 of borrowed capital.

The second major subsidiary land company was the Wanotan Land Company. It was incorporated on April 16, 1900, with a capital stock of $75,000. The articles of incorporation stated its purpose was "to buy, sell, and improve lands, buy and sell grain, loaning of money on real estate and personal property." The directors were H. F. Chaffee, president and major stockholder; Carrie T. Chaffee, director; Walter R. Reed, secretary-treasurer; and James B. Vail, vice president. H. F. Chaffee and Walter R. Reed pledged their shares in Wanotan to the Amenia and Sharon Land Company in return for additional capital necessary to get the new company started. With the backing of the parent company, Wanotan could buy large amounts of land with a very small down payment and pledge most of the future crops as annual payments.

In 1900 it purchased its first section of land from the M. J. Woodward and Sons Company for $12,800. With no down payment and interest at 7 per cent, the contract required that 400 acres be in wheat and that the entire crop be delivered as payment. Half of the crop was to be applied to the farm contract and the other half toward advances made for operating expenses. The deed was to be delivered when the balance due was reduced to $7,000. After operating the farm for two years, the Wanotan Company sold this land to Andrew Nelson for $16,000.[79]

Wanotan continued to buy land each year. To broaden its financial base, former governor John Miller and his wife were invited to invest in it and become directors. They purchased sixty-seven shares in 1904. With this and other additional capital gained from private sources, Wanotan was able to purchase considerable acreage. In April, 1905, it purchased two and one quarter sections of land from the Fenton sisters for $42,060. The total down payment was only $3,432.28 with the balance to be paid $2,000 annually. Low annual payments enabled Wanotan to use the additional income for the purchase of more land.[80]

In April, 1905, Wanotan made a purchase of 6,243 acres north of the town of Mapleton for $187,290. This farm was owned by M. T. Dill of Wisconsin. The initial payment of $7,290 was not required until January 1, 1906, well after the first crop was harvested. Subsequent annual payments of $18,000, plus interest, were to be made from three-fourths of the crop which was delivered for such purposes until $97,290 was paid.[81] Wanotan was required to spend $10,000 on permanent farm improvements within a year. Its annual report indicated that it held 11,805 acres of land secured at a total cost of $354,150. Its total investment after two years of operation was $46,733.11. Only a company with strong financial backing could secure and hold property with such a limited down payment. Strong credit to enable marginal buying proved to be one of the really great factors in the accumulative growth of the parent company. In July, 1906, the Wanotan Land Company assigned its rights and property to the Miller-Chaffee-Reed Company. Wanotan outwardly did not appear financially successful because of the excessive interest load it had in the early years. It actually lost $2,216.15 during its existence. It was, however, a very successful start for its successor subsidiary, the Miller-Chaffee-Reed Company.[82]

A new and very unique aspect of farm financing was introduced with the creation of the Chaffee-Miller Land Company. This company, which later absorbed the Red River Valley Land and Investment Company, was incorporated on January 16, 1902, with a capital stock of $250,000. To enlarge the financial base, a special stock was created and sold to the members of the M. J. Woodward and Sons Company of Watertown, Wisconsin. The purpose of the company, according to its articles, was to "deal in all phases of real estate and real property, deal in securities and in stocks and to do any and all things connected with, and incidental to the cropping of lands, the conducting of farming operations." Its headquarters, as was true of most of the subsidiary organizations, was at Amenia, North Dakota. The common and voting stock of the company was held by members of the "inner circle" of the parent company. H. F. Chaffee held 887 shares, Carrie T. Chaffee 1 share, John Miller 99 shares, his wife, Adele S. Miller, 1 share, and Walter R. Reed 50 shares. Their holdings represented 1,038 shares of common stock out of the total of 1,250 provided for under the articles of incorporation.

The M. J. Woodward and Sons Company and various members of that company purchased 1,038 shares of special non-voting stock. All stockholders served as directors but again the leadership of the new company was in the hands of H. F. Chaffee as president and Walter

R. Reed as treasurer. Two of the Woodwards served as vice-president
and secretary. The special stock was subject to purchase at any time
by the common stockholders. A $100 share of the special stock could
be purchased any time prior to 1907 for $105 plus simple interest of
6.5 per cent, less any dividends that had been paid during that period.
After January 1, 1907, the price of the special stock was set at $112.50
per share plus simple interest of 6.5 per cent less any dividends paid.
Floating special stock was one way of raising money without having
to list it as a liability, because the special stock, although in effect
actually a loan, was treated as stock.[83]

In March, 1911, the stockholders agreed to purchase all special
stock outstanding. The company had been very successful and had
paid 6.5 per cent or $13,494 dividends each year of its existence, so in
1911 it was obligated to pay only the face value of the stock which
amounted to $105,186.88. The parent Amenia and Sharon Land Com-
pany floated a $100,000 bond issue with the Minnesota Loan and
Trust Company to redeem the special stock. The Woodwards all resigned as directors and officers and the Chaffees, Reeds, and Millers
made up the slate of officers after September, 1911.[84]

In 1903, shortly after its formation, the Chaffee-Miller Land Company owned 10,880 acres contained in 22 farms, 16 of them near
Amenia and 6 near Chaffee, chiefly lands of the Guernsey trusteeship.
Additional land was purchased so that it owned 12,000 acres when
absorbed by the parent firm in 1911.

The company rented all of its land out on shares. The company, like
its parent firm, had standardized note and order forms and loaned
operating capital to its tenants.[85] The Chaffee-Miller Land Company
was extremely successful financially. Table 9 illustrates the complete
financial story of this organization.

A conservative financial picture is portrayed in the annual company statement because the lands were carried at purchase price and
not the market price. In 1907 H. F. Chaffee made a secondary statement which carried all lands at market value of $30 per acre. This
increased the surplus from $42,455.46 to $160,455.46. In 1909 the
statement carried as an asset a note receivable from the parent company for $45,920.85. This loan was originally made in 1908. An in-
ternal revenue statement on the 1909 income revealed a taxable
profit of $23,824 contrary to the $3,560.84 indicated in the annual
report. It is safe to assume that the larger figure is the correct one
because the company would not willingly be taxed on more than it
earned.[86] The tax statement also indicated that the net assets of the
company were $627,274.43 with 1,038 shares of preferred stock re-

TABLE 9[a]. The Financial Growth of the Chaffee-Miller Land Company 1902-1910
A subsidiary of the Amenia and Sharon Land Company
Paid in Capital $207,600.00.

Year	Cash Profit	Salaries To Officers	Dividends Paid	Surplus[b]
1902	$14,952.72	$1,339.13	$13,494.00	$ 7,018.99
1903	15,270.67	2,175.72	13,494.00	13,859.53
1904	13,512.90	2,138.78	13,494.00	32,849.07
1905	14,408.47	2,221.65	13,494.00	38,541.00
1906	10,358.21	2,248.21	13,494.00	33,197.53[c]
1907	14,938.28	2,141.20	13,494.00	42,455.46
1908	41,436.04	2,410.03	13,494.00	60,790.96
1909	3,560.84	2,056.83	13,494.00	71,674,43
1910	373.36	2,399.19	13,494.00	63,032.89

[a] Annual Report or Internal Revenue Statements, Chaffee-Miller Land Company, A & S Papers, File 134.
[b] Surplus represents undivided funds in excess of the $207,600 capital stock.
[c] Loss in surplus due to a fire loss of $5,343.47.

tireable at a par of $103,800. On the basis of this statement, common stock rose from $100 paid-in value in 1902 to $504.31 per share in 1909. On July 1, 1911, the Amenia and Sharon Land Company paid to the stockholders of the Chaffee-Miller Land Company $108,000 in cash plus stock certificates in the parent company worth $460,-989.24. In all, the Chaffee-Miller Land Company stockholders received $568,989.24 in cash or stock from an initial investment of $103,-800 nine years previously. This was in excess of an annual 6.5 per cent dividend and salaries drawn from the company throughout its existence.[87]

Like the Red River Valley Land and Investment Company, the Wanotan Land Company also had a more vigorous and durable successor. Wanotan merged into the Miller-Chaffee-Reed Company which was incorporated January 8, 1906, with a capital stock of $250,000. The articles of incorporation gave it a broader scope of operation than its sister subsidiaries. Its general business was to deal in farming, elevators, and real estate and to finance cattle, machinery, and storage. H. F. Chaffee, Walter R. Reed, and John Miller were the three chief common stockholders, with the members of the Woodward family holding special non-voting stock identical to that which they held in the Chaffee-Miller Land Company.[88] The new company owned 11,805 acres in 12 separate farms, all rented out on shares. Its financial growth was very similar to that of the Chaffee-Miller Land Company. The surplus did not build up quite as rapidly but after paying 6 per cent annual dividends and salaries to the officers, its net assets of $170,000 in paid-in capital had climbed to $203,999.11 by

1913. Total assets of the company that year were $375,448.94[89] An interesting aspect of the financial reputation of the local people involved appeared when the North Western Mutual Life Insurance Company of Milwaukee loaned money to the company on the basis of the personal signatures of H. F. Chaffee, Walter R. Reed, and John Miller.[90]

The Miller-Chaffee-Reed Company had two outstanding North Dakota personalities serving as its officers. Both men, leaders in the early history of the State, died during their period of service to the Company. John Miller, the State's first governor, died in late 1908 and was replaced on the board by his wife, Addie S. Miller. H. F. Chaffee, the financial genius among bonanza farmers in North Dakota, lost his life in his early forties when the *Titanic* sank in 1912. Walter R. Reed was then elected to serve in a double capacity as president and treasurer. Because of the death of Chaffee, the directors of the company decided to reduce their holdings and pay off the indebtedness. The Murray Brothers and Ward Land Company of Minneapolis was contracted to sell several farms at $52 to $59 an acre net to the Miller-Chaffee-Reed Company.[91] Many of the farms were sold, and the remnants of the company were absorbed by the parent company in 1917 as the process of liquidation speeded up in the decades of World War I and after.

Change to a Tenant System of Operation in 1893

The land had been operated primarily as a single farm from 1876 to 1892 when E. W. Chaffee, the powerful and respected leader, resigned from active management. At that time the stockholders felt that there was no one in their ranks who could continue to handle the big single-farm operation, so they decided to divide. H. F. Chaffee, however, was determined to hold the farm together, yet he seemed to be convinced that it was more economical to operate it on the basis of individual units rather than one big farm. Therefore it was decided to subdivide the entire operation into a series of farms of 320 to 640 acres. Tenants could take the farm which best suited their labor supply and capital. The company furnished the land and seed and the renter the labor and operating capital. This tenant system had been started gradually in 1889 and had worked quite satisfactorily up to 1893.

After the shift to the tenant system, the labor problem still remained large for the company because of the great expansion of its many auxiliary operations. Table 10 includes labor expenses from 1877 to 1923. It is difficult to imagine what the labor bill would have

Year	Labor	All Taxes	All Expenses[b]	Dividends	Gross Income[c]
1877	$ 3,339.64	....	$ 24,204.23	....	$ 5,495.83
1878	6,933.34	$ 794.87	19,198.66	....	14,934.62
1879	6,914.91	1,811.32	18,866.90	....	17,798.85
1880	10,960.61	1,639.96	27,964.00	....	33,785.78
1881	14,210.83	1,438.76	32,585.80	$ 5,964.00	38,330.10
1882	....	1,070.35	....	....	73,535.37
1883	16,044.57	1,070.40	48,308.13	10,934.00	59,242.13
1884	5,795.54	1,976.71	78,935.88	....	82,839.92
1885	12,651.26	1,854.45	62,128.45	....	64,404.58
1886	9,460.11	2,150.86	73,509.06	42,245.00	115,754.06
1887	11,857.34	....	84,303.14	9,940.00	94,243.14
1888	8,847.92	7,170.64	119,560.00	....	45,088.74
1889	14,379.94	2,204.85	51,424.76	....	102,559.04
1890	....	58.26	83,229.62	....	70,892.35
1891	27,800.22	2,985.79	74,799.75	....	72,523.48
1892	27,581.70	3,882.46	81,377.33	....	86,850.66
1893	24,998.40	3,492.28	69,668.00	....	75,176.90
1894	21,531.74	3,963.08	64,397.28	....	67,063.30
1895	18,548.85	3,516.31	310,490.49 [d]	....	313,600.69
1896	17,607.76	3,296.87	288,529.03	....	282,307.11
1897	15,095.73	6,213.24	352,946.06	....	364,946.06
1898	18,426.04	2,016.16	455,252.70	....	455,252.73
1899	19,995.69	2,551.62	560,237.27	....	555,736.22
1900	17,874.81	....	321,315.27	....	321,315.27
1901	17,667.29	2,626.32	363,067.64	....	363,067.64
1902	18,242.34	5,937.09	405,901.54	....	390,901.54
1903	....	2,594.55	520,489.86	....	520,489.86
1904	19,851.25	3,085.01	435,992.15	....	447,169.52
1905	21,759.21	3,883.02	403,135.82	....	498,135.82 [e]
1906	31,219.40	3,428.80	522,601.27	....	533,447.81
1911 [f]	....	....	....	29,136.00	....
1912	....	9,098.23 [g]	....	29,136.00	....
1913	12,174.65	....	....	29,136.00	....
1914	....	....	....	29,136.00	....
1915	23,906.20	12,087.19 [h]	151,567.50	29,136.00	255,691.47
1916	....	12,107.27	71,552.97	29,136.00	164,068.38
1917	....	43,354.83	80,576.89	29,136.00	328,537.22
1918	....	45,848.15	104,295.24	34,064.00	261,296.98
1919	98,230.88	54,592.07	389,640.88	85,160.00	441,059.36
1920	48,158.24	41,673.01	140,671.57	34,064.00	108,334.05
1921	59,395.14	....	115,875.15	34,064.00	54,039.61
1922	....	....	....	68,128.00	....
1923	....	....	....	68,128.00	....

ᵃ Annual statement, tax receipts, and minutes of stockholders meetings, A & S Papers, File 134.

ᵇ Does not include dividends.

ᶜ Does not include borrowed funds.

ᵈ Elevator expenses included from 1895 to 1906.

ᵉ Fire insurance payment of $80,300.02 on elevator.

ᶠ Unable to locate information for years 1907-1910.

ᵍ First U. S. Corporation tax.

ʰ Federal income tax started.

been if all the labor had been hired on a cash basis, and the farm operated as one unit. The tenant system probably was one of the reasons why the company proved to be more durable and long lasting than any of the other great bonanzas. In addition to the great cash outlay, the efficient management of such a large number of laborers would have presented a nearly impossible task. As it was labor strife for the company was virtually non-existent.[92] Many local farmers worked on the lands of the Amenia and Sharon Land Company. They were often hired along with their teams which served a dual purpose for the company in that it did not need to keep extra horses. The company hired men, horses, and binders or other equipment to help complete the work more rapidly on the tenant farms and on the privately worked land. In the first years of operation, hiring of that nature was very common and easy because such employment was one of the few sources of cash income for the small farmer in the area. As late as 1908 the company hired full rigs; men received $2.50 per day, a man and a team drew $5.00 per day, a man with horses and a binder was paid $7.50 daily.[93]

It is not too difficult to study the wage pattern of the company and therefore of the entire area from the labor records available. The wages paid grew from $6,833.34 in 1878 to $98,320.88 in 1919, an abnormally high figure. Even in that year it represented only about one-fourth of the gross operating expenses. Because the company was large, it was able to set a labor schedule based on job classifications. Table 11 is an example of the schedule for different classifications of employees. It is particularly significant in the emphasis that is placed on wages during certain months of the year.[94]

It is apparent that members of the Chaffee family were proportionately much better paid than any other employees. For as managers and stockholders they had a right to receive a greater income because they were responsible for the success of the farm. On the other side it became quite evident, especially after 1912, that in general the major interest of many of the stockholders was not promoting a bigger and better farm, but in using its resources for personal ventures.[95]

In evaluating the financial statement it has to be considered that, especially in later years, attractive salaries were drawn by certain stockholders. In 1877 E. W. Chaffee started out with a salary of $750 per year; by 1880 he was drawing $1,500 annually. His salary did not increase after that date; it was no longer an important part of his overall income. In 1891 four of the family were drawing a combined salary of $3,900 as follows: E. W. Chaffee, manager, $1,500; H. F. Chaffee, assistant manager, $1,000; C. V. A. Reed, engineer, $950; and

TABLE 11ᵃ. Wage Schedule of the Amenia and Sharon Land Company for 1903

Month	Man & Wife Sec. 25	Herders	Teamsters	Laborers
January	$22	$20	$17	...
February	22	20	17	...
March	22	20	17	...
April	27	30	25	$25
May	27	25	20	20
June	27	25	17	17
July	27	25	17	17
August	35	30	25	25
September	45	40	40	40
October	35	35	35	35
November	35	30	21	21
December	22	20	17	...
Full year bonus	54	30	32	16
	$400 ᵇ	$350 ᵇ	$300 ᵇ	$216 ᵇ

ᵃ A & S Papers, File 134.
ᵇ Includes room and board.

Walter R. Reed, bookkeeper, $450. By 1898 H. F. Chaffee and Walter R. Reed were each drawing $2,250. By 1918 Walter R. Reed with $5,000, Robert B. Reed with $3,000, and H. L. Chaffee with $2,000 salaries were doing well considering dividend income plus houses and other benefits. The salaries grew rapidly, so that in 1919, five members of the family drew a combined salary of $19,200; by 1921 this had jumped to $27,971.98. It appears that this was all part of the process of liquidation, a method in which funds were transferred from the company to the individuals. Had there been a sincere desire to hold the farm together, these salaries as well as the dividends could have been reduced during the early 1920's when farming was not too profitable.

After the change from a single-farm operation to a tenant-lease system, the tenants were held responsible for getting the work done properly under strict company supervision. The tenant problem was not entirely free of difficulties for the total number of individuals involved in this type of operation was great. In 1904 there were 131 separate leases.[96]

After the reorganization in 1912, the company attempted to confine all operations to 60 units, of which 58 farms containing 28,456.83 acres were rented on a crop-share basis. W. W. Brown, the husband of Katherine Reed Brown and a major stockholder, had one section on cash rent, and the experimental farm (referred to as Section 25) consisting of 945.09 acres, was operated by the company.[97] In 1920 the company had seventy-seven tenants holding eighty-five separate leases. Sometimes farm leases were changed; sometimes the company operated more land on its own. Occasionally tenants did not make a go of it, and the company would manage for them until they were back on their own. For many years some sections were rented on a cash basis. All these arrangements were very flexible.

Each farm was plotted, and the crops to be seeded were determined by company headquarters. If a tenant wanted certain crops not specified by the company, he was permitted to plant them but had to pay his rent in the form of wheat on an acre-average determined by the company. The company paid for new land broken and extra duties performed by the tenant. Tenants were required to keep a specified amount of wheat in storage on the farm each year until all the land was plowed. This was particularly true of short-term leases with renters who were not known as a protection for the company. If summer fallow was required, the type of green manure crop and the date of plowing was specified by the company. There was also a great deal of flexibility in the contracts; sometimes the tenant furnished seed and received a greater share of the crop. One contract even had a variable crop-share payment based on yield.[98]

Individual records were kept of each farm so that any weakness in the land or operations could be quickly detected. Company practices on each farm as to crops, summer fallow, and restrictions on the renter were all determined by the yearly report. A card was sent to each tenant annually making an appointment at headquarters for settlement of finances and discussion of farm practices. In earlier years the management went to the farms to take inventory and make settlement.[99] An example of farm records showed N. E. ¼ Sec. 30, T. 141, R. 51 on 50-50 basis, 1907, total income $809.13, expenses $262.26, operating profits $546.87. In 1908 gross income was $551.76, operating expenses $227.59, operating profits $324.17.

Tenants apparently did not object too much to the strict company management, for most of them had long periods of tenure. If the tenant followed company orders, right or wrong, he could rely upon it for help during poor years. Availability of financing from the company proved a blessing to many tenants who started with nothing. A study on tenant tenure with the company by Alva H. Benton indicated that of sixty-five tenants in 1921, thirty-six had been with the company seven years or more and twenty had been with the company ten years or longer.[100] The company was very business-like but also very fair.[101]

The Experimental Farm and Progressive Farming

The experimental farm was an important part of the success of the Amenia and Sharon Land Company. It was a pet project of H. F. Chaffee whose interest in new agricultural methods was equaled only by that of James J. Hill and James B. Power. The Section 25 farm was more of a testing than an experimental farm. It did not do any plant breeding but only tested new varieties on a competitive basis with proven grains. The objective of the farm was to search for new varieties and more profitable farming techniques. It served to test all new and old cultural practices before forcing them upon the renters. When the company found a seed or practice that paid off on the experimental farm, it "inflicted that idea on the tenants." [102] H. L. Chaffee stated that the company office was "very arrogant about that type of thing." It wanted no controversy from the tenants. "Sometimes we made mistakes. The two best examples," said Chaffee, "were that we hung on to Hanes Blue Stem wheat and some old types of oats." The company insisted on its way. It furnished the seed and made the plot of the farm and tenants were simply told, "If you don't want to farm the way we want, if you don't agree with our way of operating then it is a mistake for us to keep on trying to work together." [103]

The experimental farm was very important to the economy of the company. It not only made the tenant farms more profitable but produced a profit of its own. The varieties that the company approved were sold at its elevators and were quickly adopted by the farmers in the area. The experimental farm was also important in making the elevator at Amenia one of the large independents in the state. The closeness of the experimental farm and the elevators is illustrated in a contract with Fred Meir who was hired in 1907 to be manager of the seed-grain department. Describing the progressive philosophy of the company, the contract read:

for improving the quality and yield of the products of said farms, and of changing and improving the kinds of seed grain used in and on said farms, and in that connection to make investigations and experiments to devise methods and means of eradicating weeds and other noxious growths, and in other respects to better and improve the methods of husbandry in effect on said farms.

For his services Meir was paid $100 per month and 50 per cent of the profits of the experimental farm. The contract specified that particular attention should be paid to wheat, flax, oats, rye, barley, corn, timothy, clover, and grass seeds. [104]

Robert B. Reed stated that from the start the company sought to select the best and latest varieties and types of seed grains and grasses. It was a leader in adapting corn to North Dakota, making Northwestern Dent corn a specialty of the company.[105] Each year eight or nine varieties of corn were planted and tested very scientifically. Amenia White Flint and Amenia Northwestern Dent were two varieties of seed corn that advertised their point of origin.[106] In 1881 seventy acres of corn were planted along the Rush River with a hand planter. This was believed to be the first corn in the State, but at this time there was no commercial market for it. When others saw the "rejuvenating effect on the crops that followed," they began planting corn also. The company later had the first corn drying plant in North Dakota.[107]

In 1917 and 1918, in response to war-time needs, the company contracted to raise hemp for the International Harvester Company. This was quite profitable. Net income on thirty acres in 1918 was $954.24 which was more than the gross income from some grain crops.[108]

The Amenia and Sharon Land Company, which had an intensive record system, was more conscious of the value of records than the other bonanza operations with the exception of those of J. B. Power. They were kept in neat order and used as the basis of adopting more profitable procedures. Each farm was completely laid out by field with long-term crop records kept of the fields. Diagrams of farm places and buildings were on file with paint and repair records of each. Tractor expenses were kept on each farm as were plots showing the exact location of Canadian and sow thistle patches.[109] When a crop stopped being a consistent money maker, it was replaced by a more profitable one. In 1912 and 1913 flax was reduced from 4,647 to 977 acres while oats, which proved more profitable, was increased from 1,284 acres in 1912 to 4,020 in 1913. The net profit from flax in 1912 was $0.702 per acre contrasted to a net from oats of $3.078. In 1913 the flax net dropped to $0.387 per acre while that of oats was $2.627. On the basis in shift of several thousand acres, the company made about $7,000 more profit in 1913 than it would have if the records had not been kept.[110] Plainly these practices paid off. From 1893 to 1921 company farms outyielded the Cass County average twenty-two years, equaled them one year, and fell below only five times. Concentrated drought and intense hail damage were responsible for the five below average years. Table 12 is an example of detailed company records. The year 1913 was average in yield and profits and it clearly indicates that good record keeping was essential to maintain a respectable operating margin. With the large acreage involved, any

TABLE 12[a]. The Amenia and Sharon Land Company Crop Summary of Share-rented Farms for 1913.

Crop	Acres[b]	Bushels[b]	Average[b] Yield	Income[c]	Expenses[c]	Net Earnings[c]	Net Per[c] Acre
Wheat	10,560.7	138,954.30	13.16	$ 54,737.37	$17,989.11	$36,353.92	$3.442
Other wheat	249.3	......	....	......	......	......	....
Oats	4,019.9	114,793.25	28.56	17,839.66	7,637.19	10,560.81	2.627
Flax	977.6	3,209.13	3.28	2,127.76	1,749.14	378.62	.387
Barley	4,149.9	88,705.41	21.38	18,698.62	6,510.53	12,188.10	2.937
Corn rented	2,324.0	......	....	3,336.60	1,014.37	2,322.23	.999
Corn, 50-50	1,783.9	......	....	4,780.07	3,065.62	1,714.45	.961
Winter rye	1,067.8	19,049.51	17.84	4,961.26	1,684.11	3,277.15	3.069
Other crops	1,696.0	......	....	......	......	......	....
Total	26,829.1	......	....	$109,489.99	$45,150.09	$64,339.90	....
Sec. 25 farm	876.5						
Cash rented	534.4						
Other land	1,795.92						
Total	30,035.92						

[a] Annual report, 1913, A & S Papers, File 134.
[b] Total figures for company and tenant operations.
[c] Company share only.

slight increase in net income per acre resulted in a very impressive difference in final profits.

Machinery and Buildings of the Company

Like the other bonanzas, the Amenia and Sharon Land Company had its share of trouble with its acres, horses, machines, and buildings. The Chaffees, however, were never quite as interested in putting on a big display as Dalrymple was. So the company's concentration of equipment on any given farm was never so noticeable. To be sure there was a massive amount of equipment on hand at all times, but at the height of its operation the tenant system prevented any display of a hundred binders on one field as Dalrymple did.

After H. F. Chaffee secured control of the company in 1893 and had more than 18,000 acres under actual cultivation by 1895 the need for building was great in spite of the tenant system. Elevators and other commercial buildings appeared on the inventory in rapidly increasing numbers, so that by 1919 there were 10 elevators, 53 sets of farm buildings, 20 additional commercial buildings in Amenia, Chaffee, and Absaraka, plus 19 houses listed. These were only those that appeared on the rolls of the parent company and do not include any elevators and commercial buildings owned by subsidiary organizations. Its extensive holdings enabled the company to lease a well-drilling rig from H. B. Hawley of Casselton in 1918 in order to drill or clean wells on its fifty-three farmsteads.[111]

Like all other bonanzas, the company used large-scale machinery. In 1912 it purchased a Twin City "40" gas tractor with a twelve-bottom plow. It was a showpiece in that day. The officers expressed some disappointment as the cost of plowing "has proved to be somewhat higher than was expected but the machine has been invaluable this past fall, much plowing being finished which would otherwise have been left undone."[112] This tractor worked off the farm too as a custom tractor operation. One such job was building four and a half miles of road at $350 per mile for Empire Township just west of Amenia.[113] The company was using gasoline power on the farms and in the elevators prior to the purchase of the tractor above. From February through May, 1901, it purchased 5,775 gallons of gasoline for its operations at Amenia, Chaffee, and Lynchburg.[114] A remark in the 1912 statement indicates that a second innovation of the gas age was adopted: "It seems absolutely essential that someone be employed, and equipped with an automobile, to assist during the summer in measuring the land, and look after minor matters for Mr. Cure." The company had used automobiles since 1905 when the inventory listed a one-third interest in an automobile and car expenses appeared for the first time.

The problem of upkeep, repair, and construction of new buildings was great. Each farm had separate reports for repairs and new buildings. New buildings were always charged off the year in which they were built, which hurt the net profits for that year, for even the painting of all the buildings cost several thousand dollars. The annual cost of buildings and repairs from 1913 through 1920 averaged $25,000.[115] In 1911 when the company was reorganized the buildings were valued at $331,875. Additional consolidations and construction pushed the final building evaluation beyond $600,000, not including the subsidiary elevator organizations.

Livestock Operations

Big acreage, big finance, big elevators, and big machines all seem, in general, to dwarf the place of livestock in the story of the bonanzas, but this is not entirely true with the Amenia and Sharon Land Company. E. W. Chaffee had cattle and hogs from the first, although it was not until after 1893 that livestock became important in the overall operation. There were two reasons for more livestock: the tenants in many cases preferred a livestock operation because it enhanced their chances of a better income, and livestock fitted in well with the elevator operations of the company. After 1900 each annual statement revealed a tendency to encourage more livestock operations.

H. F. Chaffee was particularly interested in sheep. His records indicate that in 1901 he had 14,812 sheep out on contract feeding with 36 tenants or other farmers.[116] The sheep were a natural to a farm with elevator operations. The elevators cleaned all the grain they purchased and the screenings were ground and fed to sheep. In this way sheep were fed at an extremely low cost because the screenings were a clear profit item for this combined operation.

H. L. Chaffee said that there was considerably more livestock activity outside of the company operations than within, for various stockholders were conducting personal enterprises of that nature. H. L. Chaffee recalled that H. F. Chaffee attempted to maintain a flock of 16,000 breeding ewes on property owned in Barnes and Stutsman Counties. The company owned 11,662.62 acres, half a township, in Stutsman County which was operated by the Amenia Live Stock Company, a subsidiary wholly owned by the Amenia and Sharon Land Company. In addition, H. F. Chaffee rented 4,360 acres from James C. Young in Barnes County for grazing purposes.[117] Each fall the young sheep were brought to farms and feed lots around Amenia,

Absaraka, and Chaffee to be fattened and sold. As many as 1,500 sheep were put on a section of land to graze off the stubble; sheep also harvested corn fields which were planted for that purpose. The sheep stayed on the land as long as there was fodder and grain or until the weather got bad. Later they were finished in the feed lots on by-products of the elevator operation. A. I. Cure of Chaffee and George L. Dunning of Amenia were two farm superintendents who looked after the sheep and cattle operations. Cure and Dunning were paid $50 a month plus 50 per cent of the profits on the sheep-feeding operation. H. L. Chaffee said that his father commented many times that the company really made money on sheep but did not have any exceptional luck with cattle.[118] In 1903 the company had 16,000 ewes on the ranches and 16,800 lambs on feed in Cass County of which 8,400 were kept in 8 lots operated by the company. The other 8,400 were let out on shares to several tenants. That year the parent company netted $33,787.28 from the sale of sheep and some cattle and hogs and $12,000 from the sale of wool.[119]

The hog and cattle volume never approached that of the sheep program of the company. After 1893 silos and barns were added yearly to handle the growing livestock operations. The tenants encouraged the company in later years and the profit record was all the proof the company needed. Table 13 illustrates part of the profits derived from the livestock operations. Through its expanded livestock program the company became involved in a livestock marketing agency which operated under the management of A. I. Cure.

E. W. and H. F. Chaffee were interested in good cattle and hogs. There are several memos in the files indicating purchase of registered Shorthorn bulls as early as 1884 and nearly every year thereafter. The same applied to Holstein bulls, registered Shropshire rams, and registered Duroc-Jersey boars and sows. H. F. Chaffee was a member of the National Duroc-Jersey Record Association. The pedigree papers of many animals are in the files.[120]

A second subsidiary livestock enterprise of some of the stockholders was the Owego Land and Cattle Company which was in operation after 1898. The Owego firm had Robert B. Reed, J. H. Reed, and E. C. and F. E. Sargent as its officers and stockholders. It purchased and rented land in Richland County in what is now known as the Sand Hills region and also in Griggs and Steele counties between Hope and Cooperstown. In 1899 the Owego firm rented twelve sections of grazing land in the Sand Hills for $20 a section from James B. Power, acting as agent for the D. S. B. Johnston Land Company of St. Paul. Later it purchased several sections in that area.

TABLE 13ᵃ. Subsidiary Incomes of the Amenia and Sharon Land Company 1878 to 1921.

Year	Land Payments and Interest Received	Elevators ᵇ	Livestock and Rented Farms	Experimental Farm	Town ᶜ
1878	......	......	......	......	$ 500.00
1879	$ 469.79	......	......	......	......
1880	3,960.00	......	......	......	121.90
1881	6,400.00	......	......	......	147.27
1882	3,069.88	......	......	......	860.53
1883	4,477.61	$ 3,000.00	......	......	536.35
1884	3,917.82	2,386.50	......	......	650.64
1885	21,299.96	1,830.33	......	......	483.96
1886	45,000.00	1,830.33	......	......	1,112.74
1887	18,709.20	5,864.83	......	......	858.05
1888	8,425.09	3,199.73	......	......	646.98
1889	3,771.02	10,870.47	......	......	......
1890	5,334.54	6,162.37	......	......	614.32
1891	8,516.45	11,900.17	......	......	555.25
1892	2,859.06	11,221.68	......	......	549.45
1893	5,048.37	29,206.12ᵈ	......	......	697.26
1894	4,596.84	11,441.92	......	......	349.83
1895	3,711.55ᵉ	36,875.46ᶠ	......	......	......
1896	1,183.96	29,425.38	$ 1,687.92ᵍ	......	......
1897	1,845.06	40,231.36	3,087.34	......	213.72
1898	4,964.61	50,512.11	9,641.98	......	......
1899	5,695.10	74,775.65	29,039.77	......	234.85
1900	......	37,140.46	14,101.99	......	235.65
1901	20,073.87ʰ	25,260.75	25,923.75	......	260.25
1902	......	72,386.07	20,868.01	......	......
1903	7,879.15	29,009.32	33,787.28	......	178.90
1904	9,915.41	81,969.23	18,578.76	......	250.23

TABLE 13—Continued

Year	Land Payments and Interest Received	Elevators [b]	Livestock and Rented Farms	Experimental Farm	Town [e]
1905	$3,045.56	$64,813.13	$3,910.77 [1]	......	$317.63
1906	15,572.08	32,720.68	14,693.14	......	223.84
1907	......	......	......	......	......
1908	......	......	......	......	......
1909	......	......	......	......	......
1910	......	......	......	......	......
1911	......	......	75,307.48	3,571.28	......
1912	......	......	72,657.55	−667.25	......
1913	12,342.06	46,691.72	64,339.90	......	......
1914	12,404.31	26,109.31	67,030.68	......	......
1915	13,669.54	44,831.12	110,895.66	3,995.88	10,828.66
1916	11,059.74	40,673.80	35,498.68	6,442.89	7,473.58
1917	......	78,510.48	234,936.78	6,422.82	6,655.32
1918	21,724.17	42,470.74	247,514.36	1,932.10	8,143.43
1919	29,998.66	90,147.46	98,794.84	−5,181.03	−11,054.90
1920	14,551.40	29,618.02	77,823.77	−19,068.76	2,981.48
1921	22,811.11	26,399.54	−28,345.18	......	−12,059.50

[a] Annual statements for various years, A & S Papers, File 134.
[b] Includes feed mill and seed grain departments.
[c] Blacksmith shop, store, rebates, and garage are included. All village expenses have been charged against these enterprises.
[d] Rita elevator established.
[e] Company split.
[f] 1895–1906 are represented by gross operating profits.
[g] 1896–1906 are livestock profits only.
[h] From this date on figure is interest only.
[i] Reduced livestock income due to elevator fire and loss of screenings.

176

Cattle were grazed in the Sand Hills region and then brought to the farms in the fall to be fattened. In 1904 the Owego firm rented 2,296 acres of corn from the parent company and five subsidiary companies to be "corned off" in the fall by the cattle. This land was secured for $3,797 cash rent.[121]

The two operations described above indicate that the company raised more livestock than the other bonanzas with the exception of Grandin Farm No. 1 and Helendale. Total figures of the livestock operation are very impressive by themselves, but when compared to the entire business of the company, they never amounted to more than 25 per cent of the farm operation or 10 per cent of the total operation including subsidiaries.

FOOTNOTES

[1] Smalley, p. 164.

[2] Copy of organization meeting in company files of Amenia and Sharon Land Company. All records of this company are on deposit at the North Dakota Regional Studies Institute Library Room at North Dakota State University, Fargo. All records are under file number 134 unless otherwise designated. Henceforth all citations to this source will be A & S Papers, File 134.

[3] Minutes of Company Meeting, July 23, 1875, A & S Papers, File 134. Of the original stockholders, 24 came from Amenia, New York, 13 from Sharon, Connecticut, 1 from North East, New York, 1 from Washington, New York, and 1 from Vineland, New Jersey. The Chaffees are an old New England family which possess (1962) the only remaining piece of land in the State of Connecticut that is still in the same name as originally deeded by the English monarch in 1713.

[4] Copy of articles of incorporation, A & S Papers, File 134.

[5] Hunter, 10, A & S Papers, File 134; Journal 1, pp. 6-16, A & S Papers, File 134. The final transaction took place September 16, 1875. All the land purchased was in Cass County, Dakota Territory. It was basically divided into two main tracts. The one near the village of Chaffee contained fifteen sections and the other near Amenia had thirty-three sections with some scattered sections. The Cass County Atlas of 1876 indicates land held by the company as follows: T. 141 N-52 W. Sec. 1, 3, 5, 7, 9, 11, 13, 15, 17, 19, 21, 23, 25, 27, 29, 31, 33, 35, T. 140 N. 53 W. Sec. 1, 3, 9, and 11, and 440 acres in 7. T. 139 N. 53 W. Sec. 25, 27, 29, 31, 33, and 35. T. 138 N. 53 W. Sec. 1, 3, 5, 7, 9, 11, 13, 15, 17, 19, 21, 23, 25, 27, and 29. The township names are Amenia, Walburg, Wheatland, and Gill.

[6] Robert Reed interview, A & S Papers, File 134.

[7] Clipping from *The Record*, Dec., 1895; A & S Papers, File 134.

[8] Journal 1, pp. 14-16; A & S Papers, File 134.

[9] Hunter, p. 32; Copy of leases, A & S Papers, File 134.

[10] Journal 1, pp. 16-19; A & S Papers, File 134.

[11] Hunter, p. 14; A & S Papers, File 134. Section 35 (620 acres) produced 11,676 bushels of wheat which sold for $0.80 a bushel. All expenses including 7 per cent interest on the investment were $7,142.69 resulting in the net stated above. The yield was just short of twenty bushels per acre. Journal 1, pp. 75-82; A & S Papers, File 134. See Table 11, page 00, for gross income and dividends. H. F. Chaffee to E. W. Chaffee, July 26, 1889, A & S Papers, File 134.

[12] A & S Papers, File 134. The couple was Thomas Dailey and wife. He served as foremen of the Section 25 farm and his wife was the cook and housekeeper of the farm. In addition to the cash salary they received room and board. There were always several additional hired hands on the farm who had to be cared for in the same house. The

contract specified if additional help was needed in the house, the foreman would be responsible for pay of that person. In 1881 George Goldthorp and his wife were employed for $547.75. Wages declined in the late 1890's so that a couple was secured in 1902 for $346 with a $54 bonus at the end of a full year's service. The last contract for man and wife on the Section 25 farm was to G. A. Kvittum in 1920 who received $140 a month ($1,680 annually). This represents a tremendous increase in salaries and is a clear indication of labor shortage. Memos in files; H. F. Chaffee Remembrance Book; Letter of contract to G. A. Kvittum, March 16, 1920, A & S Papers, File 134.

[13] Journal 1, pp. 14, 63, A & S Papers, File 134. There is only one reference to having difficulty with labor. In 1889 E. W. Chaffee, in a letter to H. F. Chaffee who was in charge of operations that summer, asked, "Is there any more trouble among the men?" E. W. Chaffee to H. F. Chaffee, Aug. 14, 1889, A & S Papers, File 134, H. L. Chaffee, when asked this question, stated that he did not remember of a single labor incident in all his discussions with elders in the company or examinations of the files. The company strove to have as good relations as possible because it enabled them to get the same men back year after year, which was to the advantage of everyone involved. Sometimes, especially during and after World War I, they could not hire enough to get some of the work finished properly. Interview of Hiram Drache with H. L. Chaffee, Amenia, North Dakota, Nov. 10, 1960. Hereafter cited as Chaffee interview. H. L. Chaffee is the son of H. F. Chaffee.

[14] Journal 1, pp. 1, 8, 10, A & S Papers, File 134.

[15] Annual Statement 1892, A & S Papers, File 134.

[16] The first elevator was an engineering oddity and did not prove too practical. It was round with partitions dividing it pie-wise. It was engineered by Cornelius V. A. Reed, a brother of John H. Reed. Robert B. Reed interview, A & S Papers, File 134. In 1887 H. F. Chaffee and his bride moved into living quarters above the store. Shortly after that he was made assistant treasurer and agent of the company.

[17] Robert Reed interview, A & S Papers, File 134. Apparently a newspaper must have been started in Amenia because H. F. Chaffe referred to the "Amenia Times" in a letter to E. W. Chaffee, July 5, 1889, article regarding the Constitutional Convention.

[18] Journal 1, pp. 16, 63, A & S Papers, File 134.

[19] Interview of Leonard Sackett with H. L. Chaffee, April 2, 1953, A & S Papers, File 134.

[20] Chaffee's daughter had married John H. Reed who was later secretary of the company. John Reed had three children who inherited his share of E. W. Chaffee's estate. John Reed died before E. W. Chaffee. Reed's children were Walter R., Robert B., and Catherine I., later Mrs. W. W. Brown. Robert B. Reed became the first person to receive a diploma from the North Dakota Agricultural College, now North Dakota State University.

[21] Many letters from H. F. Chaffee to E. W. Chaffee at Bismarck, 1889, A & S Papers, File 134.

[22] Hunter, p. 18; A & S Papers, File 134.

[23] Last Will and Testament of E. W. Chaffee, Feb. 6, 1892, A & S Papers, File 134.

[24] Hunter, p. 16; A & S Papers, File 134.

[25] *Ibid.*, p. 24.

[26] James S. Chaffee to E. W. Chaffee, July 6, 1889, A & S Papers, File 134.

[27] Cass County tax receipt, Dec. 26, 1888, A & S Papers, File 134. The total real estate taxes on this 3,493 acres was $794.87.

[28] Minutes of meeting, Jan. 25, 1886, A & S Papers, File 134.

[29] A & S Papers, File 134.

[30] Journal 1, p. 46, A & S Papers, File 134.

[31] Administrator's report on the estate of E. W. Chaffee, A & S Papers, File 134. The administrators valued the stock in the company at about one-half of its book value at the time of E. W. Chaffee's death. The book value was always a conservative figure as it was the custom of the leaders of the company to keep it so. E. W. Chaffee's estate was divided as follows: Amanda Chaffee, his wife, received 480 acres of land in Amenia

Township, one third or 176½ shares of his stock in the company and real estate in Connecticut. (The farm in Connecticut is that which was deed to the family in 1713 by the king of England.) H. F. Chaffee, his son, received 176½ shares of stock in the company and 1,690 acres of land in Cass County. H. F. Chaffee's children living at the time of their grandfather's death were E. W. Chaffee and Dorothy A. Chaffee who each received 160 acres. H. L. Chaffee, who at this date (1964) manages much of what is left of the big farm, was not born at the time E. W. Chaffee's will was written. To the children of his daughter who married John H. Reed, he gave a one-ninth portion of stock in the company and 640 acres of land to each, Walter Russell Reed, Robert Birdseye Reed, and Katherine I. Reed (later Mrs. W. W. Brown.) In 1911 all the heirs consolidated their lands with the newly organized Amenia and Sharon Land Company of North Dakota. In return they received an additional $253,332.37 worth of stock in the new company. This did not include Amanda Chaffee's portion. Last Will and Testament of E,. W. Chaffee, February 6, 1892, A & S Papers, File 134. It was many years before final settlement between the company and the estate of E. W. Chaffee was made. The people mentioned in the will all had a major role in the later story of the company.

[32] *Cultivator and Country Gentleman*, Vol. 45, p. 70.

[33] Journal 1, p. 21, A & S Papers, NDIRS, File 134.

[34] *Fargo Weekly Argus*, April 7, 1880, p. 7.

[35] Journal 1, p. 23, A & S Papers, NDIRS, File 134.

[36] Crawford, *History of North Dakota*, Vol. I, p. 47. H. L. Chaffee said that most of the land that came back to the company was that in the Chaffee area. He cited several farmers who had a particularly rough time of it but for reasons of public relations the company preferred to stick with the man who was trying. In the eastern part of Walberg Township "land went out early and stayed out." Chaffee interview.

[37] Company Records, A & S Papers, NDIRS, File 134. J. W. Baker wrote a letter to E. W. Chaffee asking if Chaffee could pay a bill of Baker's for $390 at the Frank Lynch Implement Company of Casselton. This is just one of many letters in the files of this nature. The company had regular note and order forms which it provided for individuals who wanted financial backing from it.

[38] Chaffee interview. J. C. Gill both purchased and rented land from the company in the Chaffee area at an early date but drought made operation difficult for him. On July 9, 1889, he wrote to E. W. Chaffee stating that "the crop is not good" but if Chaffee would rent the land to him for another year "he may be able to pay enough of his creditors [bank and Messers Hunter and Lynch] so that they will help him through another year." If Chaffee would not allow him to carry on for another year he said he would be left "penniless and helpless for the present." J. C. Gill to E. W. Chaffee, July 9, 1889, A & S Papers, NDIRS, File 134. Many people purchased groceries, twine, and other goods from the Amenia store. The storekeeper was constantly contacting the Chaffees about whether or not additional credit should be granted to tenants or outsiders. In one such case H. F. Chaffee advised, "I think we had better let him go rather than get in any deeper with him." In another letter he wrote that the man could be given more credit if he agreed to do plowing for the company. H. F. Chaffee to E. W. Chaffee, July 16, 1889; July 20, 1889, A & S Papers, File 134.

[39] J. C. Gill to E. W. Chaffee, July 18, 1889, A & S Papers, File 134.

[40] H. F. Chaffee to E. W. Chaffee, July 18, 1889, A & S Papers, File 134.

[41] Chaffee interview. H. L. Chaffee relates that most farmers who rented or purchased land from the company started virtually without funds of their own. He cited a John Holgerson who started as a common laborer, worked up to become a company teamster. Then he married and the company set him up in business. He worked his way up to better and larger company farms until he was renting Section 25 and had a half interest in a large herd of excellent cattle. Later his son, Clarence, took over and today (1962) his grandchildren are operating the place. The Holgersons have been farming for the Chaffees from before the turn of the century.

[42] John Pagel land contract, April 8, 1879, A & S Papers, File 134.

[43] Land contracts from 1879 to 1903, A & S Papers, File 134. W. A. Wilkins, Septem-

ber 13, 1892, purchased 160 acres of which 100 was to be planted to wheat each year and one-third of that amount to be delivered to the company elevator for payment on principal and interest. Other contracts called for one-half of the entire grain crop to be delivered each year and a few even specified that the entire crop be delivered as was the case of William Henschel who purchased 320 acres on January 28, 1898. It is interesting to note that in many cases the company specified the amount of insurance and the company which should insure the buildings on the farms sold. At least one notation of H. F. Chaffee indicates that purchasers were often refinanced by the company if their payments were too difficult or for other reasons they got behind. The case of M. F. Fuller in 1904 indicates that both interest and principal were reduced to help the purchaser. Note in H. F. Chaffee Personal Papers, A & S Papers, File 134. On December 1, 1905, James H. Wills purchased 320 acres in Cass County and 160 acres in McHenry County (Sec. 34, T. 153, R. 76) from the company. He paid one-half of all the grain on the Cass County farm and all the grain on the McHenry farm. This is the only indication of the company having any land in McHenry County.

⁴⁴ A & S to Murray Bros. and Ward Land Co., June 12, 1920, A & S Papers, File 134.

⁴⁵ Minutes of Director's Meeting, May 27, 1892, A & S Papers, File 134.

⁴⁶ Hunter, pp. 27-28; A copy of the summons signed by the plaintiffs, A & S Papers, File 134.

⁴⁷ Chaffee interview.

⁴⁸ Journal 1, p. 33, A & S Papers, File 134.

⁴⁹ Last Will and Testament of E. W. Chaffee, A & S Papers, File 134.

⁵⁰ Chaffee had gotten out of the buggy and his horse went on to Amenia with the empty buggy. A search was made for his body at once.

⁵¹ Journal 11, p. 46; Hunter, pp. 22, 26; Minutes of special meeting, Jan. 5, 1895, A & S Papers, File 134.

⁵² Copy of Agreement, A & S Papers, File 134.

⁵³ Frank Lynch to H. F. Chaffee, Jan. 27, 1893, A & S Papers, File 134. Frank Lynch had persuaded E. W. Chaffee to sell all of his stock and interest in the company in order for Lynch to have a better chance of getting the eastern stockholders to sell out. This was a pencil copy of a proposed agreement of June 17, 1892, which apparently was never put into force.

⁵⁴ Journal 11, pp. 56-58, Frank Lynch to Company Directors, Oct. 5, 1893, A & S Papers, File 134.

⁵⁵ A & S Papers, File 134; Chaffee interview.

⁵⁶ Statement of costs and Articles of Incorporation of R.R.V. and W.R.R., A & S Papers, File 134; Chaffee interview.

⁵⁷ Lynch to H. F. Chaffee, May 21, 1893, A & S Papers, File 134.

⁵⁸ Lynch to H. F. Chaffee, June 16, 1893, A & S Papers, File 134.

⁵⁹ Lynch to H. F. Chaffee, June 18, 1893, A & S Papers, File 134.

⁶⁰ Lynch to H. F. Chaffee, July 19, 1893, A & S Papers, File 134.

⁶¹ Lynch to Geo. B. Chapman, April 11, 1893, A & S Papers, File 134.

⁶² Lynch to H. F. Chaffee, Feb. 23, 1894; H. F. Chaffee to Lynch, Feb. 20, 1894, A & S Papers, File 134.

⁶³ Journal 11, pp. 78-80, A & S Papers, File 134. The Guernsey group received 1,600 acres in Walburg Township, 2,880 in Gill, and 2,880 in Amenia townships. The reorganized company retained 7,520 acres in Walburg, 5,411 acres in Amenia, 1,240 in Wheatland, and 160 acres in Webster (near Buffalo) townships.

⁶⁴ Chaffee interview.

⁶⁵ H. F. Chaffee to E. W. Chaffee, Sept. 9, 1884, A & S Papers, File 134.

⁶⁶ H. F. Chaffee to E. W. Chaffee, July 20, July 25, July 26, July 31, Aug. 1, and Aug. 2, 1889, A & S Papers, File 134. Two other interesting aspects of H. F. Chaffee's early training are as follows: In a letter to his father at Bismarck, he wrote: "Going to look at Andres Johnson's bulls and if we can get him for 2¢ a pound and he is in good order as he claims I shall buy the two and kill one tonight. . . . The bull will go much further and the two will last till you get home." Having to buy cattle for a meat

supply for the labor force in such quantity clearly indicates a fairly large labor force. H. F. Chaffee to E. W. Chaffee, Aug. 14, 1889, A & S Papers, File 134. Another aspect was his careful attention to rebates which his father was in the habit of collecting. E. W. Chaffee kept a regular accounting of rebates and listed them in the annual statement. For example, April 10, 1877, rebate on wheat freight, $18.90; July 2, 1877, rebate on wheat freight, $37.65; November 19, 1877, rebate on machinery freight, $88.70, Journal 1, p. 3, A & S Papers, File 134.

[67] A & S Papers, File 134.

[68] H. F. Chaffee's love of the systematic and detailed life are well illustrated by information found in his personal file. He had a "remembrance book" which had numerous personal items for reference, most of which were clippings or notations that he had inserted. Among the memos was a table listing the annual high and lows on the Chicago wheat market from 1877 to 1907; another was a record of the annual rainfall in the Moorhead-Fargo area dating from 1881; a third table was a hand written record on the day of the first killing frost in the fall and last killing frost in the spring from 1895 to 1912. With such an interest in detail it is no surprise that the company accumulated tons of statistical information about every phase of their operation. The remembrance book contained countless records of oral agreements that he had made with individuals while away from the office. These were detailed in all respects. It even contained a diagram of the wiring for the company office in Amenia. It is of interest that the office contained four telephones, one each for H. F. Chaffee, W. R. Reed, the stenographer, and the bookkeeper. It also had an electrically controlled door opener. Remembrance book and personal notes in personal file of H. F. Chaffee, A & S Papers, File 134.

[69] Journal 11, p. 8, A & S Papers, File 134.

[70] Financial statements of H. F. Chaffee, Aug. 1, 1907 and Jan. 1, 1910, A & S Papers, File 134.

[71] Journal 11, inventory of appraisers of H. F. Chaffee estate, June 30, 1913, A & S Papers, File 134.

[72] The White Star Line paid 27 per cent of the $50,000 claim that the family of H. F. Chaffee had filed against it. In addition, Chaffee carried a considerable sum of personal life insurance with his family as benefactors. The company carried a policy on his life also. Before his estate was settled, over $200,000 in claims against it had to be withdrawn because he had signed endorsements or guarantees for individuals or companies.

[73] Brown contract, Sept. 1, 1901, A & S Papers, File 134.

[74] H. L. Chaffee stated that at one time he had his signature on over one-half million dollars worth of notes and could never have paid them if all had been demanded at once. He stated that all the major stockholders were involved in a similar way, giving them control of land far beyond the actual assets of the company. Chaffee interview.

[75] Annual report for 1910, A & S Papers, File 134.

[76] In October, 1899, Vail sold his shares to H. F. Chaffee, leaving the company virtually in his hands.

[77] Journal 1, pp. 42, 47, 48-61, 79, 99; Hunter, pp. 31-39, A & S Papers, File 134.

[78] On January 14, 1902, a note of $32,180 held by M. J. Woodward and sons of Watertown, Wis., was paid by the R.R.V.L. and I. Co. The Woodwards apparently were the source of the cash used to make the down payment on the purchase of the land. Hunter, p. 39. A & S Papers, File 134.

[79] Minutes of Wanotan Land Company, A & S Papers, File 134.

[80] Articles of Incorporation, minutes of early meetings, agreements for land contracts, Wanotan Land Company File, A & S Papers, File 134. The Fenton lands in Sections 2, T. 140, R. 51, 29, 35, and 36, T. 151, R. 41, were some of the original Dalrymple bonanza which the Fentons had purchased at an earlier date. Thus the Amenia and Sharon actually became controller of some of the lands once belonging to that other great bonanza operation. The Amenia and Sharon purchased another bonanza when H. F. Chaffee secured the Houston farm south of Hunter. It contained four sections

and was purchased for $93,000 from Annie L. and David V. Houston. Contract agreement, July 24, 1908, A & S Papers, File 134.

⁸¹ Contract copies, A & S Papers, File 134. H. L. Chaffee said that the Wanotan Land Company was purposely formed to purchase the Dill lands. M. T. Dill had other interests in Prescott, Wisconsin, and had expressed an earlier willingness to sell his Dakota lands. The Fenton lands were just what he considered a lucky break because the Amenia and Sharon Land Company had a better financial position than other interested parties. Chaffee interview.

⁸² Financial statement, Oct. 30, 1906, A & S Papers, File 134. Robert B. Reed stated that the Miller-Chaffee-Reed Company replaced the Wanotan Land Company January 17, 1907. Hunter, p. 38. A & S Papers, File 134. This may be technically correct but for practical purposes the lands exchanged hands in 1906.

⁸³ Articles of Incorporation of Chaffee-Miller Land Company, A & S Papers, File 134.

⁸⁴ Records of the Chaffee-Miller Land Company, A & S Papers, File 134.

⁸⁵ Even though the company loaned money to its tenants for working capital it was never completely out of debt. On March 1, 1909, the Chaffee-Miller Land Company borrowed $35,000 from J. L. and E. B. Grandin to pay off the loan to the J. R. Guernsey trustee holders of some of the original Amenia and Sharon Company property. Chaffee-Miller Land Co. records, A & S Papers, File 134.

⁸⁶ Income tax on corporations greatly provoked the stockholders of the Amenia and Sharon Land Company and subsidiaries. With the statement of earnings for the Chaffee-Miller Land Company for 1909 was the following protest: "1. That the United States Government has no lawful right to demand a statement of its private business matters and then spread them before the public. 2. Because the instruction of the Commissioner of Internal Revenue are not uniform, and do not properly interpret the law. 3. Because the law is unconstitutional. Signed the Chaffee-Miller Land Company, H. F. Chaffee, president, Walter R. Reed, treasurer. The tax statement for 1910 indicated a taxable income of $4,315.70 in contrast to $373.36 carried in the annual report.

⁸⁷ Minutes of company meeting, March 25, 1911, A & S Papers, File 134.

⁸⁸ Articles of Incorporation, Jan. 8, 1906, A & S Papers, File 134. The Woodwards purchased 1,000 shares of special stock and were limited to a maximum dividend of 6 per cent. Common stockholders could buy the special stock any time after January 1, 1911, and before January 1, 1917, on the following schedule. January 1, 1911, a share of $100 special stock would cost $112 plus 6 per cent interest for each year from 1906 less dividends previously paid. January 1, 1912, $110; January 1, 1913, $108; 1914, $106; 1915, $1.04; 1916, $102, and 1917, $100. The Woodwards in a sense were putting a 2 per cent per year penalty on any stock purchased prior to January 1, 1917. Articles of Incorporation, A & S Papers, File 134.

⁸⁹ Annual report for 1913, A & S Papers, File 134. These figures are again extremely conservative. A separate memo in the 1913 statement indicated that if land had been carried at market value gross assets would have been $607,551 and the $100 common stock of 1906 actually had a net value of $290.25. Cash profit on farm operation alone in 1913 amounted to $27,667.53.

⁹⁰ Minutes of special meeting, August 15, 1908, A & S Papers, File 134.

⁹¹ Minutes of special meetings, Dec. 3, 1908, May 28, 1912, and March 28, 1913, A & S Papers, File 134.

⁹² Chaffee interview.

⁹³ Statement of labor and team expense, 1908, A & S Papers, File 134.

⁹⁴ There are other interesting personal aspects to personnel salaries. In 1903 a Mr. Ballinger was hired as a foreman for $1,000 and living expenses. His contract required that he was to provide entertainment at his own house out of his own pocket. Thomas Armstrong, another man of managerial status, was hired at $225 per month in 1903. In addition, he was to receive board in the back room of the hotel and have sleeping quarters in the shop annex of the barn (hotel livery barn). Extra bonuses at the year's end seemed to be the common practice to entice employees to stay the full period. The bonus

was mentioned in most contracts and was listed on the standard schedule for all employees.

[95] Several examples of these ventures will be indicated later. In defense of the practice, it should be said that the drain on the resources was never so serious that it hurt its financial status. H. L. Chaffee agreed to this and added that it was their property, if they didn't want to promote the company because they had other personal interests, it was better that the company be liquidated. Chaffee interview.

[96] Benton, *Cash and Share Renting*, p. 39.

[97] Crop report 1913 in annual statements, A & S Papers, File 134.

[98] W. A. Wilkins contract, Nov. 15, 1889, A & S Papers, File 134. In this contract the renter furnished the seed and if the yield was less than twenty bushels of wheat per acre, he received two-thirds and the company one-third. If it was over twenty bushels per acre, the crop was split 50-50. On summer fallow the land had to be seeded to barley, flax, or millet and then replowed at least five inches in depth between July 25 and August 15. In this case the company furnished the seed and paid $2 per acre for the plowing. J. P. Helland contract, April 16, 1896 with E. W. Chaffee estate, A & S Papers, File 134.

[99] Settlement schedule 1923; annual operating statement, A & S Papers, File 134.

[100] Benton, Journal of Land and Public Utility Economics, Vol. I, p. 411.

[101] Among the personal notes found in the H. F. Chaffee file were long lists of children of the tenants, listed by age, sex, and presents given for birthday and Christmas. In 1905 the list contained 133 children under age 15 in 53 families. In 1910 there were 116 children in 49 families recorded who received gifts. Gifts for such a large number of children and handled in such an exacting way indicates much about the kindness of the Chaffees.

[102] Chaffee interview.

[103] Chaffee interview. The company view is well taken and justifiable. In former times farmers have been traditionally very backward about accepting new practices. The company was operating on a business-like basis and if they found that the new practices paid, they could expect the tenant to change or leave. Only since World War II have farmers learned to adopt quickly new practices as they have been proven.

[104] Fred Meir contract, 1907, A & S Papers, File 134. Meir's work paid dividends. That year the company submitted a new variety of wheat which the chemist and flour inspector of the Duluth-Superior Milling Co. reported was better than No. 1 for milling. Its gluten content was 33.12 per cent and weighed sixty-one pounds per bushel. Meir had been a leader in developing corn varieties and had been working with the company since 1902. The company at all times made efforts to stress quality rather than quantity of production. Inspectors report from Duluth-Superior Milling Co., Nov. 26, 1907, A & S Papers, File 134.

[105] Robert B. Reed interview; Hunter, p. 24, A & S Papers, File 134.

[106] Memos on corn experiments in H. F. Chaffee personal file, 1902–1910, A & S Papers, File 134. Kernels per pound, kernels per acre, plants per acre, yield, maturity, moisture content were all recorded for each variety. Other than the corn varieties named by the company, there was also Velvet Chaffee wheat which was quite popular shortly after World War I. Amenia Huban Annual Sweet Clover was sold nationally under the company name and was marketed by the De Graff Food Co. of De Graff, Ohio. In 1921 the company had 305 acres of this seed clover. Contract April 16, 1921, De Graff Food Co., A & S Papers, File 134.

[107] Chaffee interview. Another significant contribution of the Chaffees was the extensive tree planting operation conducted by the company. The results of that practice are still much in evidence today. The company was also a sizeable potato grower in the early days, chiefly to fill the needs of its kitchen. In 1879 there were 1,200 bushels listed on the inventory. It did not go into commercial production until about 1912 but lost heavily for several years on that crop, climaxed in 1919 with a loss of $3,354.04 on a gross crop of $5,821.97.

[108] Contracts with I. H. C., March 29, 1917, April 19, 1918; Credit memos, A & S Papers, File 134.

[109] Annual Reports, A & S Papers, File 134.

[110] Annual Report, 1913, A & S Papers, File 134.

[111] Contract for well rig lease, H. B. Hawley, May 17, 1918, A & S Papers, File 134.

[112] Annual report 1912, A & S Papers, File 134. The big tractor was on call for any of the tenants of the company. It would come out from headquarters to do heavy jobs, not unlike the machine tractor station operation of the Russian collectives.

[113] Contract with Empire Township, June 27, 1918, A & S Papers, File 134.

[114] Ledger statement, 1901, A & S Papers, File 134. The price of gas was $0.1375 and $0.1425 per gallon with a reduction of $0.015 per gallon rebate.

[115] Annual reports, A & S Papers, File 134. The building cost of $51,671 in 1918 in cluded $24,419 for a new elevator at Absaraka.

[116] Sheep records, H. F. Chaffee personal file, A & S Papers, File 134.

[117] Copy of contract, Dec. 5, 1899, A & S Papers, File 134. The Amenia Live Stock Company was formed in 1899 and capitalized at $45,000. H. F. Chaffee seemed to have sole interest in this enterprise. The livestock company went out of business in 1907 when the Stutsman County land was sold to the Maxhimer-Austin Investment Company. The Stutsman property was a complete ranch setup with bunkhouse, cook house, and barns.

[118] Chaffee interview.

[119] Wool account and sheep program notes for 1903, A & S Papers, File 134. The company had a modified version of contemporary pole barns and pre-cut buildings. They had a standardized sheep shed on all their locations. The material was all pre-cut so that the only equipment the construction crews needed was a hammer and nails. The company adopted standard buildings in 1900 and was still using the same pattern in 1918.

[120] A & S Papers, File 134.

[121] Memos in files of J. B. Power, NDIRS, File 309; Livestock account for 1904, A & S Papers, NDIRS, File 134; Power to R. B. Reed, Jan. 17, 1899; Power to D. S. B. Johnston Land Co., Feb. 2, 1899, NDIRS, File 309; Robert Reed interview, Helendale Papers, NDIRS, File 438. The account indicates this rental in 1904 to be with the N. W. Livestock Co. Whether that was the name of another subsidiary or not it is impossible to determine from company records but it appears to be the same as the Owego Land and Cattle Company. In recent years (1960) the Robert Reed farms near Chaffee have continued to operate the sand hills grazing lands in conjunction with their grain farms on a ranch-to-feed lot-to-market basis. Robert Reed recalled driving 276 cattle from Section 25 and the "Sargents" to the Sheyenne River west of Hope between May 14 and May 21, 1898. His story was a good illustration of the big cattle drives in miniature, about fifty miles.

CHAPTER VII

The Amenia and Sharon Land Company: Financial Progress, Subsidiaries, and Dissolution

THE FINANCIAL history of the Amenia and Sharon is a story of steady growth from a $92,000 investment in 1876 to a $3,000,000 organization in 1923. As already indicated this great growth is due partly to the rapid rise of land values, climaxed in the inflationary prices of the World War I era, and partly to the profits of a chain of subsidiaries, particularly elevators, which aided the farm's operation. In this form the Amenia and Sharon represents a true picture of early integrated American agriculture.

However, in spite of its financial success, the chief stockholders of the company preferred to dissolve when the nationwide farm depression of the 1920's occurred. There were several reasons for this dissolution, of which the most obvious one was the lack of a strong family leader and manager after the death of H. F. Chaffee. Other reasons were the personal interests of individuals of the company in other enterprises, the opportunity to sell the land at high prices, and the burden of increasing taxes during and after the war.

Financial Progress

Neat and detailed annual statements give a good financial history of the company. Tables 10, 13 and 14 present a condensed financial history of the company without the inclusion of the various subsidiaries. The growth in assets and total income is dramatic indeed even without the inclusion of the subsidiaries. The company grew from $92,600 invested capital in 1876 to $2,819,165.50 net assets in 1922. This excludes the subsidiary organizations started with company funds, the personal enterprises of stockholders who used company assets to get started, and the salaries, fringe benefits, and dividends paid by the company in its years of operation. The records are clearly very conservative. Land values were always stated below market price and every possible expense was charged before final results were determined.

Rising land values had much to do with the ever increasing net worth of the company. The original purchase of 27,831.66 acres actually cost $104,368.71, but the total cash paid in for the 994 shares never exceeded $92,600. In the first years only the improved land was carried on the inventory. In 1877 the 1,150 acres of improved land were carried at $6 an acre or $6,900. The buildings on that land were valued at $2,750.[1] This system was continued until the annual inventory as of December 31, 1882, when the statement indicated 4,160 acres of improved land at $20 an acre including buildings and 12,760 acres of wild land at $12.50 an acre. The values were well in line with land prices in Dakota during the '70's and '80's. The increase in land values changed the gross assets of the company from $178,394 to $408,249.90. The inventory of 1892 reflected the adverse agricultural conditions of the late 1880's and early 1890's when 15,282 acres nearest to the railroad were carried at $16 and 3,715 acres of more remote land were inventoried at $12 per acre. The return of better crops brought an increase in land values to $18 an acre in 1898 and a $70,000 rise in gross assets, even though holdings were reduced to 11,640 acres. In 1898 land represented $209,520 of the $382,120.43 in gross assets. Table 14 gives an indication of how changing land values affected gross assets.

No great change was made in acreage from 1895 until 1911 when the Amenia and Sharon Land Company of Connecticut, the Chaffee-Miller Land Company, and the estate of E. W. Chaffee merged and reorganized as the Amenia and Sharon Land Company of North Dakota. The new company owned 28,594.14 acres of land and resembled the organization as it was in 1876. On the land there were forty-eight sets of farm buildings in addition to thirty-nine dwelling and commercial buildings owned in Amenia and Chaffee. By 1911 the gross assets had increased to $1,973,295.22 of which $1,373,873.43 represented land which was valued from $40.66 to $61.33 an acre.[2] The increase in assets for 1912 was due almost entirely to $50,020.84 collected in life insurance which the company carried on the life of H. F. Chaffee.[3] Elevators, farm buildings, and commercial buildings were added each year by the parent company to increase progressively the assets of the organization which did not include the expansion of the subsidiaries. In 1917 the last major consolidation took place when the Miller-Chaffee-Reed Company merged with the parent company. By

TABLE 14[a]. The Amenia and Sharon Land Company Financial Progress 1876 to 1923

Year	Gross Assets [b]	Net Assets [c]	Profits	Surplus [d]
1876	$ 99,400.00	$ 99,400.00	. . . .	. . . .
1877	125,467.00 [e]	. . . .	$−18,708.40	. . . .
1878	140,684.00	. . . .	−4,264.04	. . . .
1879	147,184.00	. . . .	−1,068.05	. . . .
1880	155,168.00	. . . .	5,821.75	. . . .
1881	178,394.00	. . . .	. . . .	. . . .
1882	408,249.90 [f]	. . . .	. . . .	. . . .
1883	455,883.02	. . . .	10,934.00	. . . .
1884	482,619.00	. . . .	13,904.04	. . . .
1885	514,035.41	514,035.41	2,276.13	$ 414,635.41
1886	485,130.19	485,130.19	42,245.00	385,730.19
1887	373,607.91	373,607.91	9,940.00	274,207.91
1888	485,051.04	410,589.99	−74,471.26	311,189.99
1889	414,313.00	414,313.00	51,134.28	314,913.00
1890	402,356.54	. . . .	−12,337.27	. . . .
1891	386,604.35 [g]	367,528.40	−2,276.27	268,128.40
1892	416,405.84	405,695.31	5,473.33	306,295.31
1893	422,203.24	412,356.49	6,508.90	312,956.49
1894	432,124.29	430,790.70	2,666.02	331,390.70
1895	367,427.82 [h]	367,427.82	3,110.20	235,474.74
1896	325,426.29	306,830.95	−6,221.92	244,130.90
1897	312,344.39	308,928.22	14,000.00	246,228.22
1898	382,120.43 [i]	381,419.32	. . . .	318,719.32
1899	433,017.65 [j]	428,033.28	−4,501.05	365,333.28
1900	451,482.85	440,929.68	. . . .	378,229.68
1901	472,030.06	457,368.25	. . . .	394,668.25
1902	500,672.34	473,622.45	23,987.19 [k]	410,922.45
1903	552,883.36	514,672.23	43,767.59	451,972.23
1904	604,434.55	572,077.56	49,485.41	509,377.56
1905	637,111.03	603,523.44	35,447.08	504,823.44
1906	823,131.70	612,867.80	15,476.48	550,167.70
1907	713,517.30	654,792.48	46,856.87	592,092.48
1908	892,583.75	691,943.02	50,171.78	629,243.02
1909	912,150.95	718,333.02	38,256.79	655,633.02
1910	859,606.84	726,892.15	. . . .	664,192.15
1911	1,973,295.22 [l]	1,518,274.32	58,823.02	1,154,074.32
1912	2,041,757.67	1,581,876.57	42,717.41	1,217,676.57
1913	2,104,790.94	1,609,279.79	56,539.22	1,245,079.79
1914	2,097,587.36	1,621,569.94	40,831.14	1,257,369.94
1915	2,211,723.49	1,694,409.27	104,123.24	1,330,209.27
1916	2,195,932.34	1,686,235.71	20,506.65	1,322.035.71
1917	3,233,239.∪4 [m]	2,650,254.06	236,008.68	2,224,454.06
1918	3,361,075.45	2,773,191.81	157,001.75	2,347,391.81
1919	3,227,305.84	2,754,147.30	87,879.91	2,328,347.30
1920	3,276,868.24	2,715,071.19	−32,337.52	2,289,271.19
1921	3,221,476.63	2,619,171.65	−61,835.54	2,193,371.65
1922	3,365,815.49	2,819,165.50	−89,481.37	2,393,365.60
1923	. . . .	2,362,824.54 [l]	−16,064.30	1,937,024.54 [o]

[a] Annual Statements, A & S Papers, NDIRS, File 134.
[b] Gross assets includes all property owned, real estate, and personal including notes

187

the merger gross assets were increased from $2,195,932.34 to $3,233,-
239.04.[4] The company then had 42,772 acres of which 39,990 were
actually under cultivation, the remainder in farm yards, roads, and
pasture.[5]

There was no basic change in assets after 1917 until dissolution in
1923. Even though land was selling for $100 an acre, the company
continued to prefer to use the $70 figure which was established at
the time of the merger.[6] Land was valued at $2,126,585.81 out of total
assets of $3,233,239.04 in 1917. Such a high value for the land was
proof that the constantly increasing price of that commodity had a
direct bearing on the company's ability to finance other ventures that
actually proved more lucrative than farming. The important thing
is that it could not have been done without the land and the good
management to hold it together. In addition, the company was able
to do much financing on the strength of the land that it had sold on
contract-for-deed. Much of that land was repossessed representing
clear profit, and the large interest income from installment and land
sales aided the company's financial growth. These were both a direct
contribution of the original land purchase. Table 13 gives the complete
picture of principal and interest income annually received by the
company.

and monies. This does not include assets or incomes of any of the subsidiary organizations.

  [c] Net assets is the net worth of the company including capital stock after all liabilities
are deducted.

  [d] Surplus represents accumulated profits of the company. It does not include the value
of the capital stock.

  [e] Land carried at $6 per acre.

  [f] Land carried at $12.50 and $20 per acre.

  [g] Land valued at $12 and $16 per acre.

  [h] Company split into two organizations.

  [i] Land valued at $18 per acre.

  [j] Land increased to $20 per acre.

  [k] The profits for 1902 through 1909 are figured at 60 per cent of the combined net
income of the Amenia and Sharon Land Company, the Chaffee-Miller Land Company,
and the estate of E. W. Chaffee, which were as follows: 1902, $39,978.65; 1903, $72,-
945.99; 1904, $82,475.68; 1905, $59,078.47; 1906, $25,794.05; 1907, $76,428.12; 1908,
$83,619.63, and 1909, $63,761.32. A statement accompanying these figures stated that
net income was what remained after all operating expenses and "including all additions
and betterments on farm property, such as new buildings, wells, fences, ditches, etc."
Statement of combined incomes as A & S, C-M-L Co., and estate of E. W. Chaffee.
1902–1909, A & S Papers, File 134.

  [l] Consolidation of the Chaffee-Miller Land Company, the estate of E. W. Chaffee
with the newly organized North Dakota Corporation.

  [m] Consolidation with Miller-Chaffee-Reed Company and H. F. Chaffee Company.
Land values increased to $70 per acre.

  [n] Includes land only.

  [o] Capital stock of the company varied as follows: 1876 to 1894, $99,400; 1895 to
1911, $62,700; 1911 to 1917, $364,200; 1917 to 1921, $425,800.

Any attempt to determine the net profit year by year of the company's operation leads to sheer frustration. The profits in no way correlate with the dividends paid or with the change in surplus.[7] There were several reasons for this. E. W. Chaffee often used company funds for personal ventures; he took out and paid back regularly. When the company borrowed money it was generally listed as income and when it was repaid it was charged as an expense. This was due to the fact that the company operated on a cash basis both for operating funds and for capital expenditures. New buildings were charged off in full the year they were erected.[8] This procedure was particularly noticeable after 1894. When new land was purchased, it was charged as an expense against the year it was secured. For example, in 1885 the profits were reported to be $2,276.13, but $20,516.22 was paid for new land. The years 1890 and 1891 both show a loss but the company used $26,738.62 in cash those years to purchase shares from individual stockholders. The same was true in 1888 when a $74,471.26 loss included $22,618.48 spent on the purchase of stockholders' shares.[9] Tables 10 and 14 contain more details in regard to gains and losses in various years. Speculation in the grain market made a great difference in the profit and loss column. Sometimes the company would hold its own grain crop and also buy up large amounts from others in anticipation of a rise in prices. This was true during the difficult years in the late 1880's and early 1890's. In general the company profited from this speculation.

The profits indicated by the parent company do not show the profits of most of the subsidiary organizations. In most years the subsidiaries' income equaled or surpassed the parent company in profits. This was particularly true of the elevator companies. The same people drew both dividends and salaries from the various organizations.

As in most farm operations, there was more income than met the eye. Fringe benefits, such as livestock products, potatoes, and housing, were all used by those living on the farms. Although this would be a small part of the overall operations, it meant much to those who received the benefits. The company bore the burden of expenses of the towns of Amenia and Chaffee which were company towns and the home of the stockholders. This included telephone, electric power after 1912, garage, and other facilities. The company store no doubt sold its supplies to the stockholders at a discount which reduced the profits proportionately. An unusual income was from the sale of insurance. The company paid several thousand dollars in insurance premiums each year. C. V. A. Reed sold the insurance for several years. Premiums amounted to as much as $5,450.28 per year.[10] It is logical to assume that a 10 to 20 per cent commission on these premiums was paid to the licensed agent in the family. In 1900 insurance commissions of $673.46 were reported as part of the company income. The company had an agency by then.

Profits have some bearing on dividends but there were exceptions. E. W. Chaffee and H. F. Chaffee were interested in plowing back the profits to build a better organization. The eastern faction was interested in dividends and liquidation. The records are not entirely clear but at least $596,643 in dividends were paid from 1881 to 1923. Table 10 illustrates the years and amounts paid. This does not include the dividends that were taken by the J. R. Guernsey trustee group, about $100,000 between 1895 and 1902 from their portion of the operations. Dividends from subsidiary organizations also are not included in the above figures. On the basis of 994 original $100-shares alloted by the company in 1876, each would have been worth $3,537.30 by 1922, or an increase in value of $76.90 return each year on an original investment of $100.

At the March 4, 1913, meeting of the original company, The Amenia and Sharon Land Company of Connecticut, the treasurer's report indicated a net value of the stocks at $1,211,087.12. This was $484,-194.97 more than reported on the books when reorganization took place and must, therefore, be declared additional surplus. At that meeting a stock dividend of $1,675 per share was declared. This permitted the Connecticut organization to remain in existence with its original capital stock still at par value. What actually happened was that the money was transferred to the estate of H. F. Chaffee, to W. R., J. H., and R. B. Reed, and to Katherine Reed Brown who used it to purchase stock in the Amenia and Sharon Land Company of North Dakota. An additional $157,743.97 was used to purchase stock and make a loan to the Chaffee-Miller Milling Company.[11]

The Chaffee-Miller Land Company, a single subsidiary from 1902 through 1910, paid about $15,500 in salaries and dividends to stockholders each year. After nine years it had accumulated a $63,032.89 surplus. This firm was financed initially by capital obtained from the parent company which enabled it to secure additional financing from the Woodward firm. Table 10 gives the complete profit picture for this company during its brief lifetime. In 1895 the Red River Land and Investment Company was started on $20,000 borrowed for capital stock from the parent company. Before it was merged in 1908, it paid out $50,050 in dividends in addition to accumulating $60,790.-96 in surplus. At that time its capital stock loan was fully paid up, making a total of $220,840.96 accumulated capital and dividends in fourteen years from the $20,000 borrowed capital.[12]

The Miller-Chaffee-Reed Company was organized in 1906 on $250,000 borrowed capital, 50 per cent borrowed from internal sources and the rest from the Woodward firm. It paid 6 per cent dividends each year and when it merged with the parent company in 1917, had net assets of about $900,000. This was the most profitable subsidiary land company created by the men in the Amenia and Sharon Land Company. It did not, however, surpass the success of the $1,000,000 H. F. Chaffee Company which was used as a holding company for Chaffee's estate to prevent any great disturbance within the finances of the parent company. The H. F. Chaffee Company's stockholders were content with a 2 per cent or $20,000 dividend annually.

Internal financing is often difficult to follow in large organizations, but the holding company itemized, borrowed and loaned money between the parent company and the subsidiaries or individual stockholders. E. W. Chaffee started the practice in 1877 and it increased in scope each year thereafter. The Amenia and Sharon Land Company probably became one of the greatest organizations of American agriculture. Most of the internal loans were done by a simple transfer of the money, and the debtor individual or firm was held liable on an open account receivable. Sometimes, however, notes were issued for value received and were then carried as notes receivable, although they were never more than signature notes. The 1901 report had $59,397.56 as accounts receivable including $18,160.45 from the Red River Valley Land and Investment Company and an account payable to the estate of E. W. Chaffee for $14,603.90. That year $45,000 in capital stock in the Amenia Livestock Company appeared in the asset column. Very great internal activity is indicated in the inventory accounts of 1907 when the company had $287,608.18 loaned to stockholders or invested in subsidiary organizations. At the same time it had borrowed $58,724.82 from affiliates.[18]

The height of internal financing came in 1910 when the company had $394,222.92 on accounts receivable from stockholders and subsidiaries and $132,714.69 accounts payable to associate firms. There was no degree of risk for the company because it could withhold dividends or seize the stock of any stockholder who did not repay or it could absorb the subsidiary firms.[14]

The most common form of internal financing was the extension of credit to stockholders or subsidiaries for operating land independently of the company. Every spring there were seed and supply sales on credit to various individuals which were not repaid until after the crops were in. By this method the company bore the burden of financing personal and subsidiary farm operations without cost to them. Supply allocations indicate at least ten independent operations were being conducted in this manner.[15]

H. L. Chaffee, one of those stockholders who benefited from this internal financing, said, "The money was available and we were using it. The finances of the company were never hurt by it." He added that the reason most of the subsidiary organizations were formed was that they were easier to manage and less likely to affect the operation of the parent company.[16] Chaffee's statement is correct; the company finances were stronger each year, and at the same time the subsidiaries and individuals were accumulating money on their own because of the great resources available to them.

Subsidiary Organizations and Activities

The history of the Amenia and Sharon Land Company is also a history of the subsidiary organizations. The non-farming activities were justified in a letter to the collector of Internal Revenue when the company claimed exemption from the special excise tax on corporations "because they are an agricultural organization. Grain elevators, feed mill, blacksmith shop, and lumber yard are all incidental to farming for supplying their own needs."[17] These subsidiaries were important and profitable, and the company continued to expand them until it dissolved. There was never any doubt about their value to the company from the day that E. W. Chaffee became a general merchant in Amenia in the early 1880's. He ran the store until 1884 when a partnership was formed with Virgil F. McNeil who operated the general retail store. McNeil paid Chaffee 12 per cent on the $5,000 initial inventory plus rent for the building.[18] From that single store, a depot, elevators, and the thriving town of Amenia were developed. Later the town of Chaffee was started in a similar manner.

E. W. and H. F. Chaffee took strict precautions to see that Amenia and Chaffee remained company towns. A blueprint dated November 1, 1887, located the E. W. Chaffee store, Amenia and Sharon elevator, company feed mill, and a large grain warehouse. There was also an elevator owned by the St. Anthony and Dakota Elevator Company, but local resentment against the outside firm's intrusion into Amenia forced it to sell out.[19] H. L. Chaffee said that at the farm's height, Amenia was entirely a company headquarter.[20]

In the late 1890's the company built a large rooming and cook house for its labor force. This became Hotel Amenia and was the hub of considerable activity. The building was quite large with about

6,500 feet of floor area including an annex. A large hotel barn and ice house complemented the hotel. The company rented out the hotel in the early years and then paid for the room and board of the employees. There were frequent changes in its operators.[21] In later years the company assumed operations, and by 1919 the hotel operating loss was $6,363.05 on a total volume of $33,192.55. The 1920 and 1921 statements reported losses of about 10 per cent of the total operating volume.[22]

The blacksmith shop, erected in 1878, was essential to the operation of the big farm. It served as the repair center for all the farm's operations around Amenia. There was sufficient outside business so that the shop not only paid its expenses but was a consistent moneymaker. The book profit amounted to the salary of the blacksmith or more each year, but that does not take into account the savings the company made by having its own repair facilities. That business was still in operation in the 1960's. A blacksmith and wagon shop were also operated in Chaffee.

In 1896 the village of Amenia saw the installation and construction of a company telephone line called the Amenia Telephone Company. In 1906 a similar telephone company was established at Chaffee, and the company secured ten year's free phone service for its contribution.[23] The parent company leased lines from the telephone company.

L. F. Schneider and T. R. C. Crosell made an agreement with the company on September 9, 1899, to build a flax fiber mill. They had to assure the company that the mill would be in operation at least 100 days a year. The mill was carried on the inventory for many years, but operations were stopped when the company drastically reduced flax production after 1912.[24]

The advent of the internal combustion engine brought both tractors and automobiles into use on the company farms. Because it needed such a large supply of fuel for its own use, it was only natural that the company became a distributor. By 1901 it operated three retail gas stations, one each at Amenia, Chaffee, and Lynchburg.[25] The size of the buildings used for the gas stations indicate that they were far from the super service stations of today, but they did enough business to enable the company to secure a bulk-service business with the bulk plant at Amenia.

In 1896 the company constructed a large boiler plant in Amenia which was used for the elevator and other retail businesses. Lumber and coal yards, hardware stores, and stockyards were established at a later date at both Amenia and Chaffee to serve the needs of the company and the public.

A necessary expense to supplement the subsidiary enterprises was housing for the managers and employees. The 1919 inventory listed nineteen houses in Chaffee and Amenia in addition to individual houses at elevator locations in other villages. The average house was a 22-by-28-foot, one-and-a-half-story building which would have been considered very satisfactory sized homes at the time they were built.[26]

In 1912 the company installed a 300-light acetylene generator in Amenia which provided the town with lights at company expense. In 1919 a complete electrical system for the village was built. The building, equipment, and distribution lines were all contracted with Fairbanks, Morse and Company at a cost of $17,338.43.[27] The plant was operated entirely at company expense. Electrical power was no doubt furnished to the homes of the stockholders free of charge.

Village operating expenses, which appear as a total loss on the books, were actually a fringe benefit to the stockholders and subsidiary organizations. The 1919 village operating expense was $4,221.81; in 1920 it rose to $4,505.52 in addition to a light plant loss of $4,616.-58. This does not include income from house rent or commercial buildings or income from commercial operations using village facilities. Net income from the mill and elevators in 1920 was $29,618.02, from the lumberyard $226.60, from building rental $927.74, from the garage, $3,358.88, from truck operations $504.65, and from the service station $491.15. These more than made up for the loss of the expense of operating the company town.[28]

It is only natural that a company concerned with operating such a large amount of land should become interested in the implement business. The village of Amenia, in the midst of the company farms, provided a natural setting for such a business. On February 1, 1915, the Amenia Farm Implement Company was organized by W. R. and R. B. Reed, Carrie T. and H. L. Chaffee, and P. E. Stroud, a son-in-law of Mrs Carrie T. Chaffee.[29] Supplying machinery for company farms supported a fairly large retail machinery firm. By 1919 the implement company became a dealer for the Twin City tractor.[30] A side-line of the implement business was doing heavy custom work, either on farms or for the governmental units. Sometimes such work was not profitable; in 1920 tractor operation losses were $2,557.49. A company school-bus line was started in the same manner. Losses were incurred every year in the conduct of that business.[31]

In 1920 the Amenia and Sharon Land Company built its last structure in Amenia. It was a "community building" which was actually built by Charles E. Walker, a contractor who had a five-year rental contract from the company. A clause in the contract stated that the company "desires to encourage only such businesses as will be a credit to the town and community; and which will offer considerable inducement to local patrons to trade at home." This reflected the attitude so clearly stated by E. W. Chaffee forty years earlier.[32]

One of the major reasons for the success of the Amenia and Sharon Land Company was its early entry into the elevator business. The elevators not only brought in additional profits from their direct operations, but their by-products increased the profits of the farm livestock operations and through them the company was able to obtain large-scale outside financing. There were two different elevator operations within the scope of the Amenia and Sharon Land Company's finances. A small chain of ten company-owned-and-operated elevators was a lucrative enterprise. There were also three subsidiary concerns not directly operated by the company with headquarters in Casselton, Duluth, and Minneapolis.

The company-owned elevator chain was started by E. W. Chaffee in 1882 with a single elevator at Amenia known as Elevator "A." It was a round building of 20,000-bushel capacity and not much of an engineering masterpiece, but it became a familiar storage place for the "Blue Stem Wheat" which was grown for many years by the company. Later elevators "B" and "C" were built with a 250,000-bushel storage capacity, and up to 1900 they were the largest elevator plant in the State.[33] In 1894 when the railroad line to Chaffee was completed, the company erected a public elevator in that village and purchased one in Lynchburg.[34] The Chaffee-Miller Land Company erected a second elevator at Chaffee known as elevator "E" which was sold to the parent company in 1915.[35] In 1912 the company moved one of its farm elevators to a location along the Great Northern Railway line called Mason.[36] In 1914 a new elevator was built at Newman in Rush River Township. The Ripon elevator, which had been owned by the Amenia Elevator Company since 1900, was purchased in 1916. In 1917 the last of the independents to be purchased by the company was the Absaraka Mercantile Company which was a grain, coal, and lumber operation.[37]

The first business of all these elevators was company trade, but it was only natural that they should also be open to the public for greater profits. Their seed department and milling services were designed for company use only, but public demand soon made them open to all.[38] In fact, the seed department was expanded to the limit, for it proved to be the most profitable one. In 1912 out of 46,335 bushels of seed-wheat sold, 17,798 bushels were used on the company and "associated" farms, and 28,537 bushels were sold to the public at the Amenia and Chaffee elevators. All varieties of seed grains and grasses were sold.[39]

The company owned ten elevators in the immediate vicinity of Chaffee and Amenia, and all of its farms were within a few miles of one. The elevators had a 400,000-bushel storage capacity and were valued at $297,366.72 in 1920.[40] It also owned a terminal elevator in Superior, Wisconsin, which was known as elevator "R." In 1897 H. F. Chaffee secured 1,622 feet of trackage rights for the purpose of a gasoline storage tank and terminal elevator along the Eastern Minnesota Railroad. Its storage capacity was small, but it had a large handling and cleaning capacity. It served as the outlet for over a million bushels of company-handled grain annually and gave the company elevator chain status in the grain markets of Duluth and Minneapolis.[41]

The company owned seats on the Duluth and Minneapolis Grain Exchanges which were carried on the books of $3,500 inventory value for each seat prior to 1900. By 1910 the value of the two seats was placed at $25,450. As early as 1889 the company was getting ciphered telegrams from the large grain exchanges relative to market conditions. One of the deciphering books is still in the file. An interesting feature of the elevator and coal agreements with the railroad company found in a contract with the Great Northern, dated March 11, 1907, prohibited the company from charging more than $1 per ton profit on coal delivered to the station by that railway.[42]

The profits of these elevators over the years were often greater than the profits from the farms. Only in the World War I era did the farm profit greatly exceed the profits of the elevators. The elevator contribution to farm profits in the form of better markets, lower seed cost, free screenings, and other by-products should not be underestimated. The elevators were as important to the long-run financial gains as were rising land values.

The second phase of elevator operations which were of concern to the company involved three major firms: The John Miller Company of Duluth, the Amenia Elevator Company of Minneapolis, and the Chaffee-Miller Milling Company of Casselton.

The long sought for private grain outlet on the commercial market was secured when the successful John Miller Company was organized May 26, 1896, with John Miller president, H. F. Chaffee treasurer, and W. R. Reed secretary. H. F. Chaffee was the chief promoter of the new organization, for he desired to secure better marketing facilities for the Amenia and Sharon elevators. The articles of incorporation state the purpose of the John Miller Company to be the buying and selling of grain, and also the "purchasing, owning, leasing, and operating of elevators." Offices were opened in Duluth and Minneapolis. In 1895 the Amenia and Sharon had sold over a million bushels which was enough to support the best possible marketing facilities.[43] The John Miller Company grew rapidly, not only on the business from the parent company, but also from a line of elevators which it had secured. Capital stock was increased from $50,000 to $100,000 in 1913, and profits increased very rapidly as the business volume expanded. In 1916, with a surplus of $159,511.53, a dividend of $65,000 or 65 per cent was paid.[44] The finances of the Amenia and Sharon Land Company and the John Miller Company were closely linked. By lending to each other very freely, both gained from the relationship. Good dividends were paid every year, and the surplus continued to climb, reaching $272,093.42 by 1922.[45] The John Miller Company owned elevators at Dresden, Hannah, Karnak, Langdon, Pembina, Pickert, Sherwood, and Mapleton, in North Dakota, and at Felton, in Minnesota. It also owned the Clyde Elevator Company, another grain brokerage firm, and was closely associated with the Amenia Elevator Company.[46]

The second major elevator concern of the Amenia and Sharon Land Company was the Amenia Elevator Company of Minneapolis. It was incorporated in 1902 with a capital stock of $94,500, and H. F. Chaffee as president. Its articles of incorporation permitted it to deal in "public or private grain elevators and warehouses" and associated lines. P. E. Stroud, Chaffee's son-in-law and vice-president and treasurer of the John Miller Company, was made a director. The Amenia Elevator Company was a holding company. It controlled 26 elevators, 12 coal firms, and lumber yards in 19 villages in North Dakota and 8 in Minnesota.[47] It freely exchanged financial aid with the parent company to the mutual benefit of both. Dividends were paid freely, preventing any great accumulation of capital but not impairing its function as a holding company.[48]

The company got into the commercial flour milling business when it established the Chaffee-Miller Milling Company of Casselton. It was incorporated in 1906 and capitalized at $50,000. The major purpose of this firm was to mill company wheat for commercial sale. All of its stock was owned by the Amenia and Sharon Land Company and the Amenia Elevator Company. Gross assets increased to $310,-719.91 in 1911. Later the firm began to stagnate. The parent company had to lend money constantly to keep it operating. In 1914 the milling company was rented to Dwight M. Baldwin, Jr., who owned several other flour mills. Baldwin leased the mill until January 6, 1919, when it was sold to A. G. MacDonald for $100,000. MacDonald sold stock and formed the Farmers Cooperative and Milling Elevator of Casselton.[49]

The elevator firms served their purpose well. H. L. Chaffee said that one of the chief reasons for establishing them was to secure easier financing for the farms. The elevators could secure advances on grain in storage and in turn could lend this money to the farms. It was all a matter of internal bookkeeping. It was the Amenia and Sharon's way of getting big finance into its operation.[50] The chief source of finance for the company farms and for the Amenia Elevator Company was A. D. Thomson, a Duluth financier, shipping and elevator magnate. The company also had interests in the Crescent Elevator and the North Dakota Grain Company, both of which appeared to be sizeable brokerage firms.[51]

Another firm in which the Amenia and Sharon Land Company had an interest was the Chaffee-Crites Bee Farms, Incorporated, which raised bees in connection with the production of clover and other hay seeds which were sold by the company elevators. The company also had an interest in the Equity Cooperating Packing Company of Fargo, a farmer's cooperative meat packing plant which went bankrupt in the 1920's, and in the North Dakota Land and Investment Company which was the connecting link in several transactions between the parent company and the M. J. Woodward Company of Watertown, Wisconsin. There is also mention in correspondence of a Sharon and Amenia Grain Company and a Chaffee Land and Loan Company, but no records were found. In all, there were thirty-two separate firms and two company towns operated by or associated with the Amenia and Sharon Land Company throughout its history. In this count the operations of the ten company elevators are included as part of the parent company, and the individual retail establishments of the Amenia Elevator Company and the John Miller Company are not enumerated separately. The same is true for the sixty-one separate farms owned by the company.

Reorganizations of the Company

The parent company went through a reorganization between 1893 and 1895 when it was split into two separate firms. The capital stock of the original firm was reduced to $62,700, and the Guernsey trustee group was capitalized at $36,700. By 1911 the factional group had dissolved, and its lands were owned by the Chaffee-Miller Land Company which, together with the property of the E. W. Chaffee estate, were merged into a newly organized Amenia and Sharon Land Company of North Dakota. Total land holdings were then increased from 12,760 to 28,594 acres, and the capital stock was increased to $364,200. In 1917 a further reorganization took place when the Miller-Chaffee-Reed Company merged with the parent company.[52] The capital stock was increased to $425,800. Table 14 provides a fully detailed account of how the assets as they increased when mergers took place. Total land holdings after 1917 were increased to 42,772 acres which means that even at its height the Amenia and Sharon Land Company never had as large holdings as the Grandins. But in all likelihood their total cultivated area exceeded that of any of the Dakota bonanzas. The financial complex is illustrated in Table 15 which is a combined financial statement of the major associates as of July 21, 1922, just prior to liquidation. The actual figures of growth from the original investment are distorted by the fact that they are interlocked and, therefore, tend to duplicate the actual combined net worth. Closer examination of the records would indicate that the combined net would be slightly over $4,000,000. Table 15 represents only the major Chaffee and Reed stockholders in the Amenia and Sharon Land Company and its major subsidiaries.

TABLE 15[a]. Financial Statement of the Amenia and Sharon Land Company and Major Associates July 31, 1922

Name	Gross Assets	Net Assets[b]
The Amenia and Sharon Land Company	$3,221,476.63	$2,619,171.65
The John Miller Company	623,600.50	372,093.42
The Amenia Elevator Company	204,960.91	165,930.87
The H. F. Chaffee Company	1,999,040.21	1,937,130.91
W. R. Reed	471,623.78	453,923.78
R. B. Reed	311,690.62	306,690.62
Carrie T. Chaffee	984,921.12	892,411.31
H. L. Chaffee	293,551.12	260,734.37
P. E. Stroud	178,774.30	176,933.95
	$8,289,639.10	$7,185,020.88

[a] Financial statement of July 31, 1922; H. F. Chaffee Company statement of July 31, 1920, A & S Papers, File 134.
[b] Net assets are gross assets less liabilities.

Dissolution of the Company

It was clear that after the death of H. F. Chaffee in 1912 the company could not hold together indefinitely because it lacked his leadership and control over the extensive operations. As his son, H. L. Chaffee, so clearly stated it: "After the death of Dad the company lacked a dominating figure and simply had too much family politics involved."[53] Prior to his death the meetings of the stockholders were annual affairs. After his death they became more and more frequent and in the last few years there were weekly meetings.[54] The idea of an eventual breakup of the big farm and a dissolution of the company and its subsidiaries had become well established in the minds of many of the stockholders ever since Chaffee's death. H. F. Chaffee had made the company solid in all respects, but the individual interests of the family stockholders simply pulled in too many directions. It is obvious that in the later years the company was being milked by the stockholders to further their personal interests. It was their property and they could treat it as they saw fit.

The first official notice of dissolution appeared in the minutes of the company meeting of February 1, 1921, when W. W. Brown, proxy for Katherine Reed Brown, offered the following resolution:

Resolved, that it is for the best interests of this company that a division of the property of the corporation be made among the stockholders. Resolved further, that the Board of Directors is hereby authorized and directed to formulate plans for the consummation of such division, to become effective at the end of the current year or as soon thereafter as they may deem practicable.

The resolution passed and other meetings followed in rapid succession. The minutes of the meeting of March 1, 1922, provided for the distribution of company lands on a pro rata lease arrangement to individual stockholders until final details could be completed.[55] Other assets, elevators, and subsidiaries were similarly divided.

Next to the loss of Chaffee's leadership, taxes were a major influence in the dissolution of the company. Table 10 gives a partial picture of the tax load of the company. It was not until 1913 that the company had to pay taxes other than real estate and personal property taxes. The highest personal property tax to that date was $6,213.24 in 1897 when the company had an excessive amount of wheat on hand. The annual report for 1912, while expressing fairly good results, complained that some expenses had grown too fast. "The principal differences in expenses between the two years are, the item of taxes [about $8,000] paid in 1912." After the passage of the Federal Income Tax Law, correspondence with the Internal Revenue Department was frequent. In 1921 the company was asked to pay a 25 per cent penalty because it had delayed payment on the capital-stock tax.[56] Some tax relief was granted when the North Dakota Tax Department agreed that because agriculture was such a risky business, "the corporate farm cannot be taxed on the same basis as other corporations," so the state "fixed" $1,055,000 as the base rate of capital stock and the State tax was set at $522.50. This was established in lieu of the normal corporate stamp tax of 10 per cent of $2,691,830.22, the State's value of the company's net assets and capital stock.[57]

In 1919 the company was caught between two forces. Land prices were rising rapidly but at the same time, so were farm profits. High profits from the operations meant a high income tax, but high profits from the sale of land meant a high excess-profit tax (now called a capital-gains tax).[58] The company paid its biggest tax payment in 1919 with $29,412.52 in property taxes, $4,149.59 in state and federal capital-stock taxes, and $21,029.96 in corporate income taxes, totaling $54,592.07.[59] This big payment was one of the key motives for Mrs. Carrie T. Chaffee's motion that "steps be taken to formulate some plan for individual ownership of the property of the land company." [60]

Other considerations for the dissolution were the ever increasing difficulty of obtaining labor for subsidiary operations and part-time farm labor and the temptations to sell land at the high prices that followed World War I. All of these reasons together with the lack of a strong family leader prevented the great organization from continuing on the wheat fields of North Dakota.

FOOTNOTES

[1] Journal 1, pp. 8-10, A & S Papers, NDIRS, File 134.

[2] Annual report for 1911, A & S Papers, File 134.

[3] U.S. Internal Revenue Tax Statement for 1912, A & S Papers, File 134.

[4] Some consolidation with the H. F. Chaffee Company took place at this time also but the records are not entirely clear on this. The Miller-Chaffee-Reed Company was naturally free of debt so the assets brought a direct increase in the surplus of over $900,-000. Again it must be remembered this company had started from funds of the parent company. On the basis of the original 994 shares issued at organization in 1876, each share would in 1917 be worth $2,666.35 in addition to over $300,000 paid in dividends up to 1917, besides other benefits drawn from the company. On the basis of $92,600 actual paid in, a $100 investment would have been worth $2,862.04 in addition to dividends, etc. The value per share of paid-in stock in 1911 was $625.47. In all, $596,643 was positively accounted for as having been paid in dividends.

[5] Annual statement 1917, A & S Papers, File 134.

[6] A statement on file for 1922 protests carrying the land at $70 an acre and indicates if it had been increased to $100 an acre, which was the selling price of that period, the company's net assets would have increased from $2,819,165.50 to $3,833,075.50. A & S Papers, File 134.

[7] Several times the annual report differed from the income tax report. For example, in 1915 the tax return indicated a profit of $104,123.24 but the annual statement revealed a profit of $177,457.95.

[8] In 1920 the company lost $32,337.52 but in that same year $34,935.56 was spent for new buildings which were charged off in full. In 1921 it lost $61,935.54 but the books carried $48,088.37 in pre-paid operating expenses for 1922.

[9] At this time E. W. Chaffee was using company funds to purchase stock from various stockholders who disagreed with his management.

[10] Annual statement 1891, A & S Papers, File 134.

[11] Minutes of March 4, 1913 meeting of A & S of Connecticut, A & S Papers, File 134.

[12] Journal 11, pp. 48–61, A & S Papers, File 134.

[13] Annual statement 1907, A & S Papers, File 134. That year the company had outstanding accounts with W. R. Reed, $52,603.90; R. B. Reed, $23,085.50; K. R. Brown, $42,455.91; H. F. Chaffee, $48,228.33; Wanotan Land Co., $8,872.11; Red River Valley Land and Investment Co., $19,741.11. It held $27,200 capital stock in the Amenia Livestock Co. and $20,000 stock in the Chaffee-Miller Milling Co. The company owed the Chaffee-Miller Land Co. $2,363.93; the Miller-Chaffee Reed Co. $4,192.37; the John Miller Co. $12,058.51, and the E. W. Chaffee estate $29,927.03.

[14] An outsider who became very well acquainted with the operations of the Amenia and Sharon Land Company was North Dakota's first governor, John Miller. His estate in 1908 consisted of 100 shares in the Chaffee-Miller Land Co. worth $20,000, also 245 shares in the John Miller Company which got its start on Amenia and Sharon money and in addition had all its grain business which amounted to over $1,000,000 in its first year in 1896 when the company was formed. The John Miller Co. shares were worth $85,750. He had 115 shares in the Miller-Chaffee-Reed Co. worth $11,500. Outside stock consisted of 63 shares in the Dwight Farm and Land Co. valued at $18,900. John Miller Estate papers, H. F. Chaffee personal file, A & S Papers, File 134.

[15] Seed allocation statements for 1910, 1912, A & S Papers, File 134.

[16] Chaffee interview.

[17] A & S to Collector of Internal Revenue, Aberdeen, S. D., Jan. 27, 1917, March 10, 1917, A & S Papers, File 134.

[18] Partnership agreement, Nov. 7, 1884, A & S Papers, File 134. A new store building is in the location today and serves as housing for the Chaffee Mercantile, Amenia Post Office, and headquarters for the Chaffee farms under the management of H. L. Chaffee, son of H. F. Chaffee. (H. L. Chaffee has an intense interest in the history of bonanza farming and particularly the Amenia and Sharon enterprise. It is he who has been most responsible for the preservation and collecting of the great mass of material that is available at the North Dakota Institute for Regional Studies Library.)

[19] Blueprint, Nov. 1, 1887, and agreement with the St. Paul, Minneapolis and Manitoba Railway Company, A & S Papers, File 134.

[20] Chaffee interview.

[21] Hotel contract, G. L. Dunning, 1893, 1900, A & S Papers, File 134.

[22] Why the sudden large losses in the hotel operation? There were no explanations in the records. Many other enterprises had similiar heavy losses in the last years of operations. It may have been due to the times or to carelessness, but in view of the past operations, these do not seem likely. It is more probable that these losses were planned by the stockholders as a means of transferring funds from the company into personal hands, all in keeping with the process of liquidation.

[23] Telephone agreements, July 13, 1896, April 1, 1906, A & S Papers, File 134.

[24] Copy of the agreement, A & S Papers, File 134.

[25] Ledger accounts for 1901, A & S Papers, File 134.

[26] The dimensions for all the company buildings were kept on record for inventory and insurance purposes. Most were large-sized buildings.

[27] Contract with F. B. Morse and Co., June 1919, A & S Papers, File 134.

[28] Annual statement 1919, A & S Papers, File 134.

[29] Copy of organization, A & S Papers, File 134.

[30] Contract was made with the Minneapolis Steel and Machinery Company, one of the early companies, since consolidated into Minneapolis Moline.

[31] Annual statements 1920, 1921, A & S Papers, File 134.

[32] Contract with C. E. Walker, Jan. 6, 1920, A & S Papers, File 134.

[33] *The American Elevator and Grain Trade Magazine* of September 15, 1898, pp. 97–98, carried a picture of three Amenia and Sharon elevators at Amenia and the famous plowing postage stamp picture. The second elevator opened by the company was in Rita in 1893. It disappeared from the records, either by changing its name or going out of business.

[34] The elevator at Lynchburg was purchased about 1900 from E. Burgess and Henry K. Dallenbeck.

[35] Bill of sale, April 26, 1915, A & S Papers, File 134.

[36] Mason is in Cass County, Sec. 36, T. .42, R. 53 and still exists as a country elevator. Total moving and foundation costs were $5,000. Annual statement 1912, A & S Papers, File 134.

[37] Bill of Sale with G. W. Humphrey, Dec. 29, 1917, A & S Papers, File 134.

[38] Chaffee interview.

[39] Seed allocation statement 1912, A & S Papers, File 134.

[40] Report to Food Adm. Grain Corp.; Letter of estimate from Hickok Construction Co., May 17, 1920, A & S Papers, File 134.

[41] Record of agreement for spur construction, Nov. 24, 1897, A & Papers, File 134.

[42] Copy of agreement with Great Northern R.R., March 11, 1907, A & S Papers, File 134.

[43] Hunter, p. 35; Misc. John Miller Co. records, A & S Papers, File 134. In 1896 Miller resigned as superintendent of the Dwight Farm and Land Co. and became the farm's president. At that time it contained 60,000 acres. John Miller Papers, Dwight Farm Papers, NDIRS, File 84.

[44] Financial statement of July 31, 1916, A & S Papers, File 134. In three years the value of a $100 share of stock increased to $259.51.

[45] Financial statement, July 31, 1922, A & S Papers, File 134.

[46] A & S to Internal Revenue, Oct. 15, 1924, A & S Papers, File 134.

[47] Hunter, p. 36; Financial statements, A & S Papers, File 134. Original incorporators included George W. Kellogg of Grand Forks, Henry A. Thexton of Minneapolis, and Donald Morrison of Duluth, plus W. R. and R. B. Reed.

[48] Capital stock was valued at $167 per share in 1922 after 6 and 8 per cent dividends had been paid annually.

[49] Statement of Associated Companies, 1910, 1912; Contract with Baldwin, March 4, 1914; Bill of sale, Jan. 6, 1919, A & S Papers, File 134. The sale proved profitable to the original stockholders. In the transaction the trademarks of NODAK, Cassco, Redrival, and Casselton brand were all transferred to the new firm.

[50] Chaffee interview.

[51] A & S to W. C. Cook, Collector Treasury Dept.; Internal Revenue to W. R. Reed, Dec. 23, 1912, A & S Papers, File 134.

[52] The Amenia and Sharon Land Co. of Connecticut was terminated and liquidated April 9, 1920. It had no major function after 1911 when the North Dakota corporation of that name was organized.

[53] Chaffee interview.

[54] Chaffee interview. H. L. Chaffee was asked if his father could have pulled the company through the trying times of the 1920's and '30's. He answered, "There would have been no doubt that the company could have survived those trying times . . . as he proved himself as extremely foresighted, an excellent business manager, and I am sure that he would have had the business in such a state of organization that it would have been able to exist even through those extreme conditions." H. L. Chaffee to H. M. Drache, May 22, 1961. H. L. Chaffee is probably biased in his father's behalf but there is no doubt that H. F. Chaffee could have pulled the big bonanza through a most desperate era of American agriculture.

[55] Land was divided as follows: Katherine Reed Brown, 3 sections; R. B. Reed, 5½; W. R. Reed, 8½; J. H. Reed, ¾; Dorothy Chaffee Stroud, 5; Lester Chaffee 5; E. W. Chaffee, 4¼; H. L. Chaffee, 4½; Adelade Chaffee Higgins, 4½; Carrie T. Chaffee, 12⅝ sections with ½ section remaining in the company name. Gross value of the land distributed was $2,363,824.54. Liquidating statement, Feb. 23, 1923, A & S Papers, File 134. (These people were all grandchildren of E. W. Chaffee except Mrs. Carrie T. Chaffee who was a daughter-in-law.)

[56] Copy of claim for tax abatement, A & S Papers, File 134.

[57] N. D. State Tax Dept. to A & S July 20, 1921, A & S Papers, File 134.

[58] Minutes of meeting, Feb. 4, 1919, A & S Papers, File 134.

[59] Annual statement 1919, A & S Papers, File 134.

[60] Special meeting to discuss taxes and dissolution, April 8, 1920, A & S Papers, File 134.

CHAPTER VIII

Factors in the Rise and Decline of
the Bonanza Farms

No one factor can be attributed as the cause for the rise and decline of the bonanza. There were a combination of factors. Cheap land, which was the chief cause for the creation of the bonanza, rose quickly in value and became a major reason for dissolution. The demand for wheat in the 1870's and '80's, causing high prices, reversed itself in the 1890's causing lower prices while production costs rose. The weather cycle, so favorable in the late 1870's and early 1880's, reversed itself in the late 1880's and virtually "dried out" some of the bonanzas. Technological improvements, so important in giving the bonanzas an edge in efficiency in the early days, lost their importance as other farmers adopted machinery to their operations. Rising land taxes, corporation taxes after World War I, inability to get adequate labor, varied family interests, and socio-economical opposition all played their part in dissolution of the big farms.

For a time, however, the bonanzas served their intended purpose. They were created by the Northern Pacific to open the land and attract people to the region. And this they did well. Today a few scattered large holdings and many legends are all that remain of this great phase of American agriculture.

Rising Land Values

The constantly rising value of land is a well-known fact in American agricultural history. National average land values have increased from a price of $1.25 an acre established by the government for frontier land in 1820 to $115 in 1950, a ninety-fold increase in 140 years. In the case of the North Dakota bonanzas, the prices rose even more dramatically. Bonanza farmers paid from $0.16 to $3.75 per acre with the great bulk of the land being secured at $0.43 to $1.34. By

1920 the average land value in North Dakota was $40.39 per acre, a forty-fold increase in a period of only forty-six years.[1] Land in the Red River Valley averaged about $90.00 per acre at that time. Land of the Amenia and Sharon Land Company increased in value $2.50 per acre annually from 1879 to 1919. From 1896 to 1920 the value of its holdings increased 8.4 per cent each year compounded annually. In addition, the annual rentals netted 4.5 per cent. Discounting the increase in value due to improvements, the net increase from rising land values and rental income was 9.3 per cent a year compounded annually from 1896 to 1920. The Baldwin Corporation, which operated in Dickey County, purchased 75,000 acres in 1891 at prices ranging from $1.25 to $3.15 per acre. It profited even more than the Amenia and Sharon Land Company by rising land values because it was able to sell its lands during and after World War I for from $40 to $60 per acre. The net income on its operated land, based on inventory value in 1923, was 4.1 per cent after the chief stockholders paid themselves $6,000 for management.[2]

The Dalrymple lands, which were in the choicest location on the main line of the Northern Pacific and near Fargo, had a rapid increase in value. Dalrymple, who purchased land in 1876 and after for prices ranging from $0.40 to $5 per acre, found himself a wealthy man by 1884 when his land was worth from $20 to $25 per acre.[3] The Dwight Farm and Land Company, which had purchased land in Steele County in the early 1880's for $2 per acre, sold five sections in 1909 for $32.33 per acre, an increase in value of 57 per cent for each year of ownership.[4] Its lands in Richland County were valued at a higher price per acre.

In 1879 the Amenia and Sharon Land Company started to sell some of its land. The lowest price received for any of it was $10 an acre, a good profit on land that had cost $3.75 an acre in 1876. By 1882 it was receiving as much as $25 an acre for well improved land.[5] In 1903 it was receiving $30 an acre, by 1913, $60; by 1917, $74.58; and in 1920 it received a net sale price of $90 to $115 per acre.[6] The Chaffee-Miller Land Company, which had purchased most of its land in 1902 for $20 an acre, realized $57 in 1911.[7] This represents an increase of 31 per cent annually on the purchase price.

The natural rise of land prices was sufficient in most cases to make the bonanzas a financial success. An increase of a dollar in value per acre each year multiplied by several thousand acres certainly gave a good book profit. This favorable speculative factor was a major reason for the financial durability of many of the bonanzas.

Adequate Capital

One of the most consistent weaknesses of American agriculture through its history has been the lack of adequate long-range and short-term financing. In this respect the bonanzas differed from the typical farming operation, because most of them possessed or had access to sufficient funds. Large sums were poured into the big farms for several years to get them started successfully.

In 1880, as in 1960, there were many people who feared the big capitalistic farmer. An article in the *Atlantic Monthly* predicted:

Against the unlimited use of this combination of capital, machinery, and cheap labor the individual farmer either singly or in communities, cannot successfully contend and must go under. It is a combination of the most powerful social and economic forces known to man and all efforts for competition must and will fail so long as the three remain united.[8]

Adequate financial backing enabled the bonanzas to speculate on the grain and land markets to their greatest advantage. When the wheat market was low, Dalrymple and the others simply held their crop of a half million bushels or more until the price rose. This ability to hold and secure a higher price later in the season meant the difference between profit and loss.[9] The Amenia and Sharon held their wheat twice for two years during the 1890's. The big farms were also able to sell part of their land on a contract-for-deed and to collect considerable interest income. Sometimes these lands were repossessed, representing a net gain to the bonanza owners. When conditions were depressed, the bonanza operator generally had outside capital to tide him over. Even James B. Power, one of the smaller bonanza farmers, had interest income, salary income, and good bank connections that the small farmer did not have. Available capital also meant that the bonanza operators could often buy large amounts of land on a margin at little risk of losing the property because they could apply all income on the contract.[10] Because they had subsidiary incomes or were so large, even the smallest margin of profit meant a considerable income. Elevators, machinery agencies, construction companies, or banking interests all helped to improve the financial picture and also meant that services from those agencies were secured at a discount. Volume buying gave the bonanza operator a competitive advantage over the individual farmer.

Other Factors Aiding the Bonanza Farms

The value of professional management has been well stressed in regard to its significance to the financial success of the bonanzas. In addition on account of the leadership of these so-called scientific book farmers, the bonanzas were quicker to adapt new innovations in agriculture. In many cases, they were actually ahead of the agricultural experiment stations. The adoption of new techniques often made the difference between profit and loss. However, only a top-notch manager could make the big farm a profitable institution.

Many historians and economists have given reasons for the rise and success of the bonanza. John Lee Coulter and James B. Power, both of whom lived in Dakota in that era, compiled a list of several reasons why the bonanza appeared in the 1870's. Their basic points were: Cheap land available from both the government and the railroad. Flat, easy to work, treeless and stoneless prairies, easily adaptable to new labor-saving machinery. New farm implements for large-scale farming at low costs. An excellent combination of fertile soil and good wheat climate. Advertising of the area as the Nile of America or the Land of the No. 1 Hard. Availability and interest of eastern capital. Strong foreign demand for American flour and high wheat prices. Abundant labor supply because of the flow of immigrant settlers to the agricultural districts. The availability of lumberjacks from Minnesota and Wisconsin in the summer months. Eastern wheat farmers handicapped by new wheat diseases, increasing price of eastern land which was decreasing in productivity. Temporary good moisture conditions and for a time freedom from grasshoppers in Dakota. Superior flour derived from a combination of new wheat varieties, new milling methods, and ideal climatic conditions. An international market resulting from new low-cost rail and water facilities. And an ideal timing and a combination of the above factors.[11]

The rising wheat prices were a great motivating factor in the development of the bonanza. If prices had not been high, people would have been less anxious to come to Dakota to raise wheat. Wheat prices were high because of declining production in the old wheat growing region of eastern United States and because of a series of very poor wheat crops in Europe from 1879 to 1881, just the years when the Red River Valley was being opened by the Northern Pacific and Great Northern Railroads. This was all part of the "Great Dakota Boom" which saw the new lands of the public domain in Dakota Territory being transferred to private owners at a rate of 1,400,000 acres to 11,000,000 acres every year from 1878 to 1889.[12] From 1872 to 1880 wheat acreage in America jumped from 20,858,359 to 37,986,717, a 10 per cent increase each year for 8 years; seven million acres of the increase were in North Dakota.[13]

Dakota wheat was in active demand in the milling centers during that period because it graded from 77 to 88 per cent No. 1 Hard.[14] In 1882 nearly all of the wheat sold through Fargo was No. 1 Hard.[15] Good quality and active demand meant top prices for Dakota wheat. The average price of No. 1 hard wheat from 1876 to 1891 is shown in Table 16.

TABLE 16[a]. The Average, Low, and High Price of Wheat on the Chicago Market during the Bonanza Era.

Year	Average	Low	High
1876	$0.926	$0.83	$1.267
1877	1.215	1.015	1.765
1878	.952	.77	1.14
1879	.996	.816	1.335
1880	1.057	.865	1.32
1881	1.148	.953	1.432
1882	1.166	.911	1.40
1883	1.017	.90	1.135
1884	.83	.695	.96
1885	.839	.733	1.317
1886	.766	.693	.847
1887	.756	.606	.947
1888	.90	.711	2.00
1889	.855	.755	1.082
1890	.892	.742	1.082
1891	.966	.85	1.16

[a] Veblen, *The Journal of Political Economy*, Vol. I, p. 157; A newspaper clipping in H. F. Chaffee's Remembrance Book, A & S Papers, NDIRS, File 134. The average price from Veblen, the highs and lows from Chaffee.

Throughout this period yields were high in Dakota. Favorable weather from 1877 to 1883 produced good crops in contrast to the years from 1870 to 1876 when locusts and dry weather were prevalent.[16] Dalrymple's average yield for the first five years of operation was eighteen bushels with a top yield of twenty-three.[17] The Grandins' average weighed yield for a ten-year period was one pound short of seventeen bushels per acre. In 1877 on more than 4,000 acres, over 24 bushels per acre was produced.[18] Good yields and good prices meant a high return per acre. This was also true for oats and barley which utilized the identical equipment.

Chances of a high net income per acre were further enhanced by low operating costs on the Dakota prairies. Cost of production commencing with plowing and ending with delivery at the elevator (including interest on the capital investment) varied from $0.30 to $0.50 per bushel in a period when production costs for the eastern farmers were about $1.00 per bushel. The only disadvantage the Dakota farmer had was distance from water transportation. Dalrymple claimed, however, that he could deliver wheat to Buffalo and still have less than $0.50 invested per bushel.[19] James B. Power, who operated a much smaller acreage, figured his total production cost on wheat at $0.2981 per bushel.[20] Profits per acre varied with the yield and price, but the average net per acre after all possible costs ranged from $2.50 to $10 per acre with from $4.50 to $7.50 being the most common figures.

High transportation charges gave the Dakota farmer a disadvantage on the wheat market, but technological changes quickly alleviated that problem. Competition between the newly constructed Great Northern and Northern Pacific railways determined whether the wheat would go to Minneapolis or Duluth. But a reduction in steamship rates to Liverpool was just as significant. The rate from New York to Liverpool fell from $0.20 a bushel in 1867 to $0.07 in 1891 due to the overproduction of steamships.[21] The Great Lakes had been opened in 1855 and wheat could be shipped directly to Buffalo by rail and water for $0.27 per bushel. In 1881 Dalrymple chartered boats at Duluth to take his 600,000-bushel crop directly to Buffalo.[22] Minneapolis millers even came to the Dakota wheat fields to bargain for the crop rather than let it go to Buffalo. This encouraged the "liveliest kind of competition" among the transportation and milling agencies.[23] Because of the great volume of their business, most of the bonanza operators were able to secure "special rates" or rebates on all of their shipments.[24] Millers in the wheat fields, chartered ships, and private elevators simply meant that the bonanza operator had succeeded in by-passing the middleman in marketing his products which resulted in considerable additional income.[25] This was also true when the bonanza operator purchased equipment which was always at wholesale, never retail, prices.

William Allen White sensed a significant connection between the prairie and the bonanza operation and stated it well:

The monotonous exactness of the level makes me long for the undulating prairies of the midwest. Yet the very evenness of the plain has a commercial value and makes the location here of the great wheat farms possible. For in rolling country there is waste land . . . but in bonanza farming every foot of land must be productive with the least possible amount of human labor upon it. In the lexicon of the Dakota farmer there is no such word as hoe.[26]

The commercial value of the land was increased by what Veblen noted from 1867 to 1877 as "the changes for the better in the implements actually in use by wheat farmers during period [which were] very great, both in cheapness and in efficiency."[27] The self-rake reaper, first introduced in the early 1870's, was perfected so quickly that there were few changes in it until the late 1890's. Between 1872 and 1875 the harvester was introduced. It was partially replaced in 1874 by the wire-tie binder, which, although successful, was never fully accepted because of the expense and difficulty in keeping the wire out of the grain. The great success came in 1879 with the twine-tie binder which was different only in the binding material used. In 1875 the straw-burning engine was proven practical for stationary threshing power. Large grain drills of from twelve to fourteen foot widths were introduced in 1876. The year 1879 also saw the introduction of the riding double-gang plow which replaced the sulky. The first use of steam power for plowing came in Dakota in 1881. The great change in the milling industry, which particularly favored the hard wheat of the Dakotas and aided in increasing flour consumption, was the invention of the gradual reduction roller process.[28]

The bonanza came into being at a time when the Dakotas, whose economy is hinged directly on agriculture, was blessed with a favorable period in the weather cycle. Dalrymple, writing in 1907, said that in thirty-two years of operation in the Red River Valley, "but part of one crop was ever lost by summer frost; there has never been a crop lost by excessive moisture and there has never been a drought so bad but all the expenses of farming have been returned in the fall by the crops raised."[29] The Grandins had a similar experience. A severe hail storm in 1899 on eight sections caused their most widespread damage to crops by weather in twenty-one years of operation.[30] The hard winter of 1880 and 1881, while giving the state a bad reputation, helped settle it, for heavy snows left a high water table, created lakes and ponds, and suggested a fairly humid climate which was attractive to settlers.[31]

So a good combination of causes appearing at almost the same instant created this great drama in American agriculture.

The Decline of the Bonanza

There are several reasons for the decline of the bonanza just as there were several reasons for its rise. James B. Power, an advocate of diversified farming even though he was the creator of the bonanza idea, was well aware of its temporary nature. Alva Benton, a student of North Dakota agriculture in the 1920's, stated that all "men who were familiar with the farming situation recognized their [bonanzas'] temporary character."[32] The *Toronto Daily Globe* commented about the bonanza system: "Dalrymple . . . has already made one failure . . . Dakota and Minnesota will rue the day when the bonanza farms were introduced." The same article continued:

Carried to the ultimate, bonanza farming as now practiced would without doubt exhaust the soil, but the American farmer who is shrewd enough to see his opportunity in the bonanza system, will also be equal to the establishment of a different base as the occasion may require. When wheat farming fails, their immense farms will be the very thing for stock ranches . . . the rapid changes in the financial and commercial worlds, these colossal farms will become disentegrated. Death and heirs, process of law and other contingencies will divide them into smaller tracts long before the rich alluvial deposits are denuded of their productive qualities.[33]

Power, the best informed man on the bonanza era, listed five reasons why the bonanza broke down: Diversification came into the area. Outside capital often lacked good management to make farming profitable. There was a period of crop failures during the late 1880's. Labor problems increased, and many owners felt that it would be to everyone's advantage if the big units were subdivided.[34]

William Dalrymple, son of Oliver, said at the time of the Dalrymple's dispersal sale in 1917:

My brother and I have decided to give up operating the farm and divide it into small farms . . . it is better that this be done for many reasons, and we think it better for North Dakota. Big farms were good for publicity. But economic conditions in North Dakota have changed. The state is rich and prosperous, methods of agricultural operations have changed, everything is different. It will be better for the state, for the towns and cities of the state . . . to have a great many small farms in place of the one big farm.[35]

One of the earliest and most positive reasons for the decline of the bonanza was taxation. Because of their size, the bonanzas were satisfied with a small profit per acre. That small profit could be quickly wiped out by any increase in taxes. Cass, Cheney, and Billings, all on the Northern Pacific board of directors, expressed concern about what taxes could do to bonanza profits.[36] In the case of the Amenia and Sharon Land Company, it was not only real estate taxes but corporation excess profit taxes and income taxes of the World War I era that irked the stockholders sufficiently to make them desire dissolution.

Agriculture is constantly threatened either by the loss of crops due to poor weather or by a surplus and resulting low prices due to good weather. The Power correspondence provides an excellent illustration of poor crop conditions in the late 1880's and early 1890's. In 1890 Power wrote: "Dryer than Prohibition South Dakota up here, if rain does not come soon good bye to wheat again."[37] From 1889 to 1893 the only year that proved profitable was 1891. The *Minneapolis Journal* said, "Big farms probably have not paid even though the owners persist that their business is profitable."[38] Power claimed that the bad weather conditions started in 1886 and that, along with low wheat prices, made it impossible to sell land and unprofitable to own it.[39] Answering a creditor, Power wrote:

Eight bushels per acre of 45¢ wheat does not permit the payment of many bills . . . it is only from outside resources that bills can be met. It makes me feel as I was at the end of the rope. The poor crops and low prices . . . put a stop to the commencement of resumed feelings of confidence up here.[40]

In the moist years up to 1883 the prairie was broken too fast and more wheat was being raised than the market could take. It was at this time that the big Spiritwood Bonanza began to sell its lands because the farm was no longer making any money.[41] The adverse combination was just too much for some of the financially weak bonanzas. Those that survived the dry period had a new temptation for disposal when agricultural conditions improved after 1895.

Rising land prices made the bonanzas a profitable venture but as land values rose, many of the bonanza owners yielded to the temptation of quick profits through the sale of their land. In 1897 William Allen White predicted that "if land continues to rise in the market, the big farmers may follow troubador and mound builders" within one generation.[42] The rise in value of twenty-five, fifty, and a hundred-fold was more than most could foresee or resist. Much of the land was later repossessed because agricultural conditions did not merit paying the high World War I prices. John S. Dalrymple reported that only "Askew, Sinner, and Scherweit were able to hold their property" out of several dozen who had purchased land from his family. The Dalrymples decided to sell in 1916 because they felt that the interest on the money would yield more than they could make from operating the land.[43]

The bonanza farms were so large that when they were eventually sold, they had to be subdivided and financed by the sellers. The crop-payment plan was the common manner of sale. The share of the crop that had to be paid on the interest and principal each year depended upon the price paid for the land and the amount that had been paid down. It is believed that John L. Grandin originated the crop-payment plan. When the Grandins decided to reduce their holdings, they advertised it on time payments. They preferred to sell in quarter or half section blocks. If a farmer wanted to buy a farm, he was interviewed and asked for a financial statement. If he had adequate machinery, livestock, and a helpful family, he was almost certain to receive a farm on the crop-payment plan. If the farmer appeared a very good risk, the Grandins would even lend him extra money for operating expenses.

Regarding the crop-payment plan, John L. Grandin wrote:

We have faith we are selling you very productive land and believe that you are able to make a success. We will sell you the land for so much money but we will not ask you to give us your note secured by a mortgage. You are to farm the land with diligence and each year you are to put in one half of the marketable crop in the nearest elevator to our credit. You are to take the responsibility of selling the same and to advise the Elevator Company to remit to us the proceeds which will be credited to your purchase contract. You will never have to worry about any foreclosure and the rate of interest will be 6 per cent.[44]

The Grandins sold most of their land on the crop-payment plan because they could get a little more per acre. The buyer had nearly absolute security if he did a good job of farming. Although he did not possess title, he was not bound by a fixed payment.

The Grandin's crop-payment plan was an obvious success as they had to take back only two quarter sections of land prior to World War I. No down payment was required until land prices hit $40 per acre.[45] By this method the Grandins reduced their original holding of over 75,000 acres in 1878 to 3,259 acres in 1920 when the Murray Brothers Land Company purchased the remainder for $65 an acre.[46]

The Dalrymple bonanza was sold in 1917 but a great deal of the land had to be repossessed during the farm depression of the 1920's. This forced the Dalrymple family back into farming.[47] The Dalrymples had divided their farm into ten units after the dissolution of the Cass-Dalrymple partnership in 1896. After Oliver Dalrymple died in 1908 his sons continued to operate most of the big bonanza until 1917. They concluded that the interest returns would be greater than the profits from farming and, consequently, made many sales.[48]

One writer in 1900 said: "The impression has been circulated far and wide that in agriculture as in manufacturing, the big fish are eating up the little ones and that the independent small farm is a thing of the past." But after visiting the Red River Valley, he concluded: "The great estates of that region are doomed to disintegration. The great wheat ranch cannot complete with the small diversified farm."[49] Labor on the "family plan" plus the ability of the family farm to take advantage of some hidden income which was not possible on the bonanzas eventually proved the superiority of the diversified family farm. Even in the early days only the most efficient managers could make the bonanzas pay. In the later years of the bonanzas, they failed to secure outstanding managers with reputations such as Chaffee, Dalrymple, Power, Bagg, and Miller. Without these capable managers, the bonanzas lost their adaptability which had been so significant in their success in their early years. As more modern machinery was introduced, the family farm gained more than the bonanzas.[50] Labor represented a complete cash outlay on the bonanza and was the biggest single item of expense. Power complained in 1891 that "it has taken my entire crop this year to pay labor bills."[51] Dalrymple reported that the labor scarcity became the greatest difficulty after 1900. He had to diversify his crops to help reduce peak labor requirements.

Land was generally leased on a share-crop basis. The Grandins began their leasing in the 1880's by securing a large number of Dunkard families from Illinois who were placed on about 3,000 acres west of Hillsboro.[52] John Dunlop used the tenant system from the very beginning of his bonanza operation as did Major R. E. Fleming who owned several sections near Wheatland. Fleming took one-third of the gross crop and the tenant got two-thirds and furnished labor, seed, machinery, and stock.[53] One of Fleming's chief reasons for operating in this manner was to avoid what he felt was an expensive outlay for machinery. The Amenia and Sharon Land Company utilized the tenant crop-share system most effectively, maintaining it until its dissolution in 1923. The decision of H. F. Chaffee to split the Amenia and Sharon Land Company proved correct when that company switched to the tenant system of operation in 1893 and avoided much of the great labor problem, although it ended the single bonanza operation. By splitting the large farm into many individually operated farms, the Amenia and Sharon Land Company avoided another criticism that was so often levied, that of not being a "social animal."

"The bonanza farmer is not a social animal with his neighbors. He leaves the country early in the fall until spring. The silent and almost deserted farm is left in charge of the foreman; the proprietor spends his winter somewhere else," wrote the *Minneapolis Journal* in 1893. The article continued to say that immigrants would simply not move into an area where 7 families of 35 people operated 28 sections of land where there should have been 100 families with 500 people. The inability to secure schools and the proper social life prevented people from moving into the region. This was not the first time such charges were placed against the bonanzas. The *Atlantic Monthly* of

January, 1880, after extolling the virtues of the Grandin farms, charged that not one family was a permanent resident on the land that would have normally served adequately for over a hundred families. Because of that, there was virtually no society to be found in bonanza territory. More small improved farms would have meant a higher valuation and hence more tax revenue for the schools and roads necessary as the basis of social life. The settlers in the area accused the newspapers of playing up the good aspects of the bonanza but suppressing any bad aspects that might come to their attention. Such publicity, it was said, "might deter settlers from coming in and so defeat railroad advertising or spoil the land promoter's dream. We noticed it and were exasperated no end." [54] Social pressure in part caused the bonanzas in Richland County to split up and sell out about 1887. The bonanza farmer was not liked by the small, independent farmers because he often squeezed them off their quarter sections or he made life unbearable by not allowing the population to increase because of his big land holding. [55]

The bonanza owners were aware of the criticism that their farms were not conducive to a strong community life. The Dalrymples, in their statement on reasons for selling, indicated that they understood that the bonanza was not a social animal and responded in part to the social pressures. Power mentioned in his correspondence that his farm was so distant from neighbors it lacked an outlet for social life. House warmings or barn building bees never took place on the bonanzas. Much of the social life evolved around "city guests" from Minneapolis and St. Paul or eastern cities which served to separate the residents of the bonanza even further from the others.

FOOTNOTES

[1] "Farm Land Price Trends," *Doane Agricultural Digest*, XXIII (July, 1960), pp. 1011-1012.

[2] Benton, *Journal of Land and Public Utility Economics*, Vol. I, p. 409.

[3] *Cultivator and Country Gentleman*, Vol. 49, p. 839. There were actually more rapid price rises than this. In the *Fargo Argus*, Sept. 28, 1881, there were two reports of land that sold for $23 and $26.35 per acre. Land within a mile of Fargo at that time was selling for $200 per acre according to the *Fargo Argus*, Oct. 12, 1882.

[4] Annual statement 1909, Dwight Farm and Land Co., A & S Papers, NDIRS, File 134.

[5] Contracts on file, A & S Papers, File 134.

[6] Land contracts and agreements with realtors for various years, A & S Papers, File 134.

[7] Statement of transfer of Chaffee-Miller Land Co., A & S Papers, File 134.

[8] Bigelow, *Atlantic Monthly*, Vol. 45, p. 31.

[9] *Fargo Argus*, Sept. 19, 1884, p. 1.

[10] "The way things have been running with me financially the past few years culminating with the poorest crops this year that we have ever had make it necessary for me to

find something on the outside and if it can be brought about I want the place of State Land Comm. when the next administration comes in power." Power to H. R. Lyon, Nov., 1886, NDIRS, File 309. Because of his influence, Power received the position mentioned which played an important part in his ability to finance his operations.

[11] Coulter, NDSHS, *Collections*, Vol. III, pp. 582, 595, 612, 613; Benton, *Journal of Land and Public Utility Economics*, Vol. I, p. 407.

[12] Briggs, *NDHQ*, VI, p. 78. This is in contrast to 213,000 acres taken in 1877.

[13] Thorstein B. Veblen, "The Price of Wheat Since 1867," *The Journal of Political Economy*, Vol. I (1893), p. 78.

[14] *Fargo Daily Argus*, Jan. 31, 1881.

[15] *Fargo Argus*, Sept. 20, 1882.

[16] Hunter, pp. 10-11.

[17] *Fargo Argus*, Jan. 31, 1883.

[18] *Fargo Forum*, May 4, 1893; *Cultivator and Country Gentleman*, Vol. 44, p. 83.

[19] Coulter, NDSHS, *Collections*, Vol. III, p. 582; *Fargo Daily Argus*, Jan. 15, 1881, p. 4.

[20] Power to George W. Hill, March 28, 1889, NDIRS, File 309.

[21] Veblen, *The Journal of Political Economy*, Vol. I, p. 70.

[22] *Fargo Argus*, Sept. 1, 1881.

[23] *Fargo Argus*, Aug. 18, 1880.

[24] In 1884, when wheat prices averaged only $0.83, Dalrymple reported his production costs including transportation to be $0.58 per bushel. His net income on 600,000 bushels was $150,000. *Fargo Argus*, Sept. 22, 1884.

[25] *Cultivator and Country Gentleman*, Vol. 44, p. 83.

[26] White, *Scribner's Magazine*, XXII, p. 539.

[27] Veblen, *The Journal of Political Economy*, Vol. I, p. 83.

[28] Veblen, *The Journal of Political Economy*, Vol. I, pp. 78-86; Coulter, NDSHS, *Collections*, Vol. III, p. 572; Hunter, p. 10, A & S Papers, File 134.

[29] *The Farmer*, XXV, 770.

[30] MHS, *Collections*, X, Part 1, p. 21.

[31] Briggs, *NDHQ*, IV, p. 79.

[32] Benton, *Cash and Share Renting*, p. 38.

[33] Quoted in *Northern Pacific Times*, July 20, 1880, p. 11.

[34] James B. Power, "Diversified Farming," *The Record*, V (July, 1899), p. 15.

[35] *Casselton Reporter*, Jan. 19, 1917.

[36] Power to Kindred, Nov. 1, 1878, NDIRS, File 309; Power to Cheney, Nov. 17, 1878, File 309.

[37] Power to C. W. Butz, May 12, 1890, File 309.

[38] *Minneapolis Journal*, June 3, 1893.

[39] Power to Daniel Fish, Nov. 25, 1889, File 309. Fish was counsel for the Minnesota Title Insurance and Trust Co.

[40] Power to George Power, Feb. 13, 1893; Power to a creditor, Dec. 11, 1893, File 309.

[41] Walker interview, Spiritwood Papers, NDIRS, File 173.

[42] White, *Scribner's Magazine*, XXII, 540.

[43] Dalrymple interview, NDIRS, File 549.

[44] Grandin Papers, NDIRS, File 450.

[45] *The Goose*, a Traill County newspaper, carried an advertisement from the Grandins in November, 1894, advertising fifty-four and three-fourths sections of land plus some other lots. All land was to be sold with little or no down payment on the crop-payment plan. Clipping from *The Goose* found in Grandin Papers, NDIRS, File 450.

[46] In March, 1920, a two-day disposal sale was held to auction off the machinery and livestock of the Grandin farms. The Murray Brothers sold all but two sections to William Leazanby of Mt. Moriah, Missouri. In 1923 the Grandins were forced to foreclose and repossess the land purchased by Leazanby. The family rented the farm from 1923 to 1934 when it was placed in the Grandin Land Trust. The land was rented out until 1946 under the Land Trust's control when it was sold to D. E. Viker of Halstad,

Minnesota. It was most unfortunate that in 1946 at the time of the final sale all the records of the operation of the Grandin farms from 1876 to 1946 were burned. Apparently no one in charge realized the value of the records.

⁴⁷ John S. Dalrymple interview, NDIRS, File 549. A few years after the death of Oliver Dalrymple in 1908 a community of Mennonites were attempting to buy the remaining 25,000 acres of the Dalrymple farm for $65 an acre. At this time the Dalrymple farm was credited as being the largest contiguous farm in the world. Clipping from the *Oakes Times*, Oct. 31, 1912, Dalrymple Papers, File 549.

⁴⁸ Benton, *Cash and Share Renting*, p. 38. A concise account of extensive investment by a foreigner is the story of Stephen Williamson, a prominent Liverpool merchant shipper who purchased 5,627 acres at Euclid in Polk County, Minnesota. Williamson's land cost $19,805.41 but sod breaking, buildings, and other expenses ran his total investment to over $150,000. No profit was ever gained from the operation. His farms were the Argyl and Kilrenny bonanzas. Morton Rothstein, "A British investment in Bonanza Farming, 1879–1910," *Agricultural History*, XXXIII (April, 1959), pp. 72-78.

⁴⁹ Coulter, NDSHS, *Collections*, Vol. III, pp. 610-611.

⁵⁰ *Ibid.*, pp. 608-611.

⁵¹ Power to Allen, Moon, and Co., Jan. 13, 1891, NDIRS, File 309.

⁵² Hilstad interview, Grandin Papers, NDIRS, File 269.

⁵³ *Cultivator and Country Gentleman*, Vol. 41, p. 340; *Fargo Argus*, Sept. 26, 1881.

⁵⁴ Mary Dodge Woodward, *The Checkered Years* (Caldwell, Idaho; 1937), p. 27.

⁵⁵ The *Mayville Tribune*, August 25, 1887, had an article, "Big Dakota Farms" which reveals the true anti-bonanza feeling of that vicinity. A feature article in the Minneapolis Tribune, June 3, 1883, headlined, "Must Be Broken Up," "Not Enough Social Life," "Surrounding Towns Suffer," all reflections of feelings of the people in the Wheatland-Casselton area.

CHAPTER IX

The Effect of Bonanza Farming
on Agriculture

BONANZA FARMS encouraged some basic trends and characteristics of North Dakota agriculture. These trends and characteristics were: The use of large-scale capital; the large-farm concept; hiring of transient labor; extensive use of machinery; reliance on wheat; exploitation of land, and land speculation.

The eastern capitalists who secured their bonanzas through railroad stocks with the help of large-scale capital were willing to invest additional sums to profit from their investment. They actually poured thousands of dollars into their farming operations before any profits were realized. The image was established that only the man who could afford to smoke twenty-five cent cigars was a good farmer.

This concept of the economical necessity of a large farm became so well established that early North Dakotans were often all thought of as bonanza farmers. Newspaper and magazine accounts spread this large-farm image throughout the nation. Figures of the late 1950's give substance to this concept because North Dakota farms averaged 755 acres, nearly triple the national average.

Labor was a major problem of the bonanza operator. He had to hire a large labor force in the spring and fall. After the harvest the laborers had to move on for there was little livestock to care for and no industry to turn to. So the transient laborers became a feature of North Dakota farming. Traveling custom combine crews that followed the harvest from Texas to Canada were a later-day development in the transient labor pattern and continued the old pattern established earlier. Only 7 per cent of the State's farms in the 1960's hired more labor than the family provides. The much greater majority of the farms hire some seasonal labor.

Since the bonanza days North Dakota agriculture has always ranked high in mechanization. It was never a state of hoe-and-pitch-

218

fork farmers. The bonanzas started with big machines and the state's agriculture has remained highly mechanized, having 185 tractors, 117 automobiles, and 108 trucks for every 100 farms in 1954.[1]

Most bonanza farmers were not entirely dependent on farm income and, therefore, could afford to gamble everything on wheat. If they succeeded, they made a sizeable fortune; if they failed, they could wait for another year without hardship. To a great extent this attitude has remained with the North Dakota farmers. The big difference is that in years of failure of wheat they have had to suffer, unless they turn to livestock and diversified farming for salvation.[2]

The bonanza system intensively mined the soil through single cropping of wheat. When soil exhaustion appeared, the land was rotated, fallowed, or returned to its native grass. North Dakotans are still guilty of soil exploitation. Traditional single cropping of wheat, indifference to wind erosion, lack of attention to plow-down crops and fertilizers are examples of this exploitation. Recent years have seen a slight reversal of this trend but the 1960 census indicates that only 41 per cent of the state's wheat acreage was fertilized in the previous year, and 57 per cent of North Dakota farms used no fertilizer on any crop.[3]

Through speculation in railroad securities, many people foreign to North Dakota became land owners in the state. This speculation, which played an important part in the early economy of North Dakota, came near the end of the time of free public domain. North Dakota was one of the few real farm states where the railroads preceeded the farmer, thereby causing a much more rapid settlement and a sharper rise in land prices. Rising land prices have been a constantly bright factor of the American agricultural scene. And so the resulting speculation in land has not been without merit.

The contributions of the bonanza system to American agriculture in general were obviously limited. Benton, writing in the 1920's, said that the economic significance was a short and restricted one and that the chief value of the bonanza era was historical.[4] Of course there were some minor contributions that contributed to agriculture throughout America. Leading students of the bonanza system agree that these main contributions could be enumerated as the following:

Advertising the area. This is what the bonanza was designed to do according to James B. Power who created the idea. They served as great demonstration farms. More than any other factor, their success influenced people to come into the Red River Valley. They were the chief factor in the Great Dakota Boom of the late 1870's and early 1880's which was the era of rapid settlement of the region.

Large-scale mechanized farming. Lewis F. Crawford wrote: "The factory system of farming was transplanted wholesale to North Dakota. More of the instruments and methods of the machine age [came almost overnight] than penetrated to the plodding communities of the older states in a dozen years." Not only large machinery but also uniform equipment was used so that standard repairs and settings could be applied. This, more than any other factor, gave the bonanzas an economic advantage in their early years.

The introduction of a single-crop idea, or wheat monoculture. Wheat enabled them to concentrate on a single line of machinery in a highly specialized agricultural community. Livestock and other crops were all neglected in favor of wheat.[5] It was more than neglect, for the farmers of North Dakota refused to change to a diversified type of agriculture. During the two decades of difficulties following World War I, agricultural officials, politicians, newspapers, and many others attempted to swing the farmer to diversification in order for him to ease his plight, but he persisted in following the habitual pattern.

A few minor contributions of bonanza farming were important to individual families or communities. Great fortunes were accumulated in a short time by a few persons. Most of them have maintained their residence in the state and their families have played a part in its development. Mayville received its first library from the Grandins and land for a hospital. The telephone systems used by the Grandins, Dalrymples, and Amenia and Sharon were the beginnings of public systems.

However, one of the best-known contribution of the bonanzas to American agriculture and American history is that they served as a dramatic basis for innumerable tales of greatness and folklore which are matched only by Paul Bunyan achievements and which represent an interesting story in itself.

FOOTNOTES

[1] *N. D. Ag. Statistics*, p. 95.

[2] In the drought year of 1961, income from livestock surpassed wheat income by a considerable sum. George Strum, Prof. of An. Husb. at North Dakota State University, predicts that cattle will continue to produce a proportionately greater share of the farmer's income.

[3] Virgil L. Weiser, *North Dakota Fertilizer Guide*, NDSU Extension Service Circular A-350, December, 1960.

[4] Benton, *Cash and Share Renting*, p. 38.

[5] Power, *The Record*, V. 15; Crawford, Vol. I, pp. 468-483; Coulter, NDSHS, *Collections*, Vol. III, pp. 582-583; Murray, *Agricultural History*, XXXI, pp. 60-62.

*Bibliography, List of Illustrations
and Index*

Bibliography

Records in the Archive of the North
Dakota Institute for Regional Studies

Manuscripts and Records in the Archive of the North Dakota Institute for Regional Studies at the North Dakota State University contain most of the known and available information on bonanza farming in the Red River Valley region. The collection is the work of several individuals but particular credit goes to Professor Leonard Sackett executive secretary of the Institute, and to Dr. W. C. Hunter, its archivist. Sackett has conducted a large number of interviews with area residents familiar with the bonanza era. These are all on file at the Institute along with newspaper clippings and other memos of the individuals interviewed. These interviews provide much insight into the bonanza operation which is not otherwise available in the records of the farms. Dr. Hunter has assembled the large bulk of material into letter boxes under respective individuals and has arranged them by years. These boxes containing information on the bonanzas fill approximately three rooms in the library at the North Dakota State University. Complete records of two of the bonanzas, the Amenia and Sharon Land Company and the Baldwin farms, are found among them. Tons of material on the Amenia and Sharon has detailed daily and annual financial records, as well as personal memos and letters of the leading officers. The material specially used for this study from the collection and not otherwise available is as follows:

Hunter, W. C. "The History of the Amenia and Sharon Land Company." An unpublished paper by the Institute's archivist written while he was arranging the great quantity of material into a suitable collection. File 134.
"Letters from Golden Latitudes." A typewritten account of a visit to the Grandin farm, May and June, 1885. Found under Bonanza Farm Papers, File 71.

"Madson Recollections." A 200 page typewritten history by an early pioneer. G. S. Barnes Papers, File 507.

Power, James B. "Letterbooks," Vols. I-XIV, File 309. This file contains about 7,000 letters of Power, one of the most significant individuals in the bonanza movement, to Northern Pacific Railway officials and to others associated with the bonanzas. These letters are extremely valuable because they shed much light on the inside operation of the railroads and the opening of the agricultural lands in North Dakota. Power, an extremely alert individual, gives a good account of the realities of the economics of farming during the bonanza era.

Sackett, Leonard. A compilation of information on bonanza farms and interviews as follows:

Ella Bratland	File 254	John Peterson	File 308
J. Carlson	File 257	Robert Reed	File 438
H. L. Chaffee	File 134	Tollef Torgerson, August 24,	
John S. Dalrymple, August 28,		1957	File 867
1953, August 9-18, 1955	File 549	Emil Trapp	File 827
W. F. Dalrymple	File 513	John Walcher, August 13,	
Herman Deike	File 259	1954	File 214
E. B. Downing	File 197	Mrs. Sadie Walker, March 20,	
S. G. Downing	File 166	1954	File 173
Mrs. G. E. Dunwell	File 164	Elmer Ward	File 258
George Hilstad	File 269	Halbert L. Webb, November	
James McKessich	File 138	6, 1955	File 519
Emil Mecklenburg	File 607		

Interviews, newspaper clippings, letters, personal notes, memos, and business accounts from various files at the North Dakota Institute for Regional Studies are filed in the following way:

Amenia and Sharon Land Company Papers, File 134. This file, which contains the great bulk of the information used in this paper, fills more than one large room at the NDIRS library.

Barnes Papers	File 867
Bonanza Papers, General	File 71
Cloverlea Papers	Files 159 and 178
Dalrymple Papers	Files 125, 414, 513, and 549
Downing Papers	Files 166, 167, and 197
Dwight Papers	Files 84, 138, 214, 257, 258, 259, and 290
Grandin Papers	Files 148, 269 308, 450, and 760
Keystone Papers	File 607
Power Papers	Files 254, 309, and 438
Spiritwood Papers	Files 164 and 173
Tenney Papers	Files 515 and 519
Watson Papers	File 827

Personal Interviews

Byers, A. R. Moorhead, Minnesota. Personal interview with Byers, an old settler. January, 1961.

Chaffee, H. L. Amenia, North Dakota. Personal interview with Chaffee, son of H. F. Chaffee and grandson of E. W. Chaffee, the two chief figures in the Amenia and Sharon Land Company. H. L. Chaffee manages a large acreage of what was once company owned lands from the same headquarters that were used by the great bonanza. He is very interested in the history of bonanza farming and has been a great aid to the North Dakota Institute of Regional Studies in making many materials available in addition to assisting it by sharing first hand knowledge of the history, November 10, 1960.

Strum, George, Fargo, North Dakota. Personal interview with Strum, Professor of Animal Husbandry at North Dakota State University. February, 1962. Strum has a broad understanding of the agricultural background of Dakota.

Berg, Norton. Interview with William Berg, Horace, North Dakota. William Berg was employed as a stable man and harness maker on the bonanzas.

Berg, Norton. Interview with Mrs. Jack Garrett, Moorhead, Minnesota. Mrs. Garrett is a daughter of a former bonanza manager.

North Dakota State University
Experiment Station Bulletins

Benton, Alva H. *Cash and Share Renting of Farms.* North Dakota Agricultural Experiment Station Bulletin No. 171 (Fargo 1924).

Engelking, R. F., Heltemes, C. J., and Taylor, Fred R. *North Dakota Agricultural Statistics.* North Dakota Agricultural Experiment Station Bulletin No. 408 (Fargo, 1957).

Heltemes, C. J. and Kristjanson, Baldur H. *Handbook of Facts About North Dakota Agriculture.* North Dakota Agricultural Experiment Station Bulletin No. 357 (Fargo, 1957).

Kristjanson, Baldur H. *What About Our Large Farms in North Dakota.* North Dakota Agricultural Experiment Station Bulletin No. 360 (Fargo, 1950).

Weiser, Virgil L. *North Dakota Fertilizer Guide.* North Dakota State University Extension Service Circular A-350 (Fargo, 1960).

Newspapers and Periodicals

Benton, Alva H. "Large Land Holdings in North Dakota," *The Journal of Land and Public Utility Economics,* Vol. 1, No. 4 (October, 1925), 405-413.

Bigelow, Poultney. "The Bonanza Farms of the West," *The Atlantic Monthly,* Vol. 45, No. 267 (January, 1880), 23-44

Bill, Fred A. "Early Steamboating on the Red River," *North Dakota Historical Quarterly,* Vol. IX (January, 1942), 69-85.

————. "Steamboating on the Red River," *North Dakota Historical Quarterly,* Vol. II (April 11, 1928), 201-216.

————. "Steamboating on the Red River of the North," *North Dakota Historical Quarterly,* Vol. II (January, 1928), 100-119.

Blakeley, Russell. "Opening of the Red River of the North to Commerce and Civilization," *Minnesota Historical Society, Collections,* Vol. VIII (1898), 45-66.

"Bonanza Farming in the Northwest," *The Farmer,* Vol. XXV (December 1, 1907), 770.

"Bonanza Farms in Casselton—Early Reminiscenses," *The Record,* Vol. I (December, 1895), 15-17.

Briggs, Harold E. "Grasshopper Plagues and Early Dakota Agriculture, 1864-1876," *Agricultural History,* Vol. VIII (January, 1934), 51-63.

————. "The Great Dakota Boom, 1879-1886," *North Dakota Historical Quarterly,* Vol. IV (January, 1930), 78-108.

Brown, Margaret L. "Asa Whitney and His Pacific Railroad Campaign," *Mississippi Valley Historical Review,* Vol. XX (1953), 207-215.

Casselton Reporter (Casselton, North Dakota). 1917, 1955.

Coulter, John Lee. "Industrial History of the Valley of the Red River of the North," *North Dakota State Historical Society, Collections,* Vol. III (1910), 529-672.

Cultivator and Country Gentleman, Vols. 41-49 (1876-1884).

Fargo Argus, Fargo Daily Argus, and *Fargo Weekly Argus.* 1879-1885; *Fargo Forum.* 1927-1959.

"Farm Land Price Trends," *Doane Agricultural Digest,* Vol. XXIII (July, 1960) 1011-1012.

Gillette, J. M. "Study of Population Trends in North Dakota," *North Dakota Historical Quarterly,* Vol. IX, No. 3 (April, 1942), 179-193.

Harnsberger, John L. "Land, Lobbies, Railroads and the Origins of Duluth," *Minnesota History,* Vol. XXXVIII (September, 1960), 90-96.

————. "Railroads to the Northern Plains: 1870-1872," *The North Dakota Quarterly,* Vol. XXVII (Summer, 1959), 53-61.

Harnsberger, John L. and Wilkins, Robert P. "Transportation on the Northern Plains: 1. The Genesis of Commerce," *The North Dakota Quarterly*, Vol. XXVIII (Winter, 1961), 20-27.

———. "Transportation on the Northern Plains, II; Steamboating North of Fargo," *The North Dakota Quarterly*, Vol. XXIX (Spring, 1961), 57-65.

Hedges, J. B. "Colonization Activities of the Northern Pacific," *Mississippi Valley Historical Review*, Vol. XIII (December, 1926), 314-321.

Hill, James J. "History of Agriculture in Minnesota," *Minnesota Historical Society, Collections*, Vol. VIII (1898), 275-290.

Lamphere, George N. "A History of Wheat Raising in the Red River Valley," *Minnesota Historical Society, Collections*, Vol. X (February, 1905), 1-33.

Larson, Agnes. "On The Trail of the Woodsman in Minnesota," *Minnesota History*. Vol. XIII (September, 1932), 353-366.

Mayville Tribune (Mayville, North Dakota). August 25, 1887.

Minneapolis Journal. 1893.

Moorhead Daily News (Moorhead, Minnesota). 1893, 1911.

Munro, J. A. "Grasshopper Outbreaks in North Dakota," *North Dakota Historical Quarterly*, Vol. XVI (July, 1949), 147-153.

Murray, Stanley N. "Railroads and the Agricultural Development of the Red River Valley of the North, 1870-1890," *Agricultural History*, Vol. XXXI (October, 1957), 57-66.

"1958 Yield Summary: Major Crops," *Doane Agricultural Digest*, Vol. XXII (January 2, 1959), 2.

Northern Pacific Times (Jamestown, North Dakota). July 20, 1880.

Peterson, Harold F. "Some Colonization Projects of the Northern Pacific Railroad," *Minnesota History*, Vol. X (June, 1929), 127-144.

Power, James B. "Bits of History Connected With the Early Days of the Northern Pacific Railway and the Organization of its Land Department," *North Dakota State Historical Society, Collections*, Vol. III (1910), 337-349.

———. "Diversified Farming," *The Record*, Vol. V (July, 1899), 15-16.

———. "The First Wheat Farm," *The Northwestern Farmer and North Dakota* (May, 1905), 4-5.

Rogers, George D. "History of Flour Manufacture in Minnesota," *Minnesota Historical Society, Collections*, Vol. X (February, 1905), 35-55.

Rothstein, Morton. "A British Investment in Bonanza Farming, 1879-1910," *Agricultural History*, Vol. XXXIII (April, 1959), 72-78.

Thompson, C. W. "The Movement of Wheat Growing: A Study of a Leading State," *The Quarterly Journal of Economics*, Vol. XVIII (1904), 570-584.

Upham, Warren. "The Settlement and Development of the Red River Valley," *Minnesota Historical Society, Collections*, Vol. VIII (1898), 11-24.

Veblen, Thorstein B. "The Price of Wheat Since 1867," *The Journal of Political Economy*, Vol. I (1893), 68-103.

White, William Allen. "The Business of A Wheat Farm," *Scribner's Magazine*, Vol. XXII (November, 1897), 531-548.

Articles

Edwards, Edward E. "American Agriculture—The First 300 Years," *Yearbook of Agriculture, 1940: Farmers in a Changing World*, ed. Gove Hambidge (Washington, 1940), 171-276.

Goodhue, James M. "The Treaty of Traverse des Sioux 1851," *With Various Voices, Recordings of North Star Life*, ed. Theodore C. Blegen and Philip D. Jordan (St. Paul, 1949), 45-60.

La Croix, Joseph. "1871-1890 Towards Finer Flour: The Middlings Purifier," *With Various Voices, Recordings of North Star Life*, ed. Theodore C. Blegen and Philip D. Jordan (St. Paul, 1949), 164-167.

Schmidt, Louis B. "The Westward Movement of Wheat," *Readings in the Economic History of American Agriculture.* ed. Earl D. Ross and Louis B. Schmidt (New York, 1925), 370-380.

Shepherd, J. H. "History of Agriculture in the Red River Valley," *History of the Red River Valley, Past and Present* (Grand Forks, 1909), Vol. I, 194-211.

Stuart, Robert. "How the American Fur Company Conducted Its Affairs, 1816-1834," *With Various Voices, Recordings of North Star Life.* ed. Theodore C. Blegen and Philip D. Jordan (St. Paul, 1949), 106-115.

Whipple, Henry B. "In Defense of the Sioux," *With Various Voices, Recordings of North Star Life.* ed. Theodore C. Blegen and Philip D. Jordan (St. Paul, 1949), 72-77.

Winship, George B. "Forty Years Development of the Red River Valley," *History of the Red River Valley, Past and Present* (Grand Forks, 1909), Vol. I, 73-95.

Unpublished Material

Harnsberger, John L. "Jay Cooke and Minnesota: The Formative Years of the Northern Pacific Railroad 1868-1873." Unpublished Ph. D. dissertation, Department of History, University of Minnesota, 1956. Particularly good for important local personalities connected with the railroad's construction.

Heifort, James M. "Steamboating on the Red River." Unpublished Master's thesis, North Dakota Agricultural College, 1960.

Moll, Edith S. "Moorhead Minnesota Frontier Town 1871-1915." Unpublished Master's thesis, North Dakota Agricultural College, 1957.

Robinson, Elwyn B. "A History of North Dakota." Unpublished manuscript, University of North Dakota, Grand Forks, North Dakota, 1962. Copy in possession of the author. Good background material on earliest activities and also on immigration and settlements between 1870 and 1900.

Books

Billington, Ray Allen. *Westward Expansion: A History of the American Frontier.* New York, 1949.

Blegen, Theodore C. *Building Minnesota.* New York, 1938.

Bridges, Leonard Hal. *Iron Millionaire.* Philadelphia, 1952.

Briggs, Harold E. *Frontiers of the Northwest: A History of the Upper Missouri Valley.* New York, 1950.

Crandall, Horace B. *A History of Richland County.* Colfax, N.D., 1886.

Crawford, Lewis F. *History of North Dakota.* Vol. I. Chicago, 1931.

Folwell, William Watts. *A History of Minnesota.* Vols. I, II, and III. St. Paul, 1926.

Hafen, LeRoy R. and Rister, Carl C. *Western America: The Exploration, Settlement and Development of the Region Beyond the Mississippi.* 2nd ed. Englewood Cliffs, New Jersey, 1950.

Hansen, Marcus L. *Old Fort Snelling 1819-1858.* Minneapolis, 1958.

Hibbard, Benjamin H. *A History of the Public Land Policies.* New York, 1924.

History and Biography of North Dakota. Chicago, 1900.

Jarchow, Merrill E. *The Earth Brought Forth, A History of Minnesota Agriculture to 1885.* St. Paul, 1949.

Lamar, Howard Roberts. *Dakota Territory 1861-1889, A Study in Frontier Politics.* New Haven, 1956.

Larson, Henrietta M. *Jay Cooke: Private Banker.* Cambridge, 1936.

———. *The Wheat Market and the Farmer in Minnesota 1858-1900.* "Columbia University Studies in History, Economics, and Public Law," Vol. CXXII, No. 2, New York, 1926.

Oberholtzer, Ellis Paxon. *Jay Cooke: Financier of the Civil War.* Philadelphia, 1907

Semling, C. K. and Turner, John. *A History of Clay and Norman Counties Minnesota*. Indianapolis, 1918.

Smalley, Eugene V. *History of the Northern Pacific Railroad*. New York, 1883.

Spokesfield, Walter E. *The History of Wells County North Dakota and Its Pioneers*. Jamestown, N.D., 1928.

Turner, Frederick Jackson. "The Significance of the Frontier in American History," *The Turner Thesis Concerning the Role of the Frontier in American History*. ed. George R. Taylor, Problems in American Civilization (Boston, 1949).

Winser, Henry J. *The Great Northwest, A Guide Book and Itinerary*. New York, 1883.

Woodward, Mary Dodge. *The Checkered Years*. Caldwell, Idaho, 1937.

Public Documents

North Dakota. *Commissioner of Agriculture and Labor Annual Report*. 1890, 1900, 1905-1906, and 1910-1912.

North Dakota. *Commissioner of Railroads Annual Report*. Territorial 1886, State 1892.

North Dakota Crop and Livestock Reporting Service. *North Dakota Crop and Livestock Statistics: 1959*.

Territory of Dakota. *Laws of the Thirteenth Session of the Legislative Assembly*, 1879, Chapter XLVI, Railroads, Section XXIV.

U.S. Bureau of the Census. *Census of the United States: 1960. Agriculture*. Vol. III.

U.S. Bureau of the Census. *Thirteenth Census of the United States: 1910, Population*, Vol. III.

U.S. Department of Commerce. *Statistical Abstract of the United States: 1962*, p. 609.

U.S. *Statutes at Large*. Vol. XIII.

Reports

Hagerty, Frank H. *The Territory of Dakota, An Official Statistical, Historical, and Political Abstract*. Aberdeen, 1889.

Poor, H. F. and H. W. *Manual of Railroads of the United States*. New York, 1890-1910.

List of Illustrations

(Picture credits are given in parentheses after each picture.)

(Between pages 148 and 149)

1. Mr. and Mrs. J. B. Power (NDIRS)
   John Miller (NDIRS)
   Jerome Francis Downing (Miss Florence Bagg)
   Rollin C. Cooper (NDIRS)

2. Oliver Dalrymple (John S. Dalrymple, Jr.)
   John S. Dalrymple, Sr. (John S. Dalrymple, Jr.)
   Mr. and Mrs. John S. Dalrymple, Jr. (John S. Dalrymple, Jr.)

3. Front porch of Dalrymple home 1960 (John S. Dalrymple, Jr.)
   E. W. Chaffee (NDIRS)
   H. F. Chaffee (NDIRS)

4. H. L. Chaffee (*Guns* Magazine, November, 1963)
   Robert B. Reed (NDIRS)
   N. P. ad (N.P.R.R.)

5. Land Grant Brochure (N.P.R.R.)

6. N. P. Time Table (N.P.R.R.)
   Magazine ad (N.P.R.R.)

7. Claim shanty (Clay County Historical Society)
   Settlers hauling supplies (N.P.R.R.)
   Excursion train of the N.P.R.R. (John S. Dalrymple, Jr.)

8. Railroad bridge on ice (N.P.R.R.)
   Casselton depot (NDIRS)
   N. P. Reception House (N.P.R.R.)

9. Jay Cooke House (Clay County Historical Society)
   N. P. train at Moorhead (N.P.R.R.)
   Transient farm labor (John S. Dalrymple, Jr.)

10. Dalrymple's first house (John S. Dalrymple, Jr.)
    Dalrymple home (John S. Dalrymple, Jr.)
    Dalrymple home remodeled (NDIRS)

11. Dalrymple headquarters farm (NDIRS)
    Dalrymple elevator near Casselton (John S. Dalrymple, Jr.)
    Potter home (NDIRS)

12. Presidential party at Dalrymple farm (NDIRS)
    Horse yard on Dalrymple #5 (NDIRS)
    Mule teams plowing (Cass County Historical Society)

13. Bundle teams (Cass County Historical Society)
    Shocks of wheat on Dalrymple farm (NDIRS)
    Seeding scene (NDIRS)

14. Casselton 1881 (NDIRS)
    Amenia (NDIRS)
    Amenia blacksmith shop (Cass County Historical Society)

15. Amenia elevator (NDIRS)
    Office and store building in Amenia (Cass County Historical
        Society)
    Sheep sheds at Amenia (NDIRS)

16. Headquarters building at Amenia (NDIRS)
    Chaffee house (NDIRS)
    Elevators in Amenia (NDIRS)

17. Chaffee-Miller mill (NDIRS)
    W. R. Reed in his office (NDIRS)
    Sweet clover plowing (NDIRS)

18. 18 gang plows (NDIRS)
    Postage stamp of 1898 (NDIRS)
    Sod breaking at Coopers (NDIRS)

19. Harvest scene at Cooperstown (NDIRS)
    Boarding house at Cooper farm (NDIRS)
    Barns at Ranch #7 (NDIRS)

20. Barn on Cooper farm (NDIRS)
    Cook house (NDIRS)
    Shocking scene at Coopers (NDIRS)

21. Grandin home (NDIRS)
    Grandin barns (NDIRS)
    Grandin elevator on the Red River (John S. Dalrymple, Jr.)

35. Threshing in Richland County (Almer Christensen)
     Fairview farm (NDIRS)
     Fairview farm wheat field (NDIRS)

36. 43 binders in operation (John S. Dalrymple, Jr.)
     34 binders on Fairview farm (Lloyd Fleischhauer)

Index